The Indian Consumer

One Billion Myths
One Billion Realities

The Indian Consumer

One Billion Myths
One Billion Realities

Alam Srinivas

John Wiley & Sons (Asia) Pte. Ltd.

Other Wiley Editorial Offices

John Wiley & Sons, Inc., 111 River Street, Hoboken, NJ 07030, USA

John Wiley & Sons, Ltd., The Atrium, Southern Gate, Chichester, West Sussex P019 8SQ, UK

John Wiley & Sons (Canada), Ltd., 5353 Dundas Street West, Suite 400, Toronto, Ontario M9B 6H8, Canada

John Wiley & Sons Australia Ltd., 42 McDougall Street, Milton, Queensland 4064, Australia

Wiley-VCH, Boschstrasse 12, D-69469 Weinheim, Germany

Library of Congress Cataloging-in-Publication Data

ISBN: 978-0-470-82230-2

Typeset in 11/13 point, Plantin Light by C&M Digitals (P) Ltd.
Printed in Singapore by Saik Wah Press Pte. Ltd.
10 9 8 7 6 5 4 3 2 1

To my dad who taught me to think differently,
but always with reason and logic.

Contents

Introduction

Even I was surprised by the reactions. For years, I had been thinking that consultancy firms and think tanks had it wrong. The optimists were sold on the idea of the Great Indian Middle Class. The pessimists thought it was all hype. But when I started talking to people about how I felt about the middle class, they agreed. "Yes, you are right," said a commentator who had written extensively about the consumption class. "You should pursue these angles, they seem logical," said a U.S.-based academician. "I think it is time to reflect on the bitter facts about the middle class," opined a researcher who had churned out unending statistics about this segment of the society.

As I explored further and delved deeper into the minds of middle-class people, I realized the bitter truth. There is no truth, or truths, about the Indian middle class. Its story is about varying truths, half-truths, and falsehoods. It is about a billion realities and a billion myths. In the Introduction, we have the time and space to talk about a few of them. But these are the ones that will also make the readers think and ponder about the 999 million issues that I will not address directly. So let me begin by answering a few questions that a Chinese friend asked me recently, "What is the Indian middle class all about? How big is it? And does it really exist?"

Contrary to expectations, and contrary to the state of society in Western nations, the Indian middle class is not a homogeneous segment. It actually comprises several classes. In effect, it consists of thousands of subsets. More importantly, the sum of parts in this case is much less than the whole. But I am getting ahead of the story. Let me start at the beginning—with the rise of the Neo Middle Class (NMC) in India. This is the segment of the society that has created the buzz about India's consumption class.

Mostly born in the eighties, that is, after the post-reforms era really started in 1984, when the late Prime Minister Rajiv Gandhi opened the floodgates for imports in several areas, the NMC members have seen their numbers grow phenomenally in the past two decades. (Many of them were born earlier, but grew up in the 1980s and 1990s.) Taking advantage of the opportunities, initially in global trading (imports of consumer goods, consumer electronics, and information technology (IT) hardware from the United States, Europe, and West and East Asia), then in sunrise sectors such as telecoms and financial services in the 1990s, and later in software and business process outsourcing (BPO), they became more wealthy and prosperous than any other middle-class segment.

Their incomes were higher, and most became globetrotters, acquiring the traits of typical Western middle-class consumers. Their mindsets changed; they thought and behaved differently; they were no longer a part of the traditionally conservative middle class. They became materialistic, flashy, ambitious, confident, and sometimes arrogant. Logically, they became the perfect consumption targets for marketers.

The new base of NMC had several differences, yet some similarities, with the globe-trotting Indians of the 1960s, 1970s, and early 1980s. We can witness these by analyzing the socio-economic trends within the NewGen software and BPO communities.

Most of the early Indian travelers settled wherever they went—doctors in the U.S. and U.K. low-skilled workers in Canada and U.K. They never wanted to come back to India; their only objective was to migrate out of the country. Indeed, they comprised the post-independence wave of "Quit India." Even those who came back spent long periods abroad, like the engineers in the Gulf region. Throughout their foreign stint, the returnees' purpose was largely to save money, and they never became consumers in the real sense. They cut costs, cut corners, and saved.

Toward the end of the previous century, many Indian software engineers took the H-1B visa route to land on U.S. shores, as the IT onshoring trend—outsourcing IT-related work to vendors from emerging nations such as India and the

Philippines, which supplied cheap, yet skilled, software staff—gained credence and popularity. These Indians also dreamed of living in the United States forever, or for long periods. Over time, many managed to convert their H-1Bs into green cards. But there were two differences.

The first was that the dotcom crash and a slowdown in the U.S. IT sector forced a change in the entire onshoring strategy. Most of the IT vendors immediately took the offshoring route, by which their U.S. clients' work was outsourced to campuses based in the emerging nations themselves. It forced thousands and thousands of Indian (and other) techies to come back to their home country. Some of them were forced to return because their H-1B visas were not renewed by their firms.

Simultaneously, as offshoring opportunities rose, ambitious and successful Indian engineer-entrepreneurs headed toward their country. This was coupled with an increase in domestic demand for skilled labor in many other growing sectors, such as financial services and telecoms. This led to further reverse migration. In no time, India had a huge base of NMC members, who, unlike their predecessor migrants, were classical spenders.

The new set of youngsters had imbibed the American way of life, they loved to spend on themselves, and they were self-indulgent materialists. They were visible everywhere: Delhi, Mumbai, Bangalore, Hyderabad, Chennai, and Pune. They suddenly caught the eyes of the salivating marketers. This, according to them, was the future of New India.

In 1991, after the Narasimha Rao government gave a huge impetus to economic reforms by slashing the bureaucratic red-tape and dismantling the then-existing license-quota regime, India witnessed an era of entrepreneurship. Suddenly, the urban middle-class Indian, who invariably worried about getting—and sticking to—a decent job, decided to become a businessperson. Although this was witnessed more in the technology sector, the contagion quickly spread to several other sectors.

This phenomenon led to the rise of "Brahmin Businessmen," who used their knowledge and intellectual prowess to become rich. Unlike the past, knowledge now had a wealth quotient. They added to the growing base of new-age consumers. Both these consumerist trends were evidence of an unstoppable transition of a conservative and nonmaterialistic society into a consumerist one. This signaled the rise of the modern Indian consumer.

However, the sum of these parts is not 250–350 million people, which is what experts reckon to be the size of India's middle and rich classes. It adds up to fewer than 100 million people, or 17–18 million households, according to a 2005 study by the Delhi-based National Council for Applied Economic Research (NCAER).[1]

For investors and marketers, an even more important point to remember is to make a distinction between middle-class individuals and consumers. Not all, or even maybe most, of these nearly 100 million people are consumerists in the strict Western sense. They have the socioeconomic profile to become consumers, but they haven't become spenders. Many of them are savers, who spend a major part of their income only on essentials.

A 2007 survey by NCAER and Max New York Life revealed *How India Earns, Spends and Saves*.[2] It provided insights into the consumption pattern of the Indian middle class. And the conclusions weren't encouraging, to say the least.

Both in urban and rural areas, the majority of households' incomes are spent on routine (food and nonfood) items. In many ways, such expenses are almost fixed on a monthly basis. These would include food, housing, education, transport, and clothing. It's only when households' budgets for nonroutine areas like travel, entertainment, ceremonies, and value-added education and health go up that we can safely contend that these families have joined the consumption class. And, on an average, the latter expenses are just over 12 percent of total income in the case of an average Indian household.

What is surprising is that this figure is a lower 10.37 percent in urban areas, and a higher 13.62 percent in the rural areas. This is contrary to normal perceptions that urban families spend more on "typical" Westernized consumption items, compared to rural India. (Maybe this skew proves that rural families go overboard while spending on ceremonies, especially marriages and births of male children. It may also indicate that a very miniscule percentage of urban households are the real consumers.) One can, therefore, safely say that most urban Indians don't have a consumerist streak.

This is further indicated by the expenditure budgets of Indian households, based on the profession or the education background of the main breadwinner. Among families, where the main earner gets regular salaries or is self-employed in nonagriculture businesses, a little more than 15 percent of his or her overall monthly expenditure comprises "nonroutine" expenditure. Surprisingly, the figure jumps to more than 20 percent when the chief earner is self-employed in agriculture. Yet again, this proves that the largely urban middle-class homes spend less on "consumerist" activities.

On average, rural households spend more than 55 percent of their nonroutine budgets on ceremonies; the figures in the case of urban families and all-India households are 44.9 percent and 51.5 percent, respectively. If one looks at the differences in the breakdown of nonroutine expenditure according to households' professional background, the figures are 50.1 percent in the case of regular wages, 46.1 percent for self-employed in non-agriculture, and 54.4 percent in the case of self-employed in agriculture. As one can see, it's only a matter of plus or minus 4 percent.

It may be that the educated elite spends more on so-called consumer products and services. It may be, as is the case in Western nations, that education really defines whether a family can be dubbed middle class. At an all-India level, graduate families spend less than 17 percent of their expenditure budgets on nonroutine areas; the figure in the case of those with up to higher secondary education is 15.63 percent, which should be obvious in a consumerism-ridden society. But surprisingly, yet again, families with up to primary education in the country spend just less than 18 percent of their monthly expenses on nonroutine things. This is contrary to accepted and acceptable trends in other societies.

Just one more example from the NCAER–Max New York Life survey is important, and that is about "How India Saves." This too establishes that India is unlike any other consumer nation and, therefore, the strategies of marketers and investors need to be radically different in India.

Out of an average annual household income of Rs 65,041, Rs 16,139, or a relatively high 24.8 percent, is "surplus" income or savings. In the case of the urban family, the figure is nearly 28 percent. Contrary to normal perceptions, urban Indians save much more than their rural counterparts. So how can you really term the Indian society "consumerist"? A large segment of people still believe in saving, rather than spending or going on a binge. The consumers constitute a not-too-large segment in India.

If one looks at the micro trends, the bulk of Indians—whether rural or urban—have a sizeable proportion of their savings in cash. The respective figures are nearly 15 percent and 18 percent. In the case of households that earn regular salaries or are self-employed in nonagriculture activities, nearly 70 percent of their savings are in cash. Only in the case of self-employed families in agriculture is the percentage a much-lower nearly 60 percent. In terms of education, nearly two-thirds of surplus income in the case of graduate families and those with up to higher secondary education remain in cash.

It's clear that surplus income—especially among middle-class sections—is saved in cash, and not in financial and other instruments. This too proves that Indians don't believe in Westernized middle-class saving concepts such as equities and insurance.

Even the anecdotal evidence that I have gathered over the past 15 years makes it clear that India is not really similar to other developed or developing nations when it comes to analyzing the size, behavior, and consumption patterns of its middle class. Most of the globally accepted norms don't apply in this country. So one is more likely to make mistakes than get it right. India's middle class is about a billion realities and a similar number of myths.

For instance, unlike in most other nations, ownership of consumerist products such as mobile phones and cars, or possession of a credit card doesn't indicate a spending mindset. It does hint at the making of the middle class, but one that thinks and behaves differently.

First, let me illustrate this point statistically and, once again, I will refer to the NCAER–Max New York Life study. To indicate the growing base of the middle class in India, it points out that more than 50 percent of urban Indians own a color TV and a mixer grinder. This is believed to be an indication of an expanding consumer society. But then the situation begins to look completely different when one looks at the ownership of these products in the "vulnerable" households and "nonvulnerable" ones. (The study stated that nearly a quarter of Indian families fall into the vulnerable, or poor, section.)

Almost a fifth of the vulnerable families own motorcycles and mixers grinders, and 17 percent own color TVs. What's more shocking is that 3 percent of them own a passenger car. Now there must be something wrong here. How can the poor purchase such expensive consumer goods? When they can't make ends meet, how can they spend on such products? The answers provide the key to an important fact about India's consumerism and the country's burgeoning middle class.

One of the most important factors influencing the purchase of consumer goods in India is the wannabe and aspirational attitude. The middle-class Indian, however defined, is not an instinctive consumer; he or she is driven by other emotions. So most middle-class Indian families do not change models, whether the car, color TV, or washing machine. They believe in the traditional maxim: if it ain't broke, don't fix it (or change it). So many households continue to own the car or refrigerator they purchased a decade ago. I still own a color TV that is several years old.

This mindset is not prevalent in other consumerist nations—in east Asia, people change their mobile phones every three-to-six months; in the United States the lifespan of a car is a few years; and in Europe, clothes and other fashion accessories change every season. In India, this attitude is still restricted to the rich class (which forms a minor proportion of the middle and upper classes), the small number of "rags to riches" wannabes, who wish to ape the rich people and become "page 3 personalities", and the NMC (the yuppie, Westernized, globalized, educated, suave, and well-spoken Indians, who have many things in common with their Western middle-class counterparts).

In the case of many middle-class Indians, their decision to change their models or brands is generally not theirs, but dictated, helped, and financed by others. For example, mid-level-to-senior executives in the private sector constantly change their cars and mobile phones. But not many know that in almost all the cases, the purchases are financed by their employers, so it's not the individual who's buying, but the institution. Given a choice, the middle-class Indian is happy with what he or she has (unless it is broken).

To explain how poor and vulnerable families are able to afford purchases of cars and color TVs, one needs to look at the traditional values around Indian weddings. Under the prevalent and commonly accepted practice of "dowry" (in which the bride's family gives a combination of cash, consumer durables, and automobiles to the groom), It is inevitable that even poor households will acquire such goodies. Since they don't have the money, the poor borrow heavily from either the state banks or the powerful private money lenders. But "dowry" cannot be avoided.

In the cases of both the urban and rural middle class, and the poor who possess consumer goods, ownership does not automatically lead to usage. This too is quite unique about India, where ownership is merely to show off to others that you have the products. It is a social statement that the family has arrived; it does not translate into being a "real" consumer. Let me give a few examples—from rural and urban India—to illustrate this basic fact.

Many of the personal owners of cars, who have purchased them with their own money, use public transport to commute to their office or for other work. Their "personal" car is mostly used on weekends for family trips (shopping or eating out). In many cases, the usage of the car is quite irregular. I have noticed thousands of families in which the owner merely starts the car every day (to keep it in running condition) and takes it out once or twice a month. He has a two-wheeler (scooter or motorcycle) for weekend outings.

Even mobile phones are used in a very particular manner by many Indians. Although India's population of mobile-phone owners is growing at a pace of millions of new connections every month, the usage is minimal. First, many buy a second-hand instrument (which is also true for cars). Second, a huge proportion pays the minimum amount that is required for their mobile services, which is as low as Rs 50 (US$1.25; apart from a one-time activation charge) a month. The reason is that some users don't use the instrument to make calls (which is charged), but only to receive them (which is free). I know of several mobile-phone users, who definitely hail from middle- and upper-middle-class families, who use office and home landline connections to make calls, if necessary. This is because landline charges are cheaper, so they can cut their expenses.

Hardly any poor families who own gadgets received as gifts or in dowry use them at all, especially in rural areas. One reason is that the products are meant for public display, to show friends and neighbors that they have arrived in life. Another is that, in many rural areas, electricity is only available for three or four hours a day, so there's no point in using a refrigerator. For many Indian families, who are used to eating freshly cooked food at all meals, the refrigerator is almost redundant—and they will own one only if it came free due to a marriage (or some other occasion) in the family.

What I am saying is that there is a middle class in India that's brand conscious, and obsessed with a Western-style consumerist streak. It earns, buys, and enjoys. Its lifestyle is more modern, more Western. It constitutes the middle-class consumer in the real sense. But its population is definitely not as high as is usually estimated by experts and think tanks. What marketers are excited about is an entirely different phenomenon that may or may not add to the middle-class population.

Let's go back to statistics once again. The NCAER–Max New York Life survey points out that the top income quintile in India, comprising a little more than one-fifth of households (or 230 million people at five members per household), earn an average of Rs 33,170 per annum. This translates into an income of less than Rs 2,800 (US$70) a month. Now if one assumes rightly that the really rich class, which constitutes 10–20 percent of this quintile), earns incomes that are at least 30 times higher than US$70, it will imply that almost half of the households in this quintile earn salaries that are even less than US$70 a month. It is clear from these calculations that the number of Indian middle-class households, or those that earn at least Rs 10,000 (US$250) a month, is much lower than 200 million, or 150 million.

Look at it from another perspective. The same study concludes that over 800 million people, or nearly 80 percent of the households, can be dubbed as above the poverty line (APL) families. Of these, 2.1 percent, or 17 million people, have credit cards; 6.4 percent, or a little more than 50 million, own cars; 19.1 percent, or little more than 150 million, own mobile phones; and 22 percent, or more than 175 million, own refrigerators. As we have seen, the ownership of mobile phones and refrigerators does not automatically prove that the family is part of the consumerist middle class.

Therefore, one can safely assume that the size of India's middle class is between 50 million (households with cars) and 150 million (families with mobile phones), most probably nearer the 50-million mark.

In its previous studies on the middle class, NCAER assumed that its size was 18 million households, or 90 million people. KSA Technopak, another think tank, assumed the figure to be slightly higher at 23 million households, or 115 million people.[3] But in both cases, there was a catch. While the NCAER had clubbed together households with annual incomes of Rs 200,000–1,000,000 under this category, KSA Technopak had grouped all families with incomes of more than Rs 250,000.

But both subjective analysis (at the macro level) and observations (at the micro level) will reveal that both these figures are quite exaggerated. Any family of five members earning Rs 200,000 a year, or just less than Rs 17,000 (US$425) a month, cannot be expected to be consumers in India. They can be part of the middle class, but they will tend to be more conservative in terms of spending, and will generally be savers. They will never spend on nonroutine items at regular intervals. They will save for their children's future, for those rainy days, and for their own financial security in old age. This explains the general trend of really high saving in India, and most of it in cash.

But I can think of a category whose members may be earning this kind of income and still become a part of the consuming class. These are young, single individuals who have just started work, who live with their parents, so don't need to spend on the so-called routine essentials. What they earn, they spend on themselves. They are educated, normally employed in sunrise sectors such as software, BPO, telecoms, and financial services. Their starting salaries are high, and they get promoted quite fast to become mid-level managers within less than five years. And they have no financial obligations or responsibilities until they decide to buy a car or a house. In addition, they are brand conscious and want to ape (or are used to) Western lifestyles and the consumption mindset.

So one can realistically say that India's middle class is not more than 100 million; it may be 50–75 million. So why does everyone get it wrong and put it at 250–350 million?

It is because of the sheer numbers of "aspirers," who earn Rs 90,000–200,000 per annum, but are waiting, jostling, pushing, and striving to become a part of the middle class. During the middle of the first decade of the twenty-first century, their size was estimated at 53.28 million households (or more than 260 million people). It was predicted that this would increase to more than 75 million families (or more than 375 million individuals) within a few years. If the "aspirers" do become middle class, there is bound to be a consumer revolution, and everyone's excited about it.

Will the "aspirers" join the middle class in the near future? The answer is yes and no.

First, take a look at how the members of the "aspirer" class are entering the middle class. According to NCAER, there were nearly 4.8 million middle-class households in 1995–96. Over the next five years, up to 2001–02, the number increased to 10.7 million, or an addition of nearly 6 million families. In other words, an average of 1.2 million households jumped classes every year. By 2005–06, the number went up to a little more than 18 million, or an addition of 1.8 million a year. By 2009–10, it is expected to cross the 30-million mark, more than 3 million a year more.

Obviously, given that India's economy witnessed low gross domestic product (GDP) growth rates in the second half of 1990s, and much higher rates, at 8–9 percent a year, in the first decade of the twenty-first century, the number of "aspirers" who join the middle class can be seen to depend on growth in GDP.

Not many are willing to bet that India can continue at this frenetic pace over the next decade. This growth is more likely to slow down, so the rate at which "aspirers" become middle class is likely to be less than 3 million households a year, or around the same rate. So for India to reach a middle class population of 250 million, or 50 million households, will require a minimum of 11 years from its 2005–06 levels. If GDP grows about

6 percent per annum, then it will take almost 15 years. Therefore, most marketers have to wait before they can salivate over a middle-class population of 250 million.

Furthermore, we can listen to what promoters of organized retail feel about Indian consumers. Kishore Biyani, who owns the Future Group (with retail chains such as Pantaloons and Big Bazaar), and is considered to be the father of modern retail in India, says that Indian consumers can be divided into three categories: India 1, India 2, and India 3.[4] The last comprises the poor people and has to be left out of this calculation. Kishore feels that the members of India 1 are the consumers, who buy brands, visit malls, and spend a lot on their personal entertainment and travel. India 2 consists of people who provide the basic and other services to India 1 for the latter to maintain its lifestyle. Logically, it is in the interest of India 1 not to allow India 2 to graduate to the former's level of consumption.

More importantly, says Kishore, India 1 does not want to pay enough to India 2 to enable the latter to make the "consumption-driven" transition from "aspirers" to middle class.

Within India 1, or the middle class, there are several divisions due to caste, class, religion, and other differences. Within a similar socio-economic category, mindsets and values can differ dramatically. In several cities, people from different localities, although considered part of the middle class, think and behave dissimilarly. And not to forget the regional divide: the middle class in the south of India is not the same as the one in the north. The effort of grappling with all these complexities and fragmentation is enough to make generalizations difficult.

The truth is that unlike in most of the Western world, the middle class in India is not uniform, not even remotely. It consists of hundreds and thousands of subsets, most of which cut into each other. So it is difficult to pinpoint generalized behavior or consumption patterns.

I have talked about the NMC. Even within this evolved middle-class category, there are divisions in terms of consumer behavior. Several studies have found that many Indian software engineers are conservative in their attitudes, and are more savers rather than spenders. Among the spenders, there are many who save 30–40 percent of their monthly salaries, and believe in investing in assets (such as a house), and not in conspicuous consumption. For them, earning does not equate with spending, although they spend more on their personal wishes than their parents do. The traditional values of being nonmaterialistic and not showing off are still ingrained in the younger generation.

Among the other subsets of the middle class, the fault lines are caste, class, educational, and professional differences. For instance, consider the rise of Brahmin and middle-class businesspeople over the past decade or so. Thanks largely to the efforts of India's first prime minister, Jawaharlal Nehru, to establish higher-education seats of excellence such as the Indian Institutes of Technology (IITs) and Indian Institutes of Management (IIMs), certain Brahmins (who in the Indian caste system were the intellectuals) and evolved middle-class families pressurized their children to take the educational route to success. After independence, educational reservations for other castes and classes, which were outcomes of political pressures, helped others to become well off. Many of these new educated elites winged their way to the United States and other countries, and became materialistic, consumerist, globalized souls.

Along with reservations in government jobs, people from lower castes (backward castes and Dalits, or untouchables) joined the middle class. Educational quotas in professional colleges allowed them to become engineers and doctors; the rush to start such colleges, especially in south India, added to the opportunities for the lower classes. Eyeing government jobs, great numbers turned up for the Indian Administrative Services (IAS) entrance examinations, and became part of the powerful bureaucracy. Over decades, these Dalit bureaucrats acquired both material wealth and policy clout, and were in a position to help other Dalits. However, knowing the rigid Indian caste system, one can obviously deduce that the behavior and mindset of the Brahmin middle class is totally different from those of Dalits and other backward castes.

If one looks at the middle class based on professional backgrounds, one can yet again see stark differences. Those employed by the government (central or state) or the state-owned public sector behave more like the traditional, conservative middle class. Those working for the private sector, and partly exposed to other consumer societies, are more spenders than savers. They crave brands and material possessions, and are more likely to purchase two or three cars and a similar number of color TVs, and change their mobile phones every few months. The tens of thousands of people—mostly middle class—who work for the country's defense forces are somewhere in between—they are neither fully conservative, nor have become totally materialistic; they have shades of both, and are in the process of becoming "true" consumers but still hold firm to past values.

Finally, the middle class has regional and intra-city disparities. Its members in the southern states are likely to be more conservative than their counterparts in western parts. Those in the west are likely to be more value-for-money consumers than their counterparts in the northern states. Those in the north are likely to be more show-offs than those in any other part of the country.

What is really surprising is how the tastes in brands, products, food, music, and movies change from locality to locality in India's metropolises and A-1 cities. Take the case of Mumbai, where all these factors change quite distinctly as one starts from Colaba (south Mumbai) and moves northward toward the suburbs and Navi Mumbai. Only a blind person would miss the differences among families in Worli, Dadar, Bandra, Chembur, and Navi Mumbai. The way people dress, the restaurants, and the retail outlets are strikingly different.

By now, I have established that the Indian middle class is neither as large as some suggest, nor is it uniform, nor does it behave in the manner in which similar segments behave in other Western and developed worlds. In addition, the middle class in India is a sum of hundreds of parts (or subsets), and the sum of all parts is not a straightforward addition. The Indian middle class is complex, complicated, constantly evolving, and in the process of hitherto unknown change. It's now time to take a more detailed look at all these aspects of the Great Indian Middle Class.

Endnotes

1. National Council for Applied Economic Research (NCAER) in association with *Business Standard*, "The Great Indian Market: Results from the NCAER's Market Information Survey of Households," August 9, 2005, http://www.ncaer.org/downloads/PPT/TheGreatIndianMarket.pdf
2. Rajesh Shukla, *How India Earns, Spends, and Saves*, (National Council for Applied Economic Research (NCAER) Max New York Life, 2007).
3. KSA Technopak, *Consumer Outlook*, Kurt Salmon Associates, 2004.
4. Kishore Biyani and Dipyan Baishya, *It Happened in India*, (Rupa & Company, 2007).

Chapter 1

The "I Can, So I Will" Spenders

This is the middle class that we all know and talk about. This is the segment that we get excited about. This is the young, confident, and ambitious class that earns and spends on branded products, gizmos, and other items of conspicuous consumption. This is the post-reforms generation, born in the 1970s and 1980s, which came of age after the initial economic reforms introduced in the early 1980s, when Prime Minister Rajiv Gandhi opened the floodgates for imports. They seek instant gratification. Their mottos are "One life, live it" and "You only live once."

We may call them by any number of names—the Great Indian Middle Class, the Neo Middle Class (NMC), the elite middle class, the Spenderati, Gen-S (for Spenderati), or the "I can, so I will" spenders.

Most marketers and economists think that this section represents the entire Indian middle class of 250–350 million people. Most sociologists, however, look at this class more critically, regarding it as a generation in transition, caught between tradition and modernity, between austerity and self-indulgence. More conservative social commentators worry because for them the new consumer-oriented generation represents the moral degradation and Westernization of Indian society. Most investors are convinced that this is the Great Indian Middle Class that will buy their products in millions. The truth, as usual, lies elsewhere. And all the pundits are wrong in their respective assessments.

Before we delve into these issues, let us explore the attitudes of this class.

Ramya C. (28 years old), who handles international communications for an East Asian conglomerate and shuttles between Bangalore, Kuala Lumpur, and Singapore, is a representative of this class. She belongs to a liberal, middle-class south Indian family; her father is a scientist and her mother a teacher. Ramya studied in a government-aided Central School in Kanpur, in the north Indian state of Uttar Pradesh, and later at the Indian Institute of Science, Bangalore. She graduated from a local college in Bangalore, with a first-class (over 60 percent marks) degree, having studied psychology, journalism, and English literature.

Ramya was brought up with the values typical of Indian middle-class professionals, where intellectual, not material achievements are emphasized, where saving is considered more important than spending, and where fulfilling one's responsibility toward family members is held as a sacred duty.

At 19, she walked out of a bad marriage. Her life was shattered. She was broke and homeless, but was reluctant to return to her parents. The experience had wrecked her emotionally, but she wanted to move on. She contacted an old school friend for help. The friend spoke to her former boss at a leading yellow-pages firm. Ramya did not have any work experience but, surprisingly, she was selected for a telesales job that paid her Rs 4,500 (about US$110) per month.

"I was not qualified for anything. And they were not looking for any experience, just enthusiasm. It was a sales job and I had good communication skills, a decent tele-voice, spoke good English, and was reasonably intelligent. That's all they needed in the prospective employee," says Ramya.

Nevertheless, survival was not easy. A third of Ramya's salary went toward her share of the rent for a dingy three-bedroom house she shared with five other girls. The only advantage was that it was close to her place of work. Then there were food, electricity, and transport expenses. "I really couldn't manage on that salary. I starved a lot. Those were horrible days and it wasn't pleasant. I couldn't afford to go out, or party. So I never went out," she says.

Ramya's job was a high-pressure one; everyone had stiff annual targets to meet. Initially, her target was Rs 10 lakh (US$25,000) worth of sales, and it kept increasing each year. Work started at 8.15 a.m., but there was no fixed time for it to stop. But there was a silver lining. The firm rewarded well-performing employees with cash and other incentives.

In the first year, Ramya thrice earned cash bonuses (each of Rs 15,000, or US$375) and several other incentives. She also won an all-expenses-paid trip to Bangkok, a reward for the best-performing salesperson. She could now afford to move into a better house and have a room of her own.

Eighteen months later, she moved to another job, this one a new-economy job. Within a few months, the dotcom company was sold, and its employees were given the pink slip. Yet again, a friend helped Ramya get a job with an event management company. It turned out to be a blessing in disguise. "I knew I didn't want to be in a sales job. There was too much pressure and too little peace of mind. I did it only to pay my monthly bills. But I still wasn't sure what I wanted to do. Here I realized I liked what I was doing. A year later, I joined a public relations agency, which offered me a more developed role. It was communications related. I could do events, write, and market communication. I enjoyed it. I knew this is what I wanted to do," she says.

When Ramya took up her current job with a foreign conglomerate, she got a good salary (calculated in U.S. dollars) along with many perquisites. She became a globetrotter with an expense account (including *per diem* expenses for travel, which happened regularly).

By now, she had become a part of the NMC. Ramya works hard (traveling three weeks in a month), and plays hard. On any given weekend, she can be found at a happening pub, or eating out at a fancy restaurant. On her numerous trips, she is constantly looking around for things to buy, whether clothes, jewelry, or souvenirs. (In her blog, she reveals that she once went out to buy Band-Aid and came back with twenty other things.) Ramya also loves gizmos. She carries three mobile phones, and changes the models every year. "Due to my work-related travel, my life depends on my mobile phones. I like multifunctional sets, which double up as mini-offices," she says. She plans to buy a personal digital assistant (PDA). She jokingly says that her "street value is pretty high," as at any given moment she is carrying at least two mobile phones, a digital camera, and an iPod Nano.

"My spending now is based on my wants, as opposed to my needs in the early years. I earn enough to live a comfortable life and can afford to be occasionally frivolous. So why not? I can, so I will. I think I've earned the right. My spending is more about instant gratification," she explains.

Ramya's lifestyle reveals the traits typical of the NMC.

They were not born rich. Their parents are not high profile or famous; the fathers are government employees, mid-level managers, or army personnel. They grew up in an environment where unnecessary spending was frowned upon, where individual merit counted for everything. The parents were not socially networked, so could not curry favors for their children. The children either chose, or stumbled upon, opportunity-sector jobs and climbed up the organizational ladder by virtue of their education (and their fluency in English), hard work, ambition, and discipline. Today, they earn far more than their parents ever did, so they have higher disposable incomes as well.

The NMC spend like there is no tomorrow. They are living neither in the past, nor in the future; they are part of the "here and now;" they live for the moment. They are confident that they can succeed in this dog-eat-dog world, and thrive in any crisis situation.

I have spent the past decade studying and trying to understand this new emerging class. I have met scores of people like Ramya. They are invariably found in the metros and the big cities. They are employed in either sunrise industries such as software and business process outsourcing (BPO), where India has emerged as a global leader, or in financial services, communications and media, consultancy, pharmaceuticals, and KPO (knowledge process outsourcing). They may even be self-employed individuals in the services sector, which has boomed in the past two decades and now constitutes over 55 percent of India's GDP. Most of these young people are obsessed with gadgets and technology. Most are in the 25–35 age group, which means that they have worked for at least a few years and have reached a certain critical level in terms of salary and designation in the corporate hierarchy. Most of them openly admit to being big spenders, and are not ashamed about it. They like to live life "king size." They work hard and party hard.

Ajith Chellan, who works for the software major Infosys, is a typical representative of this class. He describes himself as a "car-and-bike" freak. He owns four motorcycles (BSA B31, Thunderbird, Aquila, and Comet) and two cars (Hyundai Accent and Fiat Uno); the Accent is his sixth in the past five years. "Autos are a part of my life. I love them, and have been interested in them since my childhood. I purchased the Thunderbird especially for a Leh–Ladakh bike trip," Ajith says.

He adds that he buys so many models because there are so many options available today, and "very few have been driven so far." For him, cars and bikes are an "extension of yourself. The most wonderful invention is the bike. You sit on top of the engine, and it takes you wherever you want to go," Ajith explains.

Bhaskar Hariharan, who works for Yahoo!, is a hardware guy. His passions include graphic cards, CPUs (central processing units), and motherboards. He also buys the latest-model cameras, PDAs, and mobile phones (his latest purchase was a Sony Ericsson W700i). Bhaskar's colleague, Arvind Ramakrishnan, is a mobile-phone maniac. He has changed six handsets in the past six months, has tried nine different models, and currently owns a Nokia N70.

"There is an 'enjoy today, forget tomorrow' attitude among the young spenders," says Rajesh Shukla, chief economist at the National Council for Applied Economic Research (NCAER), a research agency based in New Delhi.[1] Preeti Reddy, vice president, KSA Technopak, based in Gurgaon, Haryana, which specializes in retail and consumer spending studies, agrees. "The mindset is changing from self-denial to self-indulgence, from saving to shopping," she observes.[2]

Praveen Purushotham, a marketing manager in a U.S.-based software firm, and Neal Avinash Daniel, a consultant in a top BPO firm, spell out the reasons for the NMC's buying spree. It is generally about lifestyle, choice, and confidence.

"Our spending is not based so much on identifying categories that are 'splurge-worthy,' but more on how it fits our lifestyle, adds value to our living experiences, and enriches our lives in some form or the other," says Praveen. He thinks that gadgets and gizmos, books and music, furniture, and art add value to one's life. Clothes and accessories, eating out and pub-hopping, travel, and vacations enhance the living experience. "I spend on things that make a difference to either my life or to that of my family members," he explains.

Neal offers the same explanation but with a twist. "My spending on clothes and accessories is lifestyle related," he says. Since he travels a lot and spends most of his time in meetings with clients, he needs to dress well. "I must admit that being well groomed gives me a kick," he says.

It is also about the choices available to Indian consumers today. "My parents have never traveled abroad, while I have crisscrossed Europe many times in the past twelve months itself. A decade and a half ago, shopping in Singapore or Dubai was the only avenue for affluent people to spend their disposable incomes. Today, you can buy just about anything—from the expensive to the exorbitant—in any Indian city. The choices available in India are now phenomenal," explains Neal.

Both Praveen and Neal, along with many others, talk about the newfound confidence so visible among Indians today, particularly among the NMC. "I can get any job I want and make as much money as I want," says Praveen confidently. This self-belief is partially the result of the booming Indian economy, which has registered an annual gross domestic product (GDP) growth of 7–8 percent in the past three years; it is expected to record double-digit growth during the Eleventh Five-year Plan (2007–12). Gone are the days when India was crippled with the "Hindu" rate of annual growth (4 percent) and buckled under long periods of 10 percent-plus inflation.

Economists add another factor to this mix: rising aspirations. "There is an aspiration to buy newer and more expensive products due to increased social interaction. Many products have become status symbols for the younger generation. It is not necessity but greed that is driving these purchases," says Shukla of NCAER.[3] This is clear from the fact that spending in small towns (population of 0.5–1 million) is higher than the national indexed average.

However, the NMC does not accept this explanation. It claims that it is neither trying to prove a point, nor doing certain things because of social pressure. It is what it is. It is doing what it does because it can afford to do so, thanks to various macro and micro trends that have swept the country since the early 1990s.

The positive impact of economic reforms has not percolated down to the lower segments of the society, nor touched the lives of a fifth of India's population, which is still categorized as "poor." Nevertheless, economic liberalization has opened up windows of opportunity in sunrise sectors such as telecoms, retail, and financial services. The global worry about the Y2K bug in the year 2000, which, it was claimed, would have ruined all software programs, was responsible for the growth of Indian software service and BPO sectors. Both outsourcing (and off-shoring) and the boom in these new sectors led to limited growth in high-paying jobs, even as many others were lost in manufacturing.

Even the manufacturing sector has created its own islands of prosperity and privilege in the form of industrial townships. Economic growth has raised the standard of living of those employed in metros and large cities due to regular hikes in salary and compensation. Competition has lowered the prices of products like mobile phones, personal computers, and other consumer durables, making them affordable for many more people.

Social changes have led to the mushrooming of nuclear families. Many of these families are double income, no kid (DINK) or double income, single kid (DISK). Those who are single often migrate to other cities in search of better jobs; many of them do not have to support families back home. The combined result of these developments is that more disposable income is available to a class that has managed to grab the new opportunities available in India today. This is seen clearly in the case of Ramya and her ilk.

The recent revolution in mass media—cable and satellite television, broadband connections, increasing Internet usage—has brought the latest information about products and services to a larger proportion of the population. Information is now more readily accessible than ever before. This change has enhanced buying desires. The entry of new players in the marketplace has increased the number of products that can be picked off the shelves. The rising credit culture and cheap finance options have whetted this desire. In a nutshell, India is ready for a period of rapid and intense consumerism.

Economists and other experts have a mine of data to prove this trend. For a decade, researchers and consultants have churned out annual surveys and studies that show rising consumption patterns, consistent increase in average disposable income, changing values of urban Indians (from saver to spender), and a resultant demand–supply boom in several product categories.

In 2001–02, NCAER estimated the size of the Great Indian Middle Class (including the rich class) as 64 million, and predicted that it would go up to 175 million by 2009–10.[4] The middle class comprised 6.1 percent of India's 1 billion-plus population in 2001–02. The number of people aspiring to join the middle class was 223 million in 2001–02, and this number was expected to increase to more than 400 million by 2009–10.

What is important to note in the NCAER survey is the consumption patterns of the middle and rich classes. The ownership per household for two-wheelers, color TVs, and refrigerators was high, ranging between 0.62 and 0.99. Similar statistics for cars and air-conditioners were decent, ranging between 0.15 and 0.83.

The problem lay with the "aspirers" group, whose ownership ratios were between 0.34 and 0.47 for two-wheelers, color TVs, and refrigerators, and were abysmally low for air-conditioners (0.02) and cars (0.04).

To the optimist, this meant that there was a huge demand potential as the aspirers graduated to the middle class. NCAER analysts predicted that penetration levels would grow 240 percent for air-conditioners, 300 percent for cars, and 400 percent for motorcycles by 2009–10.

Government surveys have found that India's private consumption expenditure was approximately US$425 billion in 2004–05, of which retail sales (both organized and unorganized) constituted nearly 55 percent. More importantly, categories such as leisure and entertainment and communications (which account for disposable income expenditure) grew at nearly 29 percent and 22 percent, respectively.

Other indicators of growing affluence are mobile phone subscribers (whose number exceeded that of owners of fixed phone lines) and the number of credit cards issued has zoomed from 3.2 million to 12.2 million in the past five years. ICICI Bank has grown its base by 40 percent annually in the past couple of years.

A study by American Express (Amex) in 2006 provides other insights into the growing middle class in India.[5] In 2005, there were more than 700,000 affluent individuals with liquid wealth of more than US$100,000 each. This number was estimated to grow to 1.1 million by 2009, with their cumulative liquid wealth increasing from US$203 billion to US$322 billion during the same period. The study described the mindset of these people as

"I've made it." Further analyzing their thinking and behavior patterns, the study found that to be branded as affluent, people thought they had to have the "right" possessions and the "right" attitude, to have "simply the best" things and to adopt the "If I want it, I can get it" attitude.

To tap the growing affluence of this group, Amex launched the Platinum Club credit card. The survey revealed that emerging affluent consumers have unique spending habits. They earn Rs 20–25 lakh (US$50,000–62,500) or even upwards a year, are in the 30–45-year age bracket, travel abroad at least three times a year, and entertain and dine out three times more than average consumers. What was a particularly encouraging finding for Amex was that these affluent consumers had annual average credit card spending of Rs 360,000 (US$9,000), or ten times that of average consumers.

Here are some more statistics that shed light on India's consumption growth:

❑ Spending on mobile phones (population: over 300 million in May 2008) has trebled in the past three years, as teledensity (per capita telephone coverage) went up from 8.8 percent to 11.7 percent in the period January 2005–January 2006.
❑ The US$10 billion FMCG (fast-moving consumer goods) sector in 2005 is expected to treble by 2010. Most of the growth in the foods segment will come from packaged basic items like cooking oil, wheat, and rice, indicating a penchant for commodity branding among consumers.
❑ In 1995, 2.6 million Indians had a mortgage. The figure rocketed to over 20 million in eight years. Indians withdrew US$50 billion from ATMs in 2005.

One may cite endless figures and statistics to show India's emergence as a major consumer market. Indeed, such number crunching has become a favorite pastime with consumer firms and researchers. Every economist and marketer worth his or her salt has his or her own set of unique numbers to prove the trend. There are hundreds of ways of calculating these figures using different methodologies.

More than consumption, these figures indicate another critical change. Slowly but steadily, the power base of the NMC has been increasing. Recognizing this trend, this segment of the middle class has indirectly entered the public-policy arena and is now influencing policy making.

This may sound like a contradiction because one of the traits of this middle class is its political apathy and lack of engagement with the political system. It believes that politicians have failed to deliver the goods in the 60 years since India's independence. It knows that the system is riddled with corruption, staffed by nonperforming employees, and dominated by people who are solely concerned with advancing their individual interests and priorities. The system has left millions of people out of the circle of prosperity. This section of the middle class has opted out of the political process. It rarely participates in elections, does not care about who is in power, and pursues its needs on its own. Most surveys of the urban middle class prove this.

However, critics point out that this is not always the case. When this middle class is faced with issues close to its heart, or when it deals with problems that will affect it negatively, it is ready to shake off its apathy and cynicism and become more politically engaged. To protect its turf, material or otherwise, this middle class will try to influence politics, if only indirectly.

Nothing proves this point better than what has happened in Bangalore, India's technology hub, which has spawned hundreds of software firms, including giants like Infosys. To understand this situation better, let us see the work done by the managing director of Infosys, Nandan Nilekani, who hails from an upper-caste, middle-class family.

Nandan became the chairman of one of the most powerful Indian—and global—organizations, and an internationally respected manager on the basis of his education, merit, hard work, and intellect. Today, he is one of the leading minds on issues such as IT, software, BPO, and the knowledge economy.

Nandan has also spearheaded an elite group that affects urban policies in Bangalore. This group comprises some eminent members, including a clutch of younger people. Among them is Ramesh Ramanathan, a former Citibank employee who now runs an investment firm and works on social empowerment through his NGO, Janaagraha, and V. Ravichandar, who heads Feedback Marketing Services, a research-based consulting firm.

Until 2004, all of them were part of the Bangalore Action Task Force (BATF), which was initiated by the Karnataka state government with a "single-minded mission to modernize Bangalore by the end of 2004." This goal was to be achieved by improving the city's infrastructure and raising the people's standard of living. BATF's aim was to transform Bangalore into a world-class city by 2004–05.

However, in 1999, when the idea first germinated, the driver behind it was the possible effect of poor urban infrastructure on the future of Bangalore as a hi-tech city. The trigger was the lack of proper road connectivity to the city's hi-tech core on the Hosur Road, which houses the campuses of most software majors. In the past, software company CEOs led a protest on the same road against the fragile and inadequate infrastructure that was rendering their campuses and operations uncompetitive. Industry leaders felt that if the situation did not improve, the software development business would be compelled to shift to competing centers like Hyderabad (in Andhra Pradesh) and Pune (in Maharashtra).

Using their clout with S.M. Krishna, then the chief minister of Karnataka, Nandan and his friends lobbied the government for the setting up of BATF, with its lofty objectives. Ravichandar, a key member of BATF, describes the beginnings of the group:

> The CEOs and the citizens were in a trade union mold, with a "*hamari maange poori karo*" ("fulfill our demands") mindset. They felt that the government needed to deliver, as they paid taxes and bribed state officials (in order to get their work done). The state, in turn, felt that it did not have the resources to include all the projects (and especially the ones demanded by the CEOs). It said that everything will vaporize without inclusive growth. So most of the money had to be spent on the poor, and not the elite (middle class). It indicated that any money spent on a flyover, which was what the software CEOs wanted, would leave the poor with that much less money.
>
> I told the CEOs that one option was to continue with their trade union-like demands. The other option was to engage with the state government by understanding the language of such an engagement. We should form a corpus of Rs 2–3 crore (US$0.5–0.75 million) to get professional planners involved. For us the most worrisome thing was the lack of capacity in urban planning. While Kerala has 25 urban planners, Karnataka has none. Involving professionals was the cheapest way to

put a foot in the "planning" door, and spending the Rs 2–3 crore could yield a return of Rs 30–40 crore (US$7.5–10 million).

This was the way to influence public policy. Here was a need to change the mindset of CEOs, to make them acknowledge the existence of the state. Since the state could not do things on its own, we had to create spaces where the CEOs had the strength [to do so]. The political system can decide, but the CEOs should deliver some bits in the urban infrastructure space. The reality is that one needs a few people to do this.

When we met in December 1999, we realized that the bureaucrats were not going to listen to us and we had zero credibility in the public infrastructure space. In a public–private partnership model, we said that the state should build the projects and that BATF would collaborate and report to the civic authorities. We thought we should adopt three or four projects and drive them in order to gain credibility.[6]

As expected, in 2004, when the chief minister, S.M. Krishna, lost the state elections, the new regime disbanded BATF. During its existence, the organization had made little progress thanks to bureaucratic intransigence and the lack of adequate expertise among the task force members and their inability to implement their program. BATF blamed other factors for its lack of success. In doing so, the members revealed certain traits of the NMC. Even when it wants—or gets—power, or when it assumes a policy-making role, the NMC does not want to own responsibility. It is the ideator, not the implementer. It will tell others how things can be fixed, but it is the others who will have to accomplish the task. (However, when it comes to their own individual pursuits and interests, they are doers and action oriented.)

Nandan Nilekani and his friends did not want to give up their idea. "We are urban junkies who feel *kuch karna hai* (have to do something)," says Ravichandar. Nilekani came up with the idea of peddling the model in the corridors of power in the capital. Ravichandar describes the birth of the National Urban Renewal Mission (NURM):

We met Montek Singh Ahluwalia (deputy chairman, Planning Commission, who has the ear of the prime minister) and told him that the time for urban India had come. We said that urban renewal was a part of the manifesto of the current central government, so was it an important issue or just a statement? We even met Sonia Gandhi (president of the Congress Party) and Rahul (her son). Within three months, the Prime Minister's Office gave the green signal for NURM. Ours was the fourth-biggest mission, and it was linked to reforms. We managed to get on to the (urban infrastructure) train.[7]

The Indian polity, as usual, has a way of maintaining the status quo. Despite the fact that Nandan Nilekani and his colleagues claim credit for NURM, the bureaucrats have kept them out of it. At present, they are peripherally attached with the mission.

The example of Nandan Nilekani and his friends proves that apart from becoming an economic force, the NMC is gaining political clout as well. Its economic power is publicly known; its policy-making power is still unclear, and not as effective.

Nevertheless, the combination of economic and political power gives this class the confidence to take chances—of any kind. To this claim, the members of the NMC are likely to respond by saying that they merely seize opportunities and do not give up, even after failing in the specific endeavors that they take up.

To understand this aspect, we have to first understand why Gautham Gopal, 35, gave up cricket. Since his childhood he had worked towards fulfilling his dream of playing for India. In 1994, he joined the Steel Authority of India Ltd (SAIL), a public sector undertaking (PSU), which nurtured cricketers. As a wicketkeeper–batsman, he regularly played in the Ranji Trophy, the state-level annual tournament, for Orissa state.

"When I crossed 30, I realized it just wouldn't happen. I had no chance. Playing for your country partially depends on luck, and I have no grudges," recalls Gautham. He called it quits, took voluntary retirement, and became an entrepreneur. As he says philosophically, "One has to carry on with one's life."

Gautham, who is based in Chennai (formerly Madras), the capital of Tamil Nadu state, is now a buying agent for firms in the United States and Europe, and sources woven and knitted garments. He took a risk in entering an industry about which he knew nothing. "It was a totally new area and I had to start from scratch. I am still learning," he says. More importantly, he knew he would not be doing a 9-to-5 job. Finally, he wanted his work to be challenging. "The garments business is extremely competitive. It's like being on the cricket field all over again," he notes.

Like Gautham, scores of Indians are chasing their own entrepreneurial dreams. That is one explanation for the growth of the services sector, where entrepreneurship produces almost instant rewards. As in many other nations, this trend in India also started in the dotcom years with a string of New Economy startups, and has continued into the twenty-first century.

Nearly a fifth of Indians in the age group of 18–64 years are engaged in some form of entrepreneurial activity, according to a recent joint study by the London Business School and Babson College, Massachusetts, U.S. which surveyed 40 nations accounting for 60 percent of the world's population and 70 percent of its output.[8] India ranked seventh in terms of entrepreneurs, and was above the United States, China, Japan, Germany, and France. The report revealed that Indian startups created 17 million jobs in 2003, the second highest after China.

A similar trait can be seen at the workplace as well. Younger Indians are willing to experiment with their jobs, change organizations, and shift sectors either for more money, greater responsibility, or a better environment. One such person is Chetan Bhagat, 33, an IIT graduate who now works for Deutsche Bank.

For several years now, Chetan has been planning to quit his cushy job in Hong Kong and move to Mumbai to work in the Hindi film industry (popularly called Bollywood, in imitation of the USA's Hollywood). He wants to work as a full-time film scriptwriter. The reason for this was the runaway success of his first two books, *Five Point Someone,* a fictional account of life at an IIT campus, and *One Night @ the Call Center,* a story about the work pressures in the life of call-center employees. Both books have been picked up by Mumbai's big filmmakers as film scripts, which are also being written by Chetan. "This might become a career option," he says, especially after the release of his third book about cricket fanaticism in the country.

Interestingly, Chetan credits his literary achievements—and hence his wish to change professions—to the rise of the NMC. Analyzing the success of his books, he says:

> Ten years ago, no one would have read my first book, which was based on middle-class frustrations and aspirations. It worked only in 2004, when the values of this class changed. They don't feel inferior to their western counterparts. They take pride in being Indians, and they want

to read simple and interesting things about people like themselves. The second one worked because there are hundreds of thousands of young people who are employed with call centers, and a similar number who wish to join. But their travails and troubles haven't been highlighted in the BPO hype, which bases the future prosperity of the country on its competitive edge in the outsourcing sector.[9]

Within specific jobs, too, the NMC is prone to do things differently.

A senior corporate communications manager, who wishes to remain anonymous, tells of her experiences as a crisis management expert. When her company's franchisees in Nepal were imprisoned, someone had to track the legal developments and find out what was happening there. She volunteered to go, sneaked in and out of the country, stayed at nondescript hotels and moved from one to another every now and then, never revealed her name in public, and visited the jail regularly to talk and smuggle food to the franchisees. She did all this despite the fear of being arrested.

If this were not enough, she also went to northern Sri Lanka, which was, and still is, under the control of the Liberation Tigers of Tamil Eelam (LTTE), a group that has been fighting the government for a separate homeland for Tamils in the country's northeastern province. Despite the dangers (the area witnesses regular battles and outbreaks of violence), she met a few customers who were facing trouble. They told her that LTTE members were waiting outside the building, and warned her that there could be trouble. She immediately fled through the back door, and drove through the night to reach Colombo, the capital. It was dangerous as the highway had been laid with landmines by the separatist group, but she managed to reach her destination safely.

"I had no stakes. I wanted to prove myself. Somehow I thought that nothing would happen to me. Maybe if I were married and/or had kids, I wouldn't have done it," she explains. Years later, she is still employed with the same organization, and travels to difficult areas to handle crises. She is still single (although engaged) and has no children.

The willingness to take risks and a fierce sense of independence are not confined only to the workplace. The desire to chart one's own path is also found in the personal lives of this middle class. In India, a conservative nation when it comes to marriage, there are thousands of women who either have not married (even though they are in their late 30s and early 40s) or who are separated or divorced and living alone with their children.

One such remarkable woman is Anisa Begum, a woman in her mid-40s. She has been separated twice, cheated by both her husbands. She has four children. She has suffered various setbacks and hardships but has clawed her way back to re-emerge as a good mother and a successful entrepreneur. Although she is not technically a member of the NMC, Anisa Begum's story is important because she wants to be a part of this middle class, and her adult children already are members of this generation of consumers.

Anisa Begum was married at 16. Soon after, her husband ran away to Pakistan. He divorced her when she was 21. "That was the first time I stepped out of the house without a *burqa*," she recalls, sitting in her two-room house in Batla Chowk, near Delhi's Jamia Millia Islamia university.[10] A year later, she set up a small embroidery unit at her house, supplied garments to an export house, did a course in poultry farming, and became a minority partner in a poultry farm in a village near Noida, in the neighboring state of Uttar Pradesh. She learned on the job, as she did not study beyond the ninth standard. Years later, she decided to marry again. "That was the worst decision of my life. My second husband was unemployed and forbade me to work too," Anisa Begum says. But when they ran out of money, she defied his wishes and began working again because, she says, "my children's education was at stake."

Anisa Begum hails from a family of *hakims* (traditional healers who prescribe natural medicines and remedies), and it seemed natural for her to get into the business of herbal products. Business picked up. She caught the attention of government officials who asked her to participate in an exhibition, where her products sold out. She was referred to the Bharatiya Yuva Shakti Trust, run by India's premier business association, the Confederation of Indian Industry (CII). Anisa received an aid of Rs 50,000 (US$1,250) and used the money to set up a factory in Okhla, an area in Delhi. In 1996, she won the J.R.D. Tata Award for Best Entrepreneur.

Life seemed good, but who can fight fate? Anisa Begum's factory was gutted in a fire. She alleges that her jealous husband destroyed the evidence required to claim Rs 3 lakh (US$7,500) in insurance compensation. "I found the strength to fight back and divorced my second husband," she says. She managed to secure a claim of Rs 85,000 (US$2,125) and used the money to start all over again. She built a new factory in Bawana, in the neighboring state of Haryana. "My eldest son runs a restaurant in Japan and my other son wishes to become a software professional. Only the two daughters are interested in the business," she says. As the muezzin from a mosque calls out for the evening prayers, she adds, "I want to sell my products in big malls."

It is not surprising that the lives of the NMC seem to converge at the malls, or in pubs and entertainment centers. But does this observation hold true in all cases? Not really. Even within this middle class, spending patterns can be diverse. Even those who spend lavishly on personal consumption can be frugal and conservative in other areas. This may seem an odd observation. Are they not spenders? Do they not spend on themselves? Do they not hanker after branded products? The answers to these questions are not straightforward, nor black or white. The answers are complex, in varying shades of grey. Consumption, even among the NMC, is fairly nuanced, something that escapes the notice of most experts.

The first, and most important, fact is that the NMC saves as well. Most people, even those who seem to be on a buying binge, save 30–50 percent of their monthly salaries. The reasons are not hard to guess. Whether they are DINKs or DISKs, their combined disposable incomes are so high that they still manage to make short-term and long-term investments. More importantly, they have little option but to save in order to get relief from the income tax burden, since the highest individual income tax rates are more than 30 percent. Even if they are single, they are able to save because, unlike the previous generation, they generally do not have to take care of parents or children or the extended family. Single men and women generally do not have any other financial responsibilities.

Second, apart from personal consumption, many middle-class people invest in assets like residential or commercial property.

They consider even cars and consumer durables as assets. In a sense, such investments turn out to be savings and the mortgages they pay act as tax breaks. Most people say that real estate (an apartment or a house) is one of the first things they buy.

This is true of software professionals in Bangalore, which is home to more than 300,000 of them. A 2006 study found that the difference between them and their parents was that at a very early age, most of them "already own, or were planning to purchase, flats or plots of land, whereas their parents could afford to do so only close to retirement age."[11] In the study sample, 42 percent already owned an apartment, or a house, or a plot, while another 21 percent were planning to buy one of these. According to this study:

> The ability to achieve this conventional middle class goal early in life, which their fathers could do only after working for many years, is for them an important marker of generational difference and progress. But while the ability to invest in property and save money at a young age marks this generation off from the previous one, it is significant that the goals themselves have not changed (own your own house, plan for economic security, and invest in whatever is required for [the] family's security and upward mobility, such as children's education). ... Their orientation to consumption and life planning remains much the same.[12]

The study highlights how software engineers compare themselves with their BPO or call-center colleagues:

> Interestingly, even 26-year-old software engineers and 30-year-old managers regard 20-year-old call-center workers as a different generation: they are the "cable TV generation," who grew up being exposed to the new consumer culture available on satellite TV and whom they see as individualistic and excessively fashion conscious. The BPO crowd is said to have imbibed new norms of sexuality and American culture, they earn easily and spend freely, and "they do not know the value of the basic struggle of life," as one informant puts it.[13]

Software engineers feel they are different. They regard themselves as responsible consumers "who plan for the future, save and invest money wisely, buy their own houses as soon as possible, and take responsibility for the financial security of their families." Therefore, "the culture of the 'new' middle class is in many ways continuous with that of the old."

Another way of looking at this paradox is to analyze the social and moral values of the NMC and compare these to those of the previous generations. One finds that there are no overriding and uniform trends that differentiate these generations. Some sections of the Spenderati are Westernized, or, as Pavan K. Varma, author of *The Great Indian Middle Class*, describes it, "morally rudderless ... and socially insensitive to the point of being unconcerned with anything but its own self-interest."[14]

Nevertheless, huge segments of this class are still rooted to the so-called traditional Indian values. The Upadhya and Vasavi study of software professionals, who are clearly the public face of the NMC, brings this out:

> Despite tremendous changes in lifestyle and socioeconomic status, software engineers interviewed were almost unanimous in asserting that these changes have not altered their "essential values and culture". ... Reproducing a strong tradition within Indian middle class culture, these young professionals profess devotion to the family, including caring for the older generation, and stress the importance of maintaining their culture and values through the medium of the family.[15]

There seems to be some subjective truth in the fact that there is a perceptible shift toward the joint family rather than the nuclear family, but in a new avatar. Traditionally, the joint family was the dominant social arrangement in Indian society (and still is in many areas), something that one could not escape. The joint family weakened in the twentieth century for a variety of reasons and the nuclear family grew increasingly common, at least in urban areas. Now family members are being forced to come together under one roof once again because of certain external factors. With both husbands and wives working long hours under extreme pressure, and with shifts that are structured to meet the demands of global time zones (especially in BPO, software, and financial services), parents have little time or energy for their children.

Many working couples invite their parents essentially to look after their children, but give the excuse that they wish to take care of their aging parents. According to the Upadhya and Vasavi study:

> This has emerged as a pattern within the transnationalized Indian middle class, where it is common for aged parents to circulate among their several married children living in India, the U.S. and elsewhere, often in order to take over childcare duties from other sets of parents. As a result, grandparents experience a second round of parenting. These reconstituted 'joint families' do not represent adherence to the traditional joint family so much as a convenient solution to the domestic problems of working couples. ... Far from liberating employees or leading to individualization at a personal level, IT appears to be shoring up family structures ...[16]

To be fair, the system does help retired parents and acts as a defense mechanism against loneliness and physical ailments that come with old age. It is also true that in many cases the children genuinely want to take care of their parents. In my own family, for example, my parents used to spend a few months every year in the United States with my married younger brother, who has no children, and in Delhi with my married elder sister, who has two. The frequency of my parents' visits to their children has lessened because they find the travel far too grueling. They are now happy to spend time at their own home in Vishakhapatnam (in Andhra Pradesh).

In India, there is indeed a growing class that is consumption driven and that is gaining both economic and political clout. But although its numbers are increasing, it is still a small component of the 250–350 million-strong middle class. It is important to recognize that the NMC (or the elite middle class, or the Spendarati, or Gen-S, or the Great Indian Middle Class) is divided into many different segments. Within this NMC, there are variations in mindset, thinking, and behavior. Many of its members spend, but only on building assets like real estate. A number of them are savers in the conventional sense; they save 30–50 percent of their monthly salary. More importantly, a huge majority is still rooted in traditional Indian values. This comes out clearly in the way software engineers regard and talk about call-center employees.

Given the segmentation of the NMC, one may well imagine the diversity of the other components of the Great Indian Middle Class.

Endnotes

1. Alam Srinivas, Arindam Mukheree et al., "Car, Caviar, and a 4-Br," *Outlook*, October 30, 2006, http://www.outlookindia.com/fullprint.asp?choice=1&fodname=20061030&fname=Spendarati+%28F%29&sid=1
2. ibid.
3. ibid.
4. National Council for Applied Economic Research (NCAER) in association with *Business Standard*, "The Great Indian Market: Results from the NCAER's Market Information Survey of Households," August 9, 2005, http://www.ncaer.org/downloads/PPT/TheGreatIndianMarket.pdf
5. American Express, *Inside the Affluent Space: Changing Lifestyle Expectations of the Affluent in India*, 2006.
6. Interview with the author, 2007.
7. ibid.
8. London Business School and Babson College, *Sixth Annual Global Entrepreneurship Monitor*, 2004.
9. Interview with the author, 2006.
10. Srinivas, Mukheree et al., op. cit.
11. Carol Upadhya and A.R. Vasavi, *Work, Culture and Sociality in the Indian IT Industry*, National Institute of Advanced Study, August 2006, p. 105.
12. ibid., p. 106.
13. ibid., p. 106 (footnotes).
14. Pavan K. Varma, *The Great Indian Middle Class*, (Delhi: 1st ed. Penguin Books, 1998).
15. Upadhya and Vasavi, op. cit., p. 109.
16. ibid., p. 110.

Chapter 2

The Other Middle Classes

The Other Middle Classes (OMCs) form the outer and larger layer of the Neo Middle Class (NMC) nucleus. The OMCs are fragmented along the lines of class, caste, region, religion, and culture. They have different historical beginnings, and their growth and evolution took different paths. They think and behave differently from each other. They have different consumption patterns, spending habits, and living standards.

As two macro entities, the OMCs and the NMC broadly represent two sides of the middle-class coin in India. The "head" represents a class that is bubbling with enthusiasm and energy. It is filled with a sense of adventure as it seeks to reach new economic heights. In contrast, the "tail," which is much longer than the head, is fearful and anxious of what the future might bring. For each step that it takes forward, it takes three steps back.

Located between these two broad classes are people who are aware of the growing opportunities now available in India, but are insecure and apprehensive about their future. They are a combination of Jekyll and Hyde, and are caught between the past and the present. Like double-faced Januses, they grapple with many contradictions. There are no full stops in the continuing journey of the Great Indian Middle Class.

Although there are many differences between the NMC and the OMCs, there is also a dynamic interaction between the two. In their aspirations, they share certain similarities, but when it comes to the manner in which they think, behave, and spend, there are many more dissimilarities. One may find an OMC who looks like an NMC, or vice versa. Or one may find shades of the NMC in an OMC, or vice versa. The Great Indian Middle Class is a chameleon-like creature exhibiting many shades, a singular entity in some ways, yet often resembling other creatures. It all depends on when, where, and how we define this class.

If we go back to the beginnings of the modern Indian middle class, to the pre-independence period, we can witness the interplay between power, money, and merit that led to the emergence and evolution of this class. This is true of Western nations too, but what complicated the process in India was the impact of social factors such as caste, class, and religion. In addition, political, economic, and social policy decisions affected many segments of the middle class in the post-independence period. Each social class and group developed with its own unique traits. Hence, the various sections of the Indian middle class (largely Hindu) were not characterized by any sort of overriding uniformity or commonality.

Viewed from an economic lens, India has several middle classes. There is one each in the bureaucracy (at the center and state levels), the Indian Railways (which is often described as the world's largest employer), the public sector (hailed by Jawaharlal Nehru as the "temples of modern India"), the defense forces (which grew rapidly as a result of India's wars with its neighbors China and Pakistan, in addition to civil wars in Kashmir and the northeastern states), and the private sector. Not to forget the millions of self-employed people (comprising 45 percent of the total labor force of more than 400 million) and the crop of new young entrepreneurs.

Similarly, seen from the political and social perspectives, the middle class has several segments. We can see the middle-class traits in sections of the upper-caste Hindus (Brahmins, or the intellectual or scholarly caste in the caste hierarchy, who traditionally enjoyed power, money, and merit), the backward classes, which have gained economic power largely for political reasons in the northern states (Uttar Pradesh and Bihar) and in the southern states (Andhra Pradesh, Tamil Nadu, and Karnataka), and the Dalits (formerly the Untouchables or outcasts, who had no social standing in the traditional caste hierarchy but who have rebounded to grab political power in recent times). Certain sections of all these classes and castes have experienced upward social mobility largely due to better education and affirmative action.

It is not easy to club these different constituents of the Indian middle class together. All of them act, feel, think, and behave differently. Nevertheless, they share two characteristics in common—their rising economic prosperity and their increasing power in the social, political, and intellectual arena.

For centuries, the Brahmins enjoyed behind-the-scenes political power because of their monopoly over education and intellectual and scholarly pursuits. Under the caste system, they enjoyed the privilege of reading and writing, so they were in a position to exploit the opportunities that opened up when the British set foot in India in the early seventeenth century, when the East India Company signed a commercial treaty with the Mughal emperor, Jehangir.

After the shock and upheaval of the Mutiny of 1857 (or the first war of independence, as some nationalist Indian historians prefer to call this event), the East India Company was dissolved in 1858 and India was brought under the direct rule of the British Crown. The British strengthened their political hold over India in the post-Mutiny period. In a sense, this marked the beginning of the British Raj. (Some historians trace the origins a century earlier, to the British victory in the Battle of Plassey in 1757.)

The immediate concerns of the new rulers were twofold and interrelated: first, to seek the help of the local people in governing the large country, and, second, to achieve this objective, to think of a strategy to impart English education to them.

Thinking along these lines had emerged two decades earlier. In 1835, Thomas Babington Macaulay, the first Law Member of the Governor-General's Council, wrote his famous "Minute on Indian Education," which stated:

> It is impossible for us, with our limited means, to attempt to educate the body of the people. We must at present do our best to form a class who may be interpreters between us and the millions whom we govern; a class of persons, Indian in blood and color, but English in taste, in opinions, in morals, and in intellect. To that class we may leave it to refine the vernacular dialects of the country, to enrich those dialects with terms of science borrowed from the Western nomenclature, and to render them by degrees fit vehicles for conveying knowledge to the great mass of the population."[1]

But, as is usual in bureaucratic circles, the minor objectives delineated in the minute were subservient to a larger and long-term game plan. For Macaulay, the bigger idea was to transform a "barbarous" society, that is, India, into a modern one in the image of Britain. He wrote:

> History furnishes several analogous cases, and they all teach the same lesson. There are in modern times, to go no further, two memorable instances of a great impulse given to the mind of a whole society, of prejudice overthrown, of knowledge diffused, of taste purified, of arts and sciences planted in countries which had recently been ignorant and barbarous.[2]

Macaulay wanted the same thing to happen in India, and the only "remedy was to teach the Indians English and through that to open their minds to modern, western learning." However, several historians now argue that the aims of British administrators were more complicated that this; they also intended to do good for Indian society, to make it "civilized," to propagate Christianity, and, last but not the least, to form a core group of Indians who would help the ruling class in the tasks of governance and administration. Or else why would the British want to form, in Macaulay's words, "a class of persons, Indian in blood and color, but English in taste, in opinions, in morals, and in intellect"?

But there was another reason for the British to demand the propagation of European language and literature and Western ideas and science among the natives of India. Sir Charles Trevelyan, a British civil servant who was also the governor of Madras Province, in his 1838 tract, "On the Education of the People of India," wrote:

> The existing connection between two such distant countries as England and India cannot, in the nature of things, be permanent; no effort of policy can prevent the natives from ultimately regaining their independence.[3]

What Trevelyan sought was a solution that would prolong British rule for as long as possible. That, according to him, lay through the medium of "reforms," as opposed to "revolution." As he explains the logic in his tract:

The only means at our disposal for ... securing the other class of results is to set the natives on a process of European improvement, to which they (Indians) are already sufficiently inclined. They will then cease to desire and aim at independence on the old Indian footing. A sudden change will then be impossible, and a long continuance of our present connection with India will even be assured to us.[4]

Whatever may have been the larger goals behind the introduction and spread of English education in India, it is clear that the British administration needed to introduce the European, or British, style of governance among the locals. Otherwise, tens of thousands of aliens in India would have absolutely no chance of controlling the millions of natives. This bitter truth became especially clear in 1857 when the British realized how woefully outnumbered they were without Indian soldiers, bureaucrats, and officials to prop up their rule.

The Brahmins, as the traditional scholarly and intellectual caste, were the first to take advantage of the spread of English-language education. Many of them became part of the British administration. Others became professionals. As legal disputes on issues like property became widespread, more Indians trained to become lawyers. Others began to work for British firms as Britain expanded its business and trade links with India. A few joined the Indian firms that had begun to spring up, largely as traders or adjuncts to their British counterparts.

Perhaps the best way to demonstrate the intellectual power of the upper caste, the mainstay of any middle class in India, is to examine the people who determined the ideology and policies of the Indian National Congress (INC), the party under which India won independence. Clearly, this had to be the party of intellectuals. Any group of Indians that sought to address or petition the British in 1885, when the INC was formed, would necessarily have to include those who had the intellectual power, or at least the appearance of possessing this advantage, to discuss and debate issues with the rulers. Such interactions had to be initiated by the educated elite, the general public could be included later to make these interactions into a pan-Indian mass movement.

According to Pavan Varma, author of *The Great Indian Middle Class*, the INC, in the beginning,

> was essentially an upper- and middle-class affair that did not seek to challenge British rule but create a forum which would facilitate a dialogue with the British on such matters as the increasing participation by members of this class in the legislative councils set up by the British Government and the progressive Indianization of the civil services and the army.[5]

Even the initial objective of the INC seems to match those of Trevelyan and Macaulay in a broad sense. If Varma is right, then the two British administrators did succeed in creating a growing class that was closer to the British than to the Indians. What could be better evidence of this development than in Nehru's own words:

> My politics had been those of my class, the bourgeoisie. Indeed, all vocal politics then were those of the middle classes, and Moderate and Extremist alike represented them and, in different keys, sought their betterment. The Moderate represented especially the handful of the upper middle class who had on the whole prospered under British rule and wanted no sudden changes, which might endanger their position and interests. They had close relations with the British Government and the big landlord class (who gave them the power in the pre-British Raj era). The Extremist also represented the lower ranks of the middle class.[6]

Even after Mahatma Gandhi returned to India from South Africa and took over the mantle of the Congress, and at least until he became the primary driving force behind the party, the Indian middle class remained resolute and fought an intellectual battle with the Britishers. Despite this, Gandhi managed to turn the Congress-led movement into a mass movement; he succeeded in ensuring the participation of other classes, including the lower classes (such as the Untouchables, renamed *Harijan*, or children of god, by Gandhi). But the policies of the Congress were still decided by the middle class, the educated minority that had largely thrived and grown because of the English-language education policy of the British.

Even in 1935, when the Congress had gained an all-India leadership, Nehru said:

Most of those who have shaped Congress policy during the last seventeen years have come from the middle classes. Liberal or Congressmen, they have come from the same class and have grown up in the same environment. Their social life and contacts and friendships have been similar, and there was little difference to begin with between the two varieties of bourgeois ideals that they professed.[7]

Ironically, this educated middle class played a major role in disseminating the nationalist message to the masses. Despite being conversant with and comfortable in English, many of its members were bilingual, and wrote and spoke fluently in their mother tongue. Many used novelistic or journalistic writings to energize the rest of the society to participate in the revolt against foreign rule. Gandhi could write in English and Gujarati. A number of pre-independence leaders from Bengal and the southern states were equally adept in their own mother tongue as well as in English. Nehru, who wrote mostly in English, was probably an exception to this predominance of bilingualism among Indian leaders.

Still, it is clear that education (merit) and social power—stemming from these leaders' upper-caste backgrounds—were responsible for the important and critical role played by this middle-class elite in the struggle for independence. Gandhi, the astute politician that he was, worked within the framework of this middle-class dominance in the Congress Party. But he realized that for the national movement to be successful, it had to attract the other classes too, which he did through mass campaigns like the Civil Disobedience movement and the Salt March. So while the middle class remained in control, Gandhi gave the masses the hope that they would be involved in the nation-building process, at least in the post-independence period.

But that did not happen.

The middle class set the immediate post-independence agenda. One of the crucial items on this agenda was the continuing, indeed increasing, focus on merit and education. But, wittingly or unwittingly, instead of concentrating on primary and secondary education, higher education was given importance.

There are two basic reasons this happened. First, the educated, urban, middle-class elite knew that the spread of higher education was crucial for its own survival and progress. Since it already had access to primary and secondary education because of historical reasons, it needed more engineering and medical colleges to prosper. So it was purely from a caste and class perspective that this decision was implemented.

Supporters of the decision, however, contend that it was taken in the "national" interest. An independent India needed many more engineers, doctors, scientists, and lawyers to ensure the country's future growth. India had to free herself of colonial shackles and be independent both politically and economically; social progress would follow automatically (although several policies were initiated on paper for the social upliftment of the backward classes and Dalits).

Perhaps a combination of these factors was at work at that time. As it happened, higher education became one of the ways for India to achieve the goals enshrined in the Constitution and become a truly democratic, socialist republic. The new government started setting up new universities and institutes across the country.

One of the most important areas at which policy makers looked was engineering. Nehru and others like him believed that rapid, consistent, and robust economic growth would come from hundreds of public sector units. For that to happen, India had to produce thousands of quality engineers every year.

In 1951, my father joined the Benares Engineering College because it was believed to be a sure-shot way of getting a good job. He reminisces:

> At that time, there were only two or three excellent colleges. There was one in Benares and another one in Guindy, which, incidentally, is one of the oldest engineering colleges, set up way back in 1794. Everyone was talking about becoming an engineer; and parents wanted the same for their sons.

Although my father joined the private sector, many of the new engineers sought employment in public sector enterprises, hailed as the commanding heights of the economy.

Any analysis of the rise and evolution of the middle class in India has to factor in the role of the state-owned public sector, as well as the impact of government policies that forced the private sector to set up factories in backward areas.

While Nehru grappled with new economic thinking (which for him had actually started decades before India's independence), he also fought against entrenched ideologies, battled powerful Congressmen, and took on his political critics, while he also sought to clear the confusion in his own mind. Before India gained freedom, Nehru did not know what he wanted; neither could anyone safely predict India's economic future.

It seems clear that Nehru was envisioning some form of economic socialism. In May 1936, he had noted the existence of an intense discussion and ongoing conflict in the world between the votaries of capitalism and socialism.

> Out of these two groups, I have no doubt that our country will side with that group which stands for independence and socialism. If there is any country in the world which stands most in need of this ... it is our own poverty-stricken country, where unemployment prevails.[8]

In the 1930s and 1940s, Nehru concretized his ideas about economic planning, rapid industrialization (especially in the areas of basic and heavy industries like capital goods, and raw materials like steel), greater public expenditure, the role of the state in guiding private and public investment in the right direction, and the adoption of science and technology to benefit the masses.

But there were many who opposed Nehru's vision. The foremost among these critics was Gandhi, whose belief in agriculture, *khadi*, and village industry clashed directly with Nehru's ideas. Gandhi openly challenged the views of his heir apparent. In a speech, Gandhi said, "Jawaharlal considers all property to be state-owned. He wants [a] planned economy. He wants to reconstruct India according to plan. He likes to fly; I don't."[9]

As late as 1945, according to journalist–author M.J. Akbar, the mentor and his disciple were arguing about the importance of the village in Indian life. In a letter to Nehru, Gandhi explained why he was convinced that "if India is to attain true freedom ... then sooner or later the fact must be recognized that people will have to live in villages, not in towns; in huts, not in palaces."[10] Nehru, who believed in an urban, modern India, responded emphatically: "A village, normally speaking, is backward intellectually and culturally and no progress can be made from a backward environment. Narrow-minded people are much more likely to be untruthful and violent."[11]

Nehru, who became India's first prime minister, had to succumb to pressure from the private sector lobby through its biggest supporter, Sardar Vallabhbhai Patel, India's first home minister. Patel was pro-business and pro-private sector, and believed in a minimal role of the state in policy making and in select sensitive sectors. Patel's influence can be seen at each stage of economic policy making in the 1940s, whether as a part of the Congress Party's agenda or as free India's industrial policy.

In 1938, the National Planning Committee, with Nehru as its chairman, did show its bias towards big industries and the role of the state, but it also talked of "encouraging cottage industries." It did not put forward any large-scale investment program for the public sector and stated that adequate compensation would be paid in case a private entity was taken over by the government. It seemed that Nehru was bowing to the demands of the private sector lobby.

Similarly, the first Industrial Policy Resolution (1948) established state monopoly over sensitive areas such as defense, atomic energy, and railways, but it only "reserved rights over any new enterprise" in other basic areas such as coal, steel, minerals, communications, and aircraft. But the resolution, writes Akbar, "assured business houses that there would be no nationalization, and that foreign firms could continue in India."

In 1948, Indian private businessmen were sure that the government was not in a position to spend huge sums to set up basic industries. So if the private firms continued their operations efficiently, they could monopolize most sectors. Second, the private sector lobby wanted controls imposed on foreign entities, hoping that these barriers would frustrate foreign companies, which would then sell their operations and leave the country. Who would be in a position to buy these foreign firms but the Indians? Finally, they were happy with Nehru's focus on basic industries like steel and coal; this left enough scope for private business monopolies in the more lucrative and profitable consumer industries like textiles and cars.

Nehru, of course, had his critics. True socialists such as Jayaprakash Narayan complained that Nehru had become a puppet in the hands of the capitalists. In December 1948, he told Nehru, "You want to build socialism with the help of capitalism. You are bound to fail in that."

Describing these ideological tensions, Sunil Khilnani writes that Indian businessmen "saw India's future progress as driven by the further expansion of the textile and consumer industries (as opposed to basic sectors) already flourishing in cities like Bombay and Ahmedabad."[12] The technocrats did believe in planning, but they wanted the task to be "entrusted to a central intellectual brain, an economic council of expert economists and businessmen that would coordinate and direct policy for the whole of Indian society."[13] The Left wished industrial policy to be "redistributive," that is, to redistribute the wealth in agriculture and industry.

It was Gandhi's death in 1948 and Patel's in 1950 that enabled Nehru to translate his vision into reality. It started with the First Five-Year Plan (1951–56), but Nehru could not do much as he had to struggle with critical problems like ensuring the country's self-sufficiency in food grain production. Morally compelled to keep in mind Gandhian views, Nehru focused on agriculture, poverty alleviation, and, to some extent, village industries in his first plan. Because Patel was also involved in the formulation of the plan document before his death, Nehru did not have the courage or opportunity to give importance to the public sector.

But the change in direction was clearly evident in the Second Five-Year Plan (1956–61). It laid down the real foundations of a new state-controlled economy for the first time in Indian history. As Akbar describes it:

> The Second Five-Year Plan would be far grander, more Nehruvian ... As a first step, Nehru ... turned the Planning Commission into something far more than just a high-status advisory body ... Planning became largely a Nehru-run show. No chief minister (or legislative heads of the various states) dared interfere with this Prime Minister's pet passion.[14]

Nehru asked Prasanta Chandra Mahalanobis, a physicist by training and the head of the Indian Statistical Institute, to translate his vision on paper. The physicist–statistician used his talents to do just that; he put forward a mathematical planning model. Lord Meghnad Desai, a development economist, explains the Mahalanobis model:

> The basic idea was that the economy is comprised of sectors. The sectors feed into each other, and you have a pivotal sector, let's say steelmaking. The amount of steel determines how much machinery for

consumer goods you're going to have, and so on and so forth. So if you concentrate on steel production, put all your money there, then that will regulate the rate of growth in the rest of the economy. You can lay it all down mathematically.[15]

On that basis began decades of planning, whereby the private sector was slowly but surely relegated to the back burner. The state, the public sector, public investment, and the basic core sectors became paramount. This shift in focus led to the establishment of hundreds of government-owned entities at both the central and state levels.

A unique middle class emerged in India over the next few decades. The growth of this middle class was the result of the rapid development of the public sector; the transformation of state-owned firms into instruments for providing employment, contractual, and other favors; lobbying by politicians for the setting up of new units in their constituencies, states, and regions; and the establishment of factories and plants in largely backward areas to provide employment and economic opportunities to the poor and the marginalized.

Most of the middle class working in public sector units resided in self-contained industrial townships, large units set up in the middle of nowhere, with their own residential complexes, schools, and hospitals, and with their own basic amenities, such as water, power, markets, and entertainment centers. Dozens of such townships were established in various parts of the country between 1950 and 1990, and became the new centers of a resurgent, modern India.

The same thing happened in the private sector. Political forces pushed it to set up factories in backward areas between the 1970s and 1990s. In turn, private firms were forced to build townships to woo skilled workers to their factories. These became islands of prosperity and privilege and contributed to the growth of the middle class.

My father was one of the thousands who lived in these townships. Obviously, in those days, they were less grand and smaller. The new townships of today are spread over thousands of acres, possess many modern amenities, and offer a lifestyle that can almost match that of a metro or a Class I city.

What aided my father, and millions of others like him, to seek employment in either the public or the private sector was the determination of policymakers in independent India to propagate higher education, as had been done by their British predecessors. In the post-independence period, Indian middle-class policymakers took this goal forward by striving to build institutes of excellence. Other political forces led to the adoption of reservation in higher education. These steps helped more people from different classes and castes to become professionals. The first of the so-called meritocratic institutes, or those where only intellectual ability mattered, was inaugurated the year my father joined Benares Engineering College. It was called the Indian Institute of Technology (IIT).

The IITs epitomize India's excellence in higher education, specifically in science and engineering. They have spawned global corporate leaders, visionary policymakers, and committed social changemakers. More importantly, they have created a culture and mindset of academic excellence that has been recognized across the world. Along with the IIMs (Indian Institutes of Management), the IITs have been responsible to a great extent for the expansion of the Great Indian Middle Class. The IITs have produced nearly 150,000 graduates, 40 percent of whom are scattered around the globe. They symbolize the efficacy of India's education policy, first formulated in 1947.

Sandipan Deb, an IIT graduate himself and group editor for RPG Enterprises' media venture, traces the history of the first IIT at Kharagpur (in West Bengal) in his book, *The IITians*. According to Deb, the common perception that the setting up of the IITs was Nehru's idea is incorrect. Nehru was only a "facilitator of the IIT dream, and he deserves great credit for recognizing a good idea and backing it to the hilt."[16] Setting up the IITs was really the brainchild of Ardeshir Dalal, an aristocratic Parsi technocrat, who was part of the country's cabinet-in-waiting during the transfer of power by Britain to India. According to Deb, Nehru's strategy for ensuring India's scientific and technological advancement was three-pronged: to produce world-class engineers; to set up a robust research infrastructure; and to create a system of scholarships so that deserving students could avail of the best postgraduate education in the world. The IITs represented the first prong of this ambitious plan.

India pursued the other two prongs too, which contributed to the growth of other sections of the middle class.

In March 1946, the Nalini Ranjan Sarkar Committee, in its interim report, recommended the setting up of four IITs, with the first one to be established in the east, in or near Calcutta (now Kolkata). Many sensed a "Bengali conspiracy" was at work behind the committee's recommendations. P.V. Indirasen, a former director of IIT Madras (now Chennai), explains:

> Sarkar was a Bengali, and many of the members of the committee were Bengali. Sarkar was also a close friend of B.C. Roy, who was Bengal's most powerful politician. And Roy was a go-getter. The moment the Sarkar committee submitted the report, Roy went to Nehru and said: I am willing to give the land, so let's have the first Indian Institute of Technology in Bengal.[17]

That is how and why the IITs were born.

Sixty years later, the details of the birth have become inconsequential. What is important is that institutes like the IITs, and the scores of engineering and medical colleges and professional and vocational institutes that have sprung up almost everywhere in India, have become a major factor in the emergence of one segment of the Indian middle class. Access to higher education has brought about increased access to better-paying and more prestigious jobs. Over the decades, the alumni of these institutions have come to be recognized for their skills and prowess. Thousands of professionals, many of whom have made their name and fortune in the US, are a critical part of the global economic village. As their economic and social stature grew, they became an integral part of the consumption-oriented middle class.

In the 1990s, the IITians finally arrived in Silicon Valley, California, and made their mark with their entrepreneurial ability, brilliance, and strategic vision. They took over senior positions in dozens of Fortune 500 companies, and their startups sold for mind-boggling sums. As the world recognized their talent and skills, they helped fulfill India's greatest middle-class dreams. First, says Deb, the IITians proved what the salaried middle class had always believed: "The only way ... that its children could get a fair chance to earn an honest living was to excel academically, do so well in their examinations that the 'pull' did not matter."[18] Second, many of the IITians went to the US, fulfilling another fantasy of the middle class. Deb writes, "The 1990s proved that the IIT system had delivered on nearly every promise it had made or implied. And there was no one left to doubt any more that 'IIT' was the biggest and the most powerful brand independent India had been able to create."[19]

However, it should be noted that recently a debate has raged over whether the IITs are indeed creating intellectually brilliant students. Some critics believe that the IITs are merely churning out intelligent robots, especially given the fact that almost 95 percent of the entrants attend coaching classes to get through the rigorous entrance examinations. Many corporations have expressed apprehensions about recruiting IIT graduates.

Whatever may be the extent of the supposed decline in academic standards, the IITs and other institutes of higher education have, nevertheless, successfully created one of the most powerful segments of the Great Indian Middle Class. We may call this elite group, empowered by elite education, the Forward Middle Class. It has become part of the NMC.

Simultaneously, members of an educated but non-elite sections were quietly joining the middle class. They, too, were the product of the focus on higher education in both pre- and post-independent India. This led to upward social mobility of the backward castes and Dalits, traditionally consigned to the lowest strata of Hindu caste society. Although their castes remained unchanged, education enabled them to join the "economic" middle class. Today, most of them are clearly a part of the middle class.

The English-language education introduced by the British brought about long-term social changes in India. The transformation was slow and the results were manifested over several decades. In the end, this education empowered the backward classes. It also helped in the formation of another category of the middle class, which we may call the Backward Middle Class (BMC), with several subsets based on caste, region, and language. Let us see how this happened.

Thanks to the efforts of British missionaries and administrators, several princely states in India opted for reservation for backward classes in schools and colleges. (In the post-independence period, the missionaries continued with their multipronged efforts to change traditional class and caste hierarchies.) Through education and conversion, they opened windows of opportunity for the backward classes and lower castes to improve their economic and social conditions.

In 1831, the Madras Presidency (most of which is now part of present-day Tamil Nadu, a state in south India) adopted reservation in education in response to petitions from several public groups. Travancore, Kochi, Mysore, and other princely states in south India followed suit. After 1947, the southern states emerged as the "reservation" leaders, especially in the area of higher education. Social groups urged, pressurized, and forced successive governments in these states to reserve higher percentages of seats in colleges and professional institutes for the backward classes and the Dalits. Eventually, reservation became an integral part of social life in Tamil Nadu, Karnataka, and Kerala. By the early 1990s, in Tamil Nadu, 69 percent of seats were reserved, and in Andhra Pradesh and Karnataka the figures were somewhat similar.

As Ravivarma Kumar, former chairman of the Karnataka State Commission for Backward Classes, observes, "Children in Karnataka are taught from the very beginning that reservation is very much part of the social justice system, so they learn to live with it."[20]

Education spread among all classes in south India for other reasons too. Due to historical and cultural factors, private education grew rapidly in south India. South Indians have always accorded great importance to academic and intellectual achievement. In the 1980s and 1990s, the burgeoning demand from students and their parents for engineering and medical colleges led to a mushrooming of such institutes.

This growth in private education is seen most clearly in Karnataka. As the state's various chief ministers were forced to sanction the establishment of more professional colleges to meet the demands of caste lobbies and to protect the vote banks of their respective parties, 45 engineering and 6 medical colleges were sanctioned in 2001 alone.

Powerful local politicians, realizing that there was money to be made in the education business, quickly became either owners or trustees of these professional colleges. During the tenure of S.M. Krishna as the chief minister (1999–2004), this was evident from the answer to a question raised in the state assembly. When Prafulla Madhukar, a legislator, asked how many of the newly sanctioned colleges were owned by politicians, the state government replied that 27 of the state-recognized colleges belonged to politicians. Of these, about a dozen were owned by the state ministers then in power (one of them even named a college after himself), 3 by members of parliament belonging to the ruling party, and 2 by leaders of the state's opposition party. Due to the political–educational nexus, the number of unaided state medical and engineering colleges increased from 7 and 25, respectively, in 1984 to 28 and 120, respectively, in 2005.

Unfortunately, over the years, the education system in Karnataka became riddled with corruption (students were asked to pay money upfront for admission in addition to the officially stated fees); excessive admissions (over and above the specific limits set for each college) became widespread; and the quality of education and control deteriorated.

Ravindra Reshme, who has chronicled the recent history of professional education in the state, explains:

> The racket of excess admissions and retrospective approval had become a norm. The crisis grew as the state bypassed university bodies and the state-level cabinets started sanctioning professional colleges.[21]

The law courts stepped in to correct the dismal situation. This led to the opening of another avenue that gave students from different social backgrounds access to higher education. In one of its judgments, the Supreme Court criticized the state and provided a framework for the administration of professional colleges, including private colleges. This led to a state-controlled centralized system, which included areas such as the admission procedure, the fee structure, the sharing of seats, and a mechanism to help children from the poorer classes. A 2006 article in *Outlook* magazine described the new system that emerged as a result of the Supreme Court judgment:

> ... it led to a ... merit-cum-roster model, ensured the democratization of professional education, at least in the southern states . . . It had a centralized common entrance test (CET) and a centralized admission process, conducted by the state, and the fee structure and allocation of seats—either based on merit in the CET, caste-based reservations, or private management quotas—were decided by the state. The private sector had little role to play in the entire process ...[22]

Under the CET system, in 1993, the seat-sharing ratio between the state and private managements was fixed at 85:15, that is, 85 percent of the seats were to be allocated by the state on the basis of CET marks and the rest were to be decided by the managements. Of the 85 percent seats, half were allocated to students based on merit rankings in the CET and the rest were reserved for the Dalits (23 percent of 85 percent) and the backward classes (27 percent).

Within the merit and backward classes quotas, there was a further 10 percent reservation for students from a rural background. The idea was to enable students from varying backgrounds to seek admission. The annual fee was fixed by the state for its 85 percent seats, and the managements could charge whatever they wished from the 15 percent students they selected.

This arrangement worked for a decade. It enabled backward-class and Dalit students to gain professional degrees. Armed with these credentials, many of them joined public or private sector firms. Their earnings rose, and soon they became part of the growing middle class. The process started decades ago with the introduction of reservation; the CET only hastened the growth of these middle-class subsets. By the beginning of the twenty-first century, these caste-based segments were growing in strength and visibility.

Direct access to higher education alone would not have been a sufficient condition for the emergence of the caste-based middle class. The backward classes and the Dalits would still have found it difficult to get jobs in a society in which the upper castes had long dominated in the government and in the public and private sectors. The upper castes could have easily stymied the growth of the lower castes. But they could not do so thanks to reservation in government and public sector jobs. This benefit accrued to the Dalits immediately after independence as they were legally accorded reservation in both employment and higher education. Within a couple of generations, many of them graduated to private economic activities. Although they still find it difficult to get jobs in the private sector, where merit apparently rules, many Dalits have become small-time entrepreneurs.

The 2001 Census reveals that 2.62 million Dalits are employed in the household sector. Obviously, these are people operating out of their homes, and hence constitute self-employed individuals or families. But in many cases, they work for an organized setup. Many Dalit and others families, for example, work out of their homes for the larger matchbox manufacturers. We may assume that a sizeable proportion of these Dalits probably earn a decent income.

In addition, there are perhaps another three million Dalits employed in trade and commerce. Again, we may safely assume that many of them are probably self-employed or part-time entrepreneurs. Some may even be well off.

A similar number probably have government employment, given the 15 percent reservation for Dalits in this sector. Many of them are found in the lower grades, but some have managed to climb the bureaucratic hierarchy and are on par with their counterparts from other castes and classes. Over the past 15 years, the composition of the Indian Civil Service has changed considerably in favor of the backwards and Dalits.

The current debate about possible reservation in private sector jobs—either mandatory or voluntary—is forcing India Inc. to absorb more people from backward castes and Dalits. Indian companies have also initiated several measures to encourage entrepreneurs from such classes. For example, two top industry associations, the Confederation of Indian Industry (CII) and the Associated Chambers of Commerce and Industry of India (Assocham), have come out with a joint action plan to push their members to opt for voluntary affirmative action for Dalits. The report set fixed targets for the first year itself. These include the adoption of a uniform code of conduct, the creation of 100 Dalit entrepreneurs, and the setting up of coaching centers for 15,000 Dalit students in various universities and helping them prepare for entrance examinations for professional courses.

Various state governments, too, are keen on being a part of the Dalit entrepreneurial movement. Digvijay Singh, a former chief minister of Madhya Pradesh, a state in central India, came up with a Dalit Agenda a few years ago. It called on the state government to buy 30 percent of its annual purchases from Dalit businessmen, suppliers, and contractors. In an interview, Singh explained the rationale behind this step:

> With the shrinking of employment opportunities in the government
> sector, other opportunities of employment will have to be created for
> Dalits in the non-government or private sector through programs such
> as the one we have conceived. It is a beginning . . . I hope other
> governments will follow. It is part of a series of measures taken for the
> economic empowerment of Dalits, the most important of them being
> the allotment of land to landless Dalits.[23]

Nevertheless, the Dalits are on a long road to prosperity. Experts believe that the private sector is a laggard in adopting the affirmative action agenda. Dalit activists like Chandrabhan Prasad claim that most of India Inc. regards affirmative action with disdain and is strongly opposed to it. Software czars like N.R. Narayana Murthy of Infosys have said that reservations or quotas in private sector jobs will have a negative impact on the country's competitive edge in sectors like software and business process outsourcing (BPO).

Here is an example of how well-meaning government projects fail. A February 2005 article in *The Hindu* describes the problems with a scheme launched by Tamil Nadu to encourage Dalit entrepreneurs in the textiles sector. In the mid-1990s, the state established, as a pilot project, a 40-hectare knitwear estate meant exclusively for Dalits. A hundred sheds (or factory spaces) were given to 54 beneficiaries, mostly professionals, who gave up their jobs in government and public sector enterprises. The state government helped by offering 60 percent loans, 15 percent capital investment subsidy, and another 15 percent toward share capital contribution. The Dalit promoters had to come up with only 10 percent of the estimated cost. However, a high interest burden, lack of working capital, and a poor understanding of market dynamics proved to be major obstacles. By 2005, 46 of the 100 sheds had closed down and most of the floating ones became converters (making knitted cloth from yarn) for the bigger manufacturers.

Despite such problems, there is a visible change among the Dalits. One can clearly see the political and economic empowerment of this downtrodden class in the past few decades.

While the Dalits have benefited from job reservation introduced soon after India gained independence, the backward castes had to wait for more than four decades for similar benefits. This change came about through the "Mandal effect." This was one of the major contributions of V.P. Singh, a former prime minister and a former finance minister, towards the advancement of the backward castes, whose destiny subsequently changed more quickly and more dramatically than that of the Dalits.

The Indian Constitution contains special provisions "for the advancement of any socially and educationally backward classes of citizens or for the Scheduled Castes and Tribes (or Dalits)." However, the backward castes had no reservation in government jobs. The Mandal Commission was set up in 1979 to address their demands and grievances. A year later, the commission recommended that overall reservations should be increased from 22 percent to 49.5 percent to include the backward classes, apart from the scheduled castes and the scheduled tribes, who already enjoyed this privilege.

The Mandal Commission report collected dust for a decade. When V.P. Singh became prime minister, he implemented the Mandal recommendations for government jobs. This step provoked widespread and violent protests from members of the meritocracy (which forms a part of the NMC), and the issue went to court. Not to be outdone, in 1991, the next Congress-led government introduced 10 percent reservation for the "poor" among the upper castes. In 1992, the Supreme Court upheld the Mandal reservation formula.

The consequences of this judgment were far reaching. The floodgates for jobs were opened up for the backward castes. They could think of climbing up the economic ladder, and doing so rapidly. The results of this judgment became clearly visible within a period of 15 years. There are more backward castes in positions of power today than ever before; they dictate and influence policy; they have succeeded in reducing the base of the upper castes; and they also earn more money. More importantly, they have helped their fellow caste members also to climb up the social and economic ladder.

And yes, all of them have become members of the Indian middle class.

In no country can the story of social and economic upliftment, or the tale of class mobility, be complete without an analysis of the role played by politics in bringing about socioeconomic change. Political power, either as a catalyst or as a consequence, pushes or aids the process. Social, economic, and political power go hand in hand, although there may be a lag between them. The delays vary in each society depending on which comes first. In most cases, the story is one of parallel progression, and it becomes difficult to delineate what happened first and what happened afterwards. The same is true of India.

Just as reservation in education helped the Dalits and other backward sections socially, reservation in government and public sector jobs benefited them economically. The process of political empowerment occurred either simultaneously (as in the southern states) or came later (as in some of the northern and eastern states). The result, however, was the same. Politics fast-forwarded the creation of the backward and Dalit middle class

In the last three decades of the twentieth century, political dynamics and equations in India shifted dramatically. In the last two decades of the previous century, as is the case even today, there was another revolution that brought them political and economic clout. This was the dramatic rise of caste politicians.

Caste-based politics has been a long-standing feature of the Indian polity, going back to the pre-independence period. Almost every leader has used his or her caste as a base, constituency, or launching pad to become a regional or national player. But until the 1970s, they had largely been subsumed within the political monolith of the Congress Party, which in its first phase ruled India from 1947 to 1977 without a break.

When the Congress split in 1969, and Indira Gandhi became the prime minister, these developments set off a different kind of chain reaction. Caste politicians who no longer found it useful to live under the shadow of the Congress now came out into the open to pursue their own ambitions. Many leaders who left the Congress started agitating against the ruling regime. They wooed the public with certain issues that resonated with the voters. Foremost among these leaders was Jayaprakash Narayan, or JP, the man behind a student movement that grew into a socialist movement across northern India. Scared by the growing power of this movement, and fearing legal disqualification of her own election to Parliament and hence her claim to the office of the prime minister, Indira Gandhi declared emergency rule in 1975.

In 1977, after the emergency was lifted and fresh elections were held, the Congress lost a general election for the first time since independence and the Janata Party came to power. Suddenly, regional caste leaders became kingmakers in the real sense. They were taken more seriously and they could directly influence the country's political course. They soon realized that they no longer needed to be merely bricks in the wall of any parent party. There was a realization among local leaders that the Congress was not invincible and that they could carve out their own niche at both the central and state levels. Using their base, they could become chief ministers of states or cabinet ministers in the central government. Although the Congress remained powerful in the period 1979–89, the cracks in the party were visible. It was only a matter of time before the party fractured.

V.P. Singh, a former Congressman and finance minister, revolted and came to power in 1989, riding the wave of a JP-like socialist movement with support from several regional leaders. For the second time, a non-Congress government assumed power at the national level. The stage was now set for a series of coalition governments in which regional, religious, and caste leaders would play a prominent role.

Although many leaders emerged with independent power bases in the 1980s and 1990s, one example should suffice to emphasize this point. This politician is Lalu Prasad Yadav, who ruled the state of Bihar, directly and indirectly (through his wife), for 15 years, and who is now the central cabinet minister handling the railways portfolio.

Like many Indian leaders, Yadav, who hails from the backward Yadav (cattle rearer) caste, emerged from the cauldron of campus politics. Riding the wave of V.P. Singh's popularity, and being naturally aligned to a party with a socialist base, he was elected to parliament in 1989. When a non-Congress government came to power in the state assembly elections in Bihar in 1990, Yadav manipulated his way into becoming the chief minister. It was possibly the best time for a backward to occupy that office.

Until 1990, the Congress had the winning electoral arithmetic in Bihar. By wooing the upper castes, Muslims, Dalits, and some other backward castes, the party easily garnered more than 50 percent of the votes. During the 1990 state elections, the votes of the backward classes were consolidated, while those of the upper castes were fragmented. Between July 1990 and June 1991, Yadav changed the electoral equation in Bihar in his favor. While keeping the backwards together, the new chief minister weaned the Muslim voters from the Congress, and had more than 50 percent of the overall votes on his side. So began a long reign by a backward leader, who promised to help his people and demolish the upper-caste stranglehold on the state. He thumbed his nose at established norms. This colorful politician with his rustic ways evoked laughter among the urban middle-class media.

Several critics contend that Lalu Prasad Yadav is largely responsible for Bihar's descent into a vortex of economic decline, poverty, and corruption. He faces many corruption charges, most notably his alleged involvement in a fodder scam worth millions of rupees. Nevertheless, as chief minister, Yadav did one important thing, which brought him great popularity. He was probably the one person responsible for instilling increased confidence among the backward castes and ensuring economic prosperity for at least one of them, the Yadavs, his own people.

Explaining this phenomenon, Sankarshan Thakur, a journalist, writes:

> Lucrative contracts (especially government ones), liquor licenses, casual and semi-permanent government jobs, chairmanships of (state-owned) boards and corporations, all began falling into [the] hands Laloo Yadav chose. They went to the influential among the new ruling class—to the privileged among the backwards and the Muslims.[24]

Even though the extremely backward castes and the less influential sections didn't get these economic benefits,

> they remained swayed by Laloo Yadav because he was able to instill in them a new sense of pride and participation, a sense that he was one among them and ruling on their behalf, that Laloo raj was their raj.[25]

Lalu Yadav helped his fellow caste members, and also members of other backward castes, to forcefully establish their identity in society. He helped them realize that they constituted the mainstream of society, and not its periphery, that they were socially and politically central to the system, and not tangentially. As Yadav told journalists:

> It used to be terrible to be born a Yadav, or any other caste that was not upper caste. (But) haven't I changed things for myself and my people? I am flying in this aircraft. I am eating the best chocolates in the land, I am wearing crisp white muslin, I can do what I want. I have changed things and I will change them more.[26]

Similarly, in the neighboring state of Uttar Pradesh, the rise of Mulayam Singh Yadav, who, like Lalu Prasad Yadav, also became the state chief minister several times (the two men are not related), changed the attitude and mindset of the backward castes.

From Bihar to Uttar Pradesh, from Andhra Pradesh to Karnataka, the backward castes began surging ahead politically, socially, and economically through a mix of education and political power.

They were all aiding the growth of the Great Indian Middle Class.

All these class- and caste-based middle classes have a few traits in common. Many of these sub-classes interact or integrate with others. Many OMCs have become part of the NMC; some NMC people have OMC-like values. But all of them, consciously or subconsciously, think of themselves as being part of the middle class.

However, in many ways, the various segments of the Indian middle class are quite different in the way they think and behave, buy and invest, consume and save, look at foreign and Indian brands. They are also influenced by their social upbringing, the regions in which they reside, the schools they attend, the professions they enter, and the extent to which they have become a part of the global village. In a sense, there is no one middle class in India. There are hundreds of subsets, some having commonalities with several others, which, in turn, may converge with certain other segments.

The NMC in the southern states is different from the NMC in the northern and western states. The NMC in Delhi is different from the NMC in Mumbai or Kolkata. The educated, professional elite is different from those who come from second-rung professional institutes. The software crowd is different from the BPO crowd. The backward castes in the south are different from those in the north. The upper castes in the north are different from those in the west. The Dalits are different from the backward and upper castes. The public sector employees are different from the private sector employees. The private sector workers in townships are different from those who work in cities.

But some members of the NMC belong to the backward castes. A number of backward castes are employed in the public sector because of the government's reservation policy. The software and BPO sectors employ people from all sections, such as the educated elite, graduates of second-rung colleges, people from cities and small towns, people from all parts of the country. The composition of the educated elite has changed—and will continue to change—with the government's imposition of reservation, which it now wishes to extend to top-notch higher educational institutions like the IITs and the IIMs.

The characteristics of these sections of the middle class will be analyzed in the following chapters.

Here it may be apt to describe the thinking of a few ambitious marketing people in the entertainment sector, where understanding the mindset of the consumer is critical for success.

Velu Shankar, content head of World Space Radio, which offers dozens of different satellite-based music and news channels on a single instrument, explains his dilemma. He is mainly concerned with two issues. The first is the fact that his consumers—essentially the middle and upper classes—are radically different in different cities and in different regions. Even though the NMC may have a similar mindset overall, the constituent sections of this class behave differently when it comes to entertainment and news. Each individual or subgroup has different preferences. The second issue is how to make the content model unique so that the consumer willingly pays for it. The only way to make this happen is to offer varied entertainment, so that each consumer is free to select what he or she wants.

So Velu Shankar has started collecting music of all kinds. While World Space initially focused on the main Indian languages, such as English, Hindi, Tamil, Telugu, and Malayalam, it has now started venturing into other, less frequently spoken languages like Himachali and Konkani. Within music genres, Velu is trying to digitize and acquire rights for niche music like folk songs in various languages or little-known classical styles.

According to him, when it comes to music, his consumer is becoming so fragmented that he or she behaves differently across different localities within the same city. The kind of music wanted by South Mumbai customers does not work with listeners in suburban Mumbai. Those in the New Mumbai areas are different from both. In suburban Mumbai, the consumer in Bandra likes a different kind of music from the listener in Chembur. As a friend of Velu's puts it, "The music played in Mumbai's auto rickshaws depends on the customer. An auto *wallah* is forced to play different music for residents of Bandra, Chembur, Andheri, or Vashi." Velu nods in agreement.

So World Space offerings have to be as diversified as possible. Velu spends most of his time finding and collecting little-known music. The strategy works also because as the repertoire grows, World Space can ask customers to pay for the service. A customer will invariably find at least one or two channels that will interest him or her.

If it is true that there is no one middle class in India, then why have economists, consultants, and policymakers got it wrong? The problem, it seems, lies in the manner in which one defines the Indian middle class. We explore this issue in the next chapter.

Endnotes

1. Lord Thomas Babington Macaulay, "Minute on Education", February 2, 1835, para. 31.
2. ibid., para. 14.
3. Sir Charles Edward Trevelyan, "On the Education of the People of India", Longman, Orme, Brown, Green & Longmans, 1838.
4. ibid.
5. Pavan K. Varma, *The Great Indian Middle Class*, 2nd ed., Penguin Books India, 2007 (Delhi p. 7).
6. Pavan K. Varma, *The Great Indian Middle Class*, 1st ed., Penguin Books India, 1998 (Delhi p. 8).
7. ibid., p. 16.
8. M.J. Akbar, *Nehru: The Making of India*, Lotus Collection, 2002, p. 465.
9. ibid., p. 468.

10. Gandhi's letter to Nehru, October 1, 1945.

11. Nehru's letter to Gandhi, October 9, 1945.

12. Sunil Khilnani, *The Idea of India*, Farrar, Straus and Giroux, 1997, p. 70.

13. ibid., p. 71.

14. Akbar, op. cit., p. 473.

15. Lord Meghnad Desai, interview by PBS, July 12, 2000.

16. Sandipan Deb, *The IITians: The Story of a Remarkable Institution and How its Alumni are Reshaping the World*, Penguin/Viking, p. 26.

17. ibid., p. 28.

18. ibid., p. 8.

19. ibid., p. 7.

20. Venkitesh Ramakrishna, T.S. Subramanian et al., "Southern Record," *Frontline*, April 22–May 5, 2006, http://www.thehindu.com/fline/fl2308/stories/20060505006400800.htm

21. Sugata Srinivasaraju, "Seat Taken," *Outlook*, July 17, 2006, http://www.outlookindia.com/full.asp?fodname=20060717&fname=Cover+Story&sid=10

22. ibid.

23. V. Venkatesan, "For a Billion Opportunities," *Frontline*, August 17–30, 2002, http://thehindu.com/thehindu/fline/fl1917/19171000.htm

24. Sankarshan Thakur, *The Making of Laloo Yadav: The Unmaking of Bihar*, HarperCollins, 2000, p. 104.

25. ibid., p. 105.

26. ibid., pp. 107–8.

Chapter 3

Redefining the Indian Middle Class

As I look around me and observe the people with whom I interact every day, I can figure out why there is so much hype about the middle class in India. My cook, Kiran, works in three houses and earns Rs 1,500–1,700 (US$38–43) a month. With her husband's monthly salary of Rs 5,000 (US$125), the combined household income is less than Rs 7,000 (US$175).

Kiran's family is considered part of the Indian middle class because she and her husband own a mobile phone each; these are nothing fancy but they work. The same is the case with my driver, Rakesh, who earns Rs 10,000 (US$250) a month and carries a fancy mobile phone. (Until I switched to a Nokia Communicator, his mobile was more impressive than mine.) Almost every driver hanging out in the basement parking area of my building has a mobile phone. They are also considered part of the middle class. On the way to my office, I see taxi and auto rickshaw drivers, cyclists, scooterists, hawkers, shopkeepers, users of public transport—and all of them have mobile phones.

Today, India has over 300 million people who own mobile sets. Based on this definition, and if we assume that both parents are mobile owners and if we add at least one dependent, the total middle-class population of India comes to 450 million. But since many people own two or three mobile sets, we may subtract 50 million, or nearly a tenth of the wireless users, from the total of 400 million. Even after this, the size of the Indian middle class is still estimated to be nearly 400 million.

However, this figure is misleading. When we analyze the situation—and mobile service providers will confirm this finding—we discover that most of the "mobile" population spends minimally on communication. For instance, Rakesh pays a sum of Rs 250 (US$6) a month for the mobile services he uses.

Millions of others pay as little as Rs 50 (US$1.25) a month. They use their mobiles only to receive calls, which is a free service. They don't use any other services like text messaging. Many of them, including Rakesh, buy second-hand sets or new models that cost less than Rs 2,000 (US$50).

If we look at other aspects of their standard of living, such as their homes, we realize that they are definitely not part of the consuming class.

Even those who can afford expensive phones, those who are perceived to be part of the consuming class, use their mobiles minimally. In my office, most people earn more than Rs 20,000 (US$500) a month, and their monthly mobile phone bills are Rs 1,000 (US$25) or less. One of them earns nearly Rs 50,000 (US$1,250) a month, and his bill is Rs 1,500 (about US$38). I know a senior editor who earns more than Rs 60,000 (US$1,500) a month, but does not own a mobile.

The truth about the "wireless revolution" is that most mobile phone owners spend less than 3 percent of their income on communication, a critical need in today's connected and networked world, and particularly for those employed in media organizations. The bills of the big spenders may amount to only 5 percent of their monthly income.

The figures released by the Telecom Regulatory Authority of India (TRAI) support these conclusions. In the quarter ending December 2006, the all-India blended average revenue per user (ARPU) per month in the case of GSM mobile services declined to Rs 316 (US$8) from an average of Rs 337 (US$8.4) in the previous quarter. The countrywide figure for CDMA services registered an even sharper fall during the same period, from Rs 215 to Rs 196 (from US$5.38 to US$4.90). Another insight can be gained by analyzing the ARPUs for the postpaid and prepaid segments for mobile phones running on both technologies. During the period under consideration, the monthly ARPU for postpaid GSM fell from Rs 643 to Rs 632 (from US$16.08 to $15.80), but the decline was bigger in the prepaid segment, from Rs 277 to Rs 262 (from US$6.9 to US$6.6). It is clear that within GSM, where blended ARPUs are nearer to the average for the prepaid segment, there are more prepaid subscribers, who tend to spend much less on using their mobile phones. Even in the case of CDMA subscribers, the blended ARPU of Rs 196 (US$4.90) is nearer to the average in the prepaid segment (Rs 159 or US$3.90), or less than half of the postpaid ARPU of Rs 456 (US$11.25).

Take the case of Vodafone Essar, formerly Hutchison Essar, which is grappling with the unique phenomenon of increasing minutes of use (MoU) and a growing subscriber base but lower ARPU. The number of subscribers has grown by leaps and bounds, from fewer than 10 million in Q3 2005 to more than 20 million in Q3, 2006. The growth in blended, or combined, MoU is also impressive—from 369 to 406 in the same period.

Surprisingly, the monthly ARPU has come down quite sharply, from Rs 518 to Rs 420 (from US$12.95 to US$10.5). And the difference between postpaid and prepaid ARPU is huge, Rs 1,066 and Rs 293 (US$26.65 and US$7.33), respectively, in Q3 2006. One of the reasons for the declining ARPU is the increasing number of prepaid customers, whose base jumped from just more than 7 million to more than 17 million between Q3 2005 and Q3 2006. In the case of postpaid subscribers, the increase in the same period was almost negligible, from 2.46 million to 3.24 million.

Another reason for the declining ARPU is the reduction in tariffs and allied charges by TRAI, which has lowered the burden on consumers. Outgoing call rates—local, within India, and international—have witnessed a steep fall. So even higher volumes have not made up for this loss of revenue. Indirectly, this has helped the private service providers because most of the impact of reduced charges has been borne by the state-owned Bharat Sanchar Nigam Limited (BSNL). (The sharpest cut has been in the access deficit charges that were paid by private companies to BSNL as the former used the latter's infrastructure for connectivity.)

Compare the Indian situation with that of the United States, one of the world's most mature and saturated middle classes. In the United States, the average monthly mobile charges are pre-fixed—US$30 or so with limits on talk time. Incoming calls are charged, just like outgoing calls. Although the cost of mobile phones is cheaper, the consumer's choice of instrument is limited to the service provider that he or she chooses. The customer can upgrade to a better phone—from the same service provider—at a discounted price, but only after a certain time, usually two years. In any case, the minimum monthly payment is US$30 or Rs 1,200.

In India, the monthly tariffs can be as low as Rs 50 (US$1.25). Incoming calls are free, so subscribers can get by with paying the minimum monthly rental in the case of postpaid accounts or they can use their prepaid cards of very low denominations for a minimum of six months. In case the prepaid card runs out of money, subscribers can still use the phone to receive calls until they are forced to recharge the card after six months. Or they can pay a one-time fee of Rs 495 (US$12.38) and keep receiving incoming calls for life (actually until the license of the service provider expires). The beauty of this scheme is that consumers are not hooked permanently to one particular mobile instrument. Because of the use of SIM cards, they can simply buy a new instrument and use it by inserting the SIM card from the older phone. So there is flexibility vis-à-vis usage and mobile instruments.

The third reason for low ARPUs in India is that the mobile phone is not perceived as an item of consumption; it is not even used as a product or service of consumption. For Indian consumers, the mobile is a status symbol, a means of making a socioeconomic statement. For them, it is a visible way of proving to the rest of the world that they have arrived. They just need to possess one mobile phone to send the signal; they do not have to spend too much to keep it.

This consumption pattern is similar to the trend concerning the purchase and use of the newly introduced Maruti 800 car model in the late 1980s and the early 1990s when Indians made a mad dash to buy it. The Maruti 800 (like the mobile phone today) was a status symbol. It did not matter that the car was used once in two weeks, or even less frequently. A middle-class family only had to have the car parked outside their house or apartment. In the 1980s, hundreds of cars (mostly Maruti 800s) used to be parked outside the houses in Delhi's middle-class colonies, especially in West Delhi. On most days, they were covered with a car cover. Only once a week, on a Sunday, the owner (always a man) would spend a couple of hours cleaning it, warming it, and checking whether everything was okay. On some rare Sundays, he would take his family for a drive, for shopping, for a movie, or to visit friends and relatives. On weekdays, the owner used his two-wheeler or public transport to commute to the office or for daily chores and errands. The women rarely used the car.

Compared with a car, the mobile phone is more of a lifestyle statement because the owner can flash it wherever he or she goes, unlike the Maruti 800, which was often parked at home, and driven only on rare occasions. More importantly, most mobile phone owners, at least in India, belong to a group that aspires to belong to the middle class. They are the Aspirerati.

Let us define this term. There is a growing segment of the Spenderati—and also the Seenarati and the Smootherati—who spend considerable amounts of money on mobiles. In the first chapter, we met consumers who splurge on the latest gizmos and gadgets, especially mobiles. Some of these people use their phones indiscriminately, running up huge bills. But not all mobile phone owners are like that. Most of them use the mobile phone to make a social statement related to status, aspiration, and lifestyle. This behavior does not imply the existence of a full-fledged consuming culture.

Let us now consider a few other myths related to the Indian middle class and its allegedly big-spending habits.

Another subjective parameter to signify the growing Indian middle class is the number of people in urban centers who regularly visit pubs. Hundreds hang out at Delhi's pubs every day, particularly on weekends. The pubgoers are like the people who hang out at the happening shopping centers and cinemas of the city—PVR Priya, PVR Saket, South Extension, and Greater Kailash in South Delhi, and the new malls in West Delhi. Many hop across three or four pubs in a single evening, starting around 7.00 p.m. and carrying on until the shutdown, which is any time between midnight and 5.00 a.m. (on weekends).

They have their favorite places. The most popular are Buzz (Saket and Gurgaon), Opus (Vasant Vihar), Shalom (Greater Kailash), Elevate (Noida), Climax (Lado Sarai), and Orange Room (Ashoka Hotel). A lawyer friend starts at Buzz at 7.00 p.m., hops across to Shalom at 9.00 p.m., and ends up at Elevate, which is open until 5.00 a.m. on weekends. A woman I know, who frequents Buzz, leaves only when the shutters are pulled down.

These young people obviously seem to spend a huge amount of money on their evening entertainment. But there is more to it than meets the eye. All of them manage to get discounts from these pubs, either because they already know the owners or managers or eventually get to know them, or because they are so regular that the pubs are obliged to offer discounts. The discounts can be as high as 50 percent. In addition, many of them hit the pubs just before happy hour ends (most pubs give 50 percent discount to attract customers during the nonpeak hours). They take advantage of the happy hour 50 percent discount and order enough drinks to last them for a few hours.

Consider the economics for a beer drinker in such a scenario. In the open market, a 650 ml bottle costs Rs 40 (US$1) in Delhi, and more in Gurgaon (one of Delhi's satellite towns). In a pub, the same bottle costs between Rs 120 and Rs 150 (US$3–3.75). At a 50 percent discount, the consumer pays Rs 60–75 per bottle (US$1.50–1.90), or Rs 20-35 (50–90 cents) more than the open market price. However, for a customer who used to frequent the cheaper clubs, going to these newer, hipper pubs is an attractive option. This is because most clubs in Delhi charge about Rs 60 for a bottle of beer, and by paying the same or just a little more at a pub, the customer enjoys a much better experience and ambience.

As a journalist, I can tell you why I shifted to pubs. I used to be a regular at Delhi's Press Club, where the liquor prices were the cheapest in the city a few years ago. (For some brands, it may still be inexpensive.) Today, a beer costs Rs 60 at the Press Club, the same price as at a pub during happy hour or at a place where customers can manage to get a decent discount. More importantly, while the Press Club is frequented by an older crowd who talk loudly, some younger journalists prefer pubs where they get to hear good music and meet interesting people. Almost the entire crop of young journalists, especially those who work for TV news channels, have stopped going to the Press Club. Pub managers, too, have become smarter; many organize a media night where the happy hour is extended for the entire evening.

In essence, the pub culture of urban India is kept alive partly by a substitution trend. Some consumers have shifted from clubs to pubs, and some from their homes to these new social hubs. However, it would be a mistake to assume that these people are drinking more or are spending more. In economic terms, whether they drink at home, or at clubs, or at pubs, they are getting almost the same bargain.

Yet another insight into the phenomenon of pub-hopping may be gained from noting that many people save money by doing so. This may sound ridiculous, but it is true. As increasing numbers of the urban middle class become self-employed (as consultants, advisors, or independent providers in the services sector), they are able to claim many of these expenses as income tax breaks. So if they drink at pubs and spend 20–35 percent more on their liquor, they still stand to gain as they save more than 30 percent income tax on the amount they have spent. They show these expenses as business expenses.

Another trend that I have noticed in Delhi, Mumbai, and Bangalore is that young people have become smarter when it comes to paying for drinks. Most of them drink at home first to save money, and then go out to a pub or a night club. Their aim is not to spend at these places but to be seen, to meet friends, to enjoy the music, and to dance. They tend to order one beer each (perhaps no more than a pint) and to draw this out for the entire evening.

These are the middle-class people who are smart Spenderati, others who are sharp Seenerati, and many more who are aching to become part of the middle-class Aspirerati. Then there are those who are the smooth spenders.

I have a few friends who graduated from Ahmedabad's National Institute of Design (NID), and are successful professionals in their respective fields (graphic design, textiles, and the media). They earn good incomes. They like their creature comforts: an air-conditioner, a DVD player, and a flat-screen TV are musts. They wear stylish clothes and accessories; even their perfumes and deodorants are trendy. They love good food and drink. They are educated, intelligent, and aware. They are an integral part of the global village. They plan to buy a house and a car as soon as they can afford it. Some already own both. They are very much part of the Indian middle class, yet they are poles apart from the seemingly similar Spenderati and Seenerati.

Bonita, a friend and former colleague, is part of this NID group. A Goan by birth, she was educated mostly in Mumbai. She hails from a typical middle-class family, where the parents work hard to give their children a good education and to inculcate Indian values and morals. Thanks to their own hard work and determination, as well as to the opportunities that opened up during the period of India's economic reforms in the 1990s, the children of these middle-class families ended up in well-paying jobs and acquired a "Westernized" mindset. All this should have made Bonita similar to Ramya, Neal, and Praveen, the individuals who appear in the first chapter, who are the Spenderati. But it did not. Bonita is different.

There is another subset of the middle class that we have not met until now—the Smootherati. They are slick, street-smart, and grounded. They know what they want and know how to get it, at least in most cases. In that sense, they behave, act, and talk like the Spenderati and the Seenerati. Most importantly, they know how to manage their money; their consumption and investment behavior is driven by contradictory desires. Bonita is a member of the Smootherati. She usually eats out two or three times a month, and visits pubs once or twice. She describes her spending habits:

> I like good food. But instead of going out regularly, I would rather cook a lavish meal at my house or at a friend's. For that, I am willing to spend money to buy branded spices and other ingredients for an Italian or a French delicacy. I want to have a drink on a weekend with friends, but in places that allow us to talk, share, and voice our concerns. I wear stylish and classy clothes, but they don't need to be branded all the time. I also buy stuff at pavement shops in Sarojini Nagar or Lajpat Nagar markets. I would rather have great taste than be loaded with money. For example, I would rather spend on books than on brands and entertainment mindlessly. My friends and I are not dictated [to] by what others around us are doing. We just want to be ourselves, and we don't want to be bracketed as a part of the Great Indian Middle Class.[1]

The Smootherati are driven by individual dreams, ambitions, and priorities; they have a strong dislike of anything pretentious or fake; they possess values that make them both open and closed; they spend their money on many different things. Their lives sometimes intertwine with those of the Spenderati and the Seenarati, yet they remain distinct. This is the "fence-sitting" middle class—conservative and liberal, extrovert and introvert, apprehensive and aspirational. At some stage, the Smootherati may become a part of the Spenderati. But then they may not.

So the subjective parameters used for assessing the amazing growth of the Indian middle class may not be the most useful or appropriate measures. As we have seen, neither mobile phone ownership nor visibility at pubs, clubs, and restaurants indicates that the middle class has also become a consuming class. Neither can we arrive at similar conclusions based on the middle class's desire to emulate some of the more materialistic aspects of the Western lifestyle. It is important to draw a clear distinction between the middle class as a sociopolitical entity and the rapid growth of the middle class as exemplifying a consumption trend, so we need to study this social group accordingly. While in some cases the two aspects of the middle class may coexist, they may not do so in many other cases.

This is even more true when we look at the objective or quantitative data—the macro picture—that define the Indian middle class in terms of socioeconomic factors and consumption behavior. This is why economists and consultants have got it wrong.

For example, let us ask a simple question. Most experts and analysts generally contend that the size of the Indian middle class is between 250 and 350 million. This figure was the estimate given by one of India's leading think tanks, the National Council for Applied Economic Research (NCAER). It was then picked up and touted by others like KSA Technopak.

Now let us look at a recent study (August 2005) by the NCAER[2] to find out what it actually said.

In 2005–06, the number of households estimated as middle class, as per NCAER's definition, was 16.40 million. Another 1.73 million families constituted the rich class. So the size of the consumption class was 18.13 million households, or just more than 90 million individuals (if one considers an average of five members per household). That is it.

The figures look less impressive when one considers the income levels of the middle and rich classes. The income of middle-class households started with Rs 2 lakh (US$5,000) a year, or less than Rs 20,000 (US$500) a month. We may assume that this category includes families where both spouses work. In such cases, the starting individual earning of NCAER's middle class is less than Rs 10,000 (US$250) a month.

Can such families be considered a part of the consuming class?

My driver, Rakesh, earns Rs 10,000 a month, and his younger brother also earns a similar amount. Since they live together, and if they pool their earnings, they should form a part of NCAER's middle class. But they do not. They are the aspirants; they want to belong to the middle class. But they have a long way to go before they become "real" consumers.

Rakesh and the other six members of his family do own a color TV and a refrigerator. But they do not buy branded clothes and accessories. They do not eat out. They do not go to the cinema regularly, nor do they pursue other forms of entertainment. For a vehicle, they have a scooter, which is used by both brothers and their father. The only branded products that the family buys are toothpastes, bathing and washing soaps, and shampoo sachets.

Neither Rakesh nor his family members have credit cards, life insurance, investments in stocks, or savings in fixed deposits. Rakesh has a bank account, which he usually maintains at the minimum level and uses rarely. Family savings take the form of a local kitty to which several families contribute a fixed amount every month; each family is allowed to bid once for the monthly collection during the kitty's tenure.

Ironically, if one were to go by the value of the family's assets, Rakesh's family probably would be considered rich. They own a brick-and-mortar (*pucca*) house in an urban village in South Delhi, and they also own enough land to enable them to grow enough grain for their needs. The value of the house and the farm runs into crores of rupees (a crore is US$250,000). Even if the family does not sell the land, it can maintain a comfortable standard of living. Nevertheless, Rakesh's family is definitely not part of the consumption class.

Another problem with NCAER's income criteria is the manner in which the organization defines the rich class. It starts with an annual household income of Rs 10 lakh (US$25,000). In 2005, an unmarried friend used to earn around that much but he was definitely not a Ferrarati (owner of a Ferrari, the modern symbol of a rich Western family). Today, he earns much more, is still single, and is still not a rich consumer. My friend was, and is, a Spenderati. But he sees himself as belonging to the middle class. At an intellectual level, he is a Westernized liberal (or a democrat), a globalized soul, and a part of the technodigital universe. He believes in individual freedom, is not judgmental, and is not unnerved by the thought of premarital sex, unmarried life partners, or the demand for private space by young Indians (although he does hang out a lot with his friends). His obsession with consumption is all about brands, techno-gizmos, enter-tainment, travel, and the pursuit of an upper-end lifestyle. But as a consumer, he will still not buy high-end products. He will purchase a good color TV but not an LCD model; a decent second-hand Hyundai Accent car (Rs 6 lakh, or US$15,000) but definitely not a Skoda (Rs 13–15 lakh, US$32,500–37,500); a Blackberry, but only after the company slashed prices. He is always looking for bargains at stores like Nike, Reebok, Marks & Spencer, Benetton, and Levi's. There is no way he will even look at luxury products like Swarovski, Tissot, or Cartier.

Households with annual incomes of Rs 10 lakh abound in Gurgaon, Delhi's satellite town to the south. Yet most of them will refuse to buy expensive brands, will never walk into Swarovski and FCUK stores, and will continue to scout for bargains. So how can households with annual incomes of Rs 10 lakh (whose individual earnings will actually be much less) fall into the rich category?

Now look at the bigger picture. Clearly, the NCAER statistics about the size of the middle and rich classes are exaggerated if one considers the socioeconomic profiles of the two segments and their spending patterns. Their combined size ranges between 50 million and 90 million, possibly closer to 50 million.

What compounds the problem is NCAER's categorization of "aspirers," or the Aspirerati, who aspire to join the middle class, who dream about owning more consumer durables, who seek to ape the lifestyle of the upper-income groups, and who are aware of the opportunities that exist for pursuing these ambitions. According to the NCAER survey, aspirers comprised more than 53 million households, or more than 265 million people (based on the 1:5 ratio). If clubbed together with the middle and the rich classes, the size of India's consumer base is more than 350 million.

Rosy predictions based on such optimistic analysis are what excite investors, marketers, economists, and sociologists. All of them are certain that the aspirers will soon graduate to the middle class, that a huge section of the middle class will become rich, that the number of the super rich will grow, and that there will be hundreds of millions of Indian consumers.

There is only one small problem with this assumption. It just does not happen that way, especially in Indian society. Only some of the aspirers will climb up the pyramid. Indeed, most will remain where they are, just as they have done for the past few years. For example, my driver and my cook will continue to be aspirants for years. As we have seen, only a few subsets, or parts of the subsets, of the middle class are consumers in the strictest marketing sense. A small proportion of the middle class will join the rich class. It will take a long time for the number of consumers to become sufficiently large enough to tempt advertisers, marketers, and producers.

A caveat is in order here. Even the lower figure discussed above is not a small number by any means. A middle–rich class of 55–70 million is larger than that found in most countries. NCAER projects the combined size of this class at more than 32 million households, or 160 million people, by 2009–10. Even if we were to discount this figure by a third, it is still impressively large at 100 million-plus.

Still, instead of taking this overall figure as a benchmark, a better way of computing the size of the middle class is on the basis of consumption according to product categories. Sandipan Deb (passages from his book appear in the previous chapter) argues that the lowest common denominator for the Indian middle class is the ownership of a color TV (CTV). He contends:

> CTV purchase isn't an impulse purchase or a necessity. It's a conscious decision by a household to buy one. It implies that this family is making an effort to spend that much extra, over and above what it considers essential items.[3]

According to the National Readership Survey (NRS), which also statistically tracks the ownership pattern of various products of readers, 64 million homes owned CTV in 2006. NCAER estimated the CTV penetration level at 21.3 percent of households in 2005–06, or around 40 million households. NRS found that the number of readers of both dailies and magazines in the 12-plus age group was 222 million. All these figures again indicate that the middle and the rich classes together comprise 200–300 million.

The problem arises when we compare CTV penetration levels with those of motorcycles (where demand is pushed by clearly consumerist forces, such as choice, style, and class) and refrigerators (which is an important convenience product for most middle-class families). NCAER statistics reveal that the penetration level is more than 30 percent lower in the case of motorcycles and 25 percent lower in the case of refrigerators.

According to conventional wisdom, in a consumerist society, or at least in the consumerist segment of a society, sales of products such as motorcycles and refrigerators should be higher than those of CTVs. This should be especially true for nations or cities that do not have an efficient public transport system, as is the case in India. So why do CTVs sell more? Can CTV be taken as the defining product for estimating the size of the middle class? Or are there any other product categories that are more relevant in this regard?

First, we need to understand what is specifically responsible for the huge demand for CTVs and TVs in general. In societies that are stressed and fractured, some form of entertainment becomes critical. This is especially true of the aspirant class, which is squeezed from both the top and the bottom of the societal pyramid. It wants to ape the middle class but does not have the economic means for doing so. At the same time, it wishes to be seen as different from the lower class. In purely materialistic terms, since it cannot consume everything that the middle class can afford, it makes its choices about the products that it should possess.

How would a typically aspirant family think about the goods it seeks to purchase? It would look at a motorcycle, or even a scooter, as an item of conspicuous consumption, simply because it has running costs attached to it. One can buy a motorcycle for Rs 30,000 and pay for it in affordable installments because of the availability of cheap financing options. But the user would have to spend at least Rs 1,500 (US$37.50) every month on petrol. Maintenance costs would be extra. So an aspirant family would rather use public transport, inefficient though it is, at less than half the cost of operating and maintaining a two-wheeler. It may still own a two-wheeler for reasons linked to social image and prestige.

A refrigerator becomes redundant for the aspirers. Even today, most Indian families like to eat freshly cooked food and to buy fresh vegetables. This is the norm—and widespread preference—across all social classes, whether the low class, upper-low (aspirant) class, middle class, or rich class. Even if both husband and wife work, the wife still cooks breakfast before leaving for office (and lunch for the office) and dinner when she returns home. Most of the food is bought, cooked, and consumed on the same day. This is especially true of low and upper-lower class Indian homes.

So where is the need for a refrigerator? Although empirical evidence does not exist to support this claim, it is probable that many of the lower- and upper-lower-class homes that do own a refrigerator received the appliance as part of the wife's or daughter-in-law's dowry (the system in which the bride's family presents cash, gifts, jewelry, clothes, various home appliances, and possibly a vehicle, to the groom's family at the time of the wedding).

Statistics can help us to understand how a refrigerator is not important for the aspiring class. According to NCAER, just more than one-fifth of households owning a two-wheeler (scooter or motorcycle) also own a refrigerator. The ratio in the case of TV-owning households is slightly better at 26.3 percent. Surprisingly, it is only 12.9 percent in the case of families possessing a credit card. It is more than 80 percent only in the case of households owning cars/jeeps and air-conditioners.

This reveals that a two-wheeler or a TV is considered more essential than a refrigerator. Second, it shows that even people with credit cards cannot qualify as middle class since they include thousands of farmers who have been given a *kisan* (farmer) card by the central and state governments. Finally, any household owning a car or an air-conditioner has to be middle class by definition, so is likely to own most white goods (household goods that traditionally came in the color white, such as refrigerators, washing machines, and microwave ovens).

Compared with the buying of a motorcycle or a refrigerator, the purchase of a CTV is a different ball game. As we have seen, the Aspirerati are caught in an unending vortex of social, economic, and emotional forces. They want to move up the socioeconomic pyramid rapidly, but are unable to do so. This failure or setback has certain psychological ramifications. Given the monetary constraints they face, the only option for such families is to seek a cheap escape route every now and then into a make-believe world where they feel that they are, or can be, a part of the middle and rich classes. A CTV offers a perfect way out, especially after the advent of cable and satellite TV. For a few hours every day, by paying a low monthly rental of Rs 100–150 (US$2.50–3.75), these families can escape from the stresses of the daily struggle by watching soap operas, films, and other entertainment programs. They are also able to peek into the homes of the middle and rich classes to see how they live and behave. They can lose themselves for a few hours in a dreamworld, in which they too can enjoy the lifestyles of the Spenderati and the Seenarati.

For instance, several families in Mumbai's slums own a CTV. The same is true for people in Delhi's urban villages, which have a mix of well-to-do and just-about-surviving households. In Mehrauli, a typical urban village in South Delhi, white plastic-coated cables carrying satellite channel signals stream into almost every home. The families all watch cable TV, and that too on a CTV. The lower and upper-lower sections of Indian society participate willingly in a kind of forced entertainment economy. They turn to their daily dose of entertainment not only because they can afford it but also because without it they are likely to suffer from withdrawal symptoms.

A better way of gauging the relationship between the middle class and CTVs is to look at the demand for high-end CTVs, and not only at the cheaper, more affordable models. The makers of CTVs claim that the demand for flat-screen TVs and LCD/plasma TVs is rising exponentially; in the case of LCD TVs, sales have increased by 400 percent. Yet the customer base is still quite small, and the bulk of CTVs sold are low-end models.

So is it better to gauge the size of the Indian middle class on the basis of the penetration levels of branded toothpastes, bathing soaps, washing powder, and shampoos? These are lifestyle-related products, indicative of a mindset that is conscious about the importance of physical attractiveness, beauty, body care, and hygiene. They signify a shift from price sensitivity to value sensitivity. Finally, the growing demand for these products reveals the Westernization of this segment of consumers, a shift to so-called modern middle-class values. The NCAER survey shows that almost half of all Indian households buy shampoo and that three-quarters purchase washing powder. The use of these two products together would put the size of the Indian middle class between 500 million and 750 million. Even the most ardent and optimistic supporters of the claim of the expanding Indian middle class would reject these figures as exaggerated.

It is true that most Indians are obsessed with looks, particularly fair skin. Most Indian women want to be fairer. They will buy fairness-increasing creams even at the cost of foregoing a meal. Advertisers and manufacturers have done their bit to reinforce the notion of the superiority and beauty of fair skin. The print and electronic media are flooded with advertisements touting the benefits of creams guaranteed to make women fairer, or more beautiful, in only a few weeks. The craze for fair skin has now also affected Indian men, who are lining up to buy fairness and skin-lightening creams.

When I visited Brazil two years ago, I found a similar trend. The beauty industry was doing a roaring business. This is not surprising in a country obsessed with good looks and beauty. Brazilian women across all classes and social groups spend a certain portion of their income on beauty products, even at the cost of foregoing other basic necessities.

Clearly, the expenditure on beautification, physical care, and hygiene in India and Brazil is dictated by reasons that cannot be defined by a consumption urge. It is more of a social phenomenon. Therefore, such consumption does not imply that the spenders belong to a specific socioeconomic spenders' class.

Perhaps a better way to get an idea of the size of the Indian middle class is to look at the ownership of cars. The cumulative figure for all car sales is just more than 10 million. Discounting this figure by 10–20 percent for households that have two or more cars, the size of the middle class should be 40–45 million. This takes us back to nearly the same figure that we had earlier estimated for the middle and rich classes.

Enthusiastic observers of the growing Indian middle class point out that ownership of a car and an apartment is increasingly becoming the characteristic feature of the Neo Middle Class. (NMC) Nandan Nilekani, chairman of Infosys, notes that consuming patterns have changed since he was a young man. "I see younger people in my campus who want to buy a car within two years of working and a house within four or five years. This is so different from our generation, which used to even think of buying them after 10–15 years of service," he says.[4] So it is logical to assume that the individuals who have entered the ranks of the middle class over the past 10–15 years will buy a car almost as soon as they can.

But when we think about this more deeply, we realize that even the car owner may not be a typical consumer, and vice versa. Several families own a car but have extremely conservative spending patterns. They do not go in for brands or high-end consumer products. Many people in Delhi, Mumbai, Kolkata, and Bangalore do not own a car but are definitely part of the middle class in terms of consumption.

NCAER itself brings out this dichotomy in its survey. It states that 30 percent of all households in Delhi, and only 20 percent in Mumbai, own a car. We may be sure that the size of the middle class in both cities, especially in Mumbai, is much larger. The reason many middle-class families refuse to buy a car in Mumbai is because of traffic congestion and the existence of a fairly decent public transport system in terms of both buses and trains.

Similar useful insights into the Indian middle class can be gained by analyzing the findings of another survey, the annual NRS.

As per the NRS definition of socioeconomic class, the size of the middle class is about a quarter of the population, or 250–300 million. In urban areas, this includes households where the chief wage earner is a skilled worker who is a graduate; a trader who has a similar educational background; a shopowner who has studied in school for several years; a businessman except one who does not employ anyone, who has not been to college, who is employed at a clerical or supervisory level, and who has finished school; a junior officer or executive who has had schooling for several years; and a mid- or senior-level officer or executive. In rural areas, it includes households that own a *pucca* or a semi-*pucca* home and whose chief wage earner has had at least several years of schooling.

But the figures change dramatically when we look at the monthly incomes of these households. Only 9 percent of Indian households earn more than Rs 7,000 (US$175) per month. That gives us a middle class of about 100 million. Even this is a slightly exaggerated figure because urban households with this income can only be described as aspirants, not the real consuming middle class.

If we look at household possessions, the figure shrinks even further, running into only a few million. Less than 6 percent of Indian households own a stereo or mono audio system. (In India, music systems with a single speaker and two speakers are sold.) One percent own a video cassette player or recorder, and less than 2 percent own a PC or laptop or hifi music system. On the basis of the ownership of music system, the size of the middle class is only 75 million.

Even if we club together households that own some sort of a music-playing device (including Walkman and Discman), the figure comes to less than 12 percent. If we discount this by 20–30 percent for households that have at least two of these items, the figure drops below 10 percent and amounts to about 100 million people. We may assume that most middle-class households will own a camera, either a digital camera or a video camera. The total number of households owning a camera is less than 4 percent. That gives us an Indian middle class of less than 50 million people.

We may also assume that a middle-class home, at least in urban areas, will have an air-cooler or air-conditioner. On the basis of this parameter only 7.5 percent of urban households constitute a middle class, that is, the urban middle class is less than 100 million. And not all of them are real consumers.

So if it is not about cars, mobile phones, CTVs, motorcycles, cameras, music systems, and refrigerators, how do we determine the size of the Indian middle class? And if it is not even about eating out and pubbing, the exercise becomes an impossible one.

The most effective way to achieve this objective is by employing the 4/6 model. Out of a basket of six consumer products—say, a car, a mobile phone, a washing machine, a CTV, a microwave oven, and a new house (as opposed to a house that was purchased by one's parents, grandparents, or great-grandparents)—if a household has bought at least four items, it should automatically fall into the middle- or the upper-middle-class category. The only problem is that there are no data to identify such homes.

A bigger problem is that even if reliable statistics were available, it is not likely that the entire base of this middle class would be the consumption class. This is why it is important for manufacturers, producers, marketers, and advertisers to make a distinction between the two classes. One cannot assume a direct correlation between them, at least not in India.

Endnotes

1. Interview with the author, 2007.
2. National Council for Applied Economic Research (NCAER) in association with *Business Standard*, "The Great Indian Market: Results from the NCAER's Market Information Survey of Households," August 9, 2005, http://www.ncaer.org/downloads/PPT/TheGreatIndianMarket.pdf
3. Interview with the author, 2007.
4. Interview with the author, 2005.

Middle-some Masala

In many ways, any society's mass—or pop—culture provides important clues about its changing characteristics and its various components and constituents. This is especially true about the middle class because, in most ways, popular culture stems from and appeals to this segment. And this is truer still for the entertainment industry, which treats the middle class as its major consumer base.

In India, the entertainment segment that captures it all is Bollywood, which makes more films every year than either Hollywood or any other nation's film industry. As *Outlook*'s film critic told me: "All Hindi movies are basically middle-class movies."

More interestingly, Bollywood films are becoming a part of the school education curriculum in India. In 2006, *Sholay (Flames),* a 1975 blockbuster, was included in the English course for Class V students. This year, there is reference to another major hit of the late 1970s, *Deewar (Wall)*. In fact, the latter one shows three clips from a scene to encourage children to understand concepts like "dignity of labor," "social equality," and a sense of pride and self-respect.

The scenes from *Deewar* show a younger Amitabh Bachchan (the hero) as a shoe polish boy who refuses to accept money thrown at him by a rich smuggler. The dialogue is: *"Saab, hum joota polish karte hain, bheek nahin mangte. Paise utha ke haath mein do."* ("Sir, I polish shoes, I don't beg. So don't throw the money at me.") The educationists hoped that the notions mentioned will be conveyed to schoolchildren through such film clips.

Since education, or access to it, is an integral part of any middle class, this implies that Bollywood does have elements that can help pinpoint some of the traits of this segment in India. Moreover, Bollywood films, over the years, can give important clues to the changes in the composition and attitude of the middle class.

So it may not be a bad idea to trace the transformation of the middle class through the manner in which it has been portrayed by Bollywood movies. It may be a great idea to pick up the nuances in these characters. More importantly, it will give us the shifting contours of the middle class over the six decades since India's independence. Through the actors, we can sketch out how "reel" and real people are almost the same. In parts, the various middle-class movie characters exist in each of us.

Raj/Raju/Raj Kapoor were among the defining personalities in the first 15 years of India's independence. The first two were reel names and the third was the real one, and together they portrayed a mix of idealism, realism, and the ironic distance between hope and actuality. In movies such as *Awara* (*Vagabond*) and *Shree 420 (Mr 420)*, Raj Kapoor—one of the all-time greats—reflected several societal ideas at the same time.

In *Awara*, he represented the bulk of the Indian society that was excluded by the then existing centers of control such as power (political and economic), family (joint families), and law (fair arbitration). Yet there is also a sense of faith in the system to transform and change India. In *Shree 420*, a vagabond tries to make a fortune in a city, and realizes the schism between the corrupt rich and the warm, loving poor. The poor were a better lot, so they were the change drivers in a country that had to rebuild itself. Here is an exchange that also shows the inherent irony within the society.

> Poor person 1: "What's your name, son?"
> Raj Kapoor: "Raj."
> Poor person 2: "See, I told you that raj ("rule" or "governance" in Hindi) will come to our house some day."

During those early years, films such as *Dharti ke Phool (Flower of the Earth)* and *Naya Daur (New Era)* conveyed the brimming socialist optimism that prevailed during the reign of India's first prime minister, Jawaharlal Nehru. As he cajoled the nation to opt for socialism and economic planning, the two movies encapsulated ideas such as collective farming, a humanist approach to remove class divisions, and the inevitable clash between tradition and modernity.

Boot Polish (Shoe Polish), although based on the lives of lower-class (not middle-class) street children, tried to convince the viewing public that even the urchins could control their own destinies, although the process of doing so was not easy. It was a message to the middle class that it too could control the destiny of the nation by initiating concrete steps and participating in the process of nation building.

However, there were several discordant notes too. It was the director or storyteller's way of saying that the change process was difficult and, in many cases, impossible. The reason: one was trying to change a system that was thousands of years old, and dismantling it was difficult because of the existing interest groups and lobbies that were powerful enough to stall the transformation.

Jagte Raho (Stay Awake), another Raj Kapoor film, was a critique on the Bengali (hailing from the state of West Bengal or Bangladesh) middle class. The so-called *bhadralok* (decent people) are perceived to be saints in white robes. But Mohan (Raj Kapoor), a poor villager who comes to the city to seek his fortune, finds that underneath the veneer of honesty and truth lies a dark side; a shadow that is expansive enough to darken the future of the country. In a comical–philosophical journey from one house to another in a middle-class residential area in search of a glass of water, the hero discovers this bare certainty about independent India. Yet again, there is hope that the poor—the majority in this country—still had the traits to put India back on track.

As a synopsis on www.upperstall.com stated:

> The film shows Mitra's (the director) pre-occupation with social justice and is a Chaplinesque denunciation of the petit-bourgeois ... *Jagte Raho* is an allegoric film about darkness and light, where darkness is the cloak of respectability under which a city supposedly sleeps but in effect thrashes around in throes of crime and evil—a civilization gone to seed. It seems a night without end, but there is an end, the coming of a dawn at which the peasant discovers that the terrible darkness of the night is only half the truth but out of the suffocating darkness itself shall be born the dawn, and a new day of truth and justice.[1]

The disillusionment with urban life, the sad state of affairs in the cities, the debasing of human characters, and the influx of dark elements into an optimistic country were issues dealt with in other movies like *Do Bigha Zameen (Two Bigha Land,* with one bigha equivalent to a little more than 840 square meters), *Afsar (Government Official)*, and *Naukri (Job)*.

In *Do Bigha Zameen*, a small landowner—or a part of the rural middle class—fights with the local *zamindar* (feudal lord) to retain possession over his two bighas of land. Forced to migrate to the city to earn money to repay the *zamindar*, Balraj Sahni (the protagonist) is forced to become a rickshaw puller. Finally, he returns home with the money, only to find that a factory is being built over his *do bigha zameen*.

Naukri and *Afsar* showed the frustrations of the urban middle class. In the latter, a government employee who has dreams of making a difference through public life finds himself embroiled in village politics with the local officials. In *Naukri*, Kishore Kumar vents his disgust with politics and the education system as he strives in vain to get a decent job to take care of his family. In an era when education was supposedly the one-way ticket to employment, this was a trendsetter.

However, the movie of that era which focused on the insecurities of the urban middle class was *Garam Coat (Warm Coat)*. It is a story of a postal clerk who goes through hell when he thinks that he has lost a Rs 100 note. His anxiety rises to a level where he thinks about the worst possible things. For instance, he feels that his wife has become a prostitute. At a philosophical level, the movie was about the middle class' financial crisis, its instinct to think about the worst for its family and, thence, society in general, and the inability to think positively—about themselves, their family, or the nation.

The most insightful aspect is that the shades and form of the middle class in these films exist even today—government officials, who are forced to become a part of the corrupt and immoral system, or get thrown out; the millions of educated youth who are unable to find decent employment, and are slowly, but surely, participating in minor civil revolutions in the country; and rural migrants who dream of making it big in the city and become rags-to-riches legends.

Despite reforms and India's rejection of socialism, one can witness shades of the latter when the country's current crop of political leaders talk about "inclusive growth," "efficient delivery systems," and "reforms with a human face."

Controversies on issues such as the Special Economic Zones (for which the states and the private sector acquired land from farmers) show that the politicians still have to go overboard and talk about protecting the rights of the poor to manage "vote banks." The debate on industrialization versus protecting local communities continues.

By the early 1960s, the middle class had given up on the grand transformation dream. It had understood the ground rules—either live within the system or opt out. The movies of that period (1962–75) showed both trends—in multicolor images of pessimism, hate, and celebration.

For one, the period saw the maturing of Bharat, a quintessential middle-class youth portrayed by actor Manoj Kumar, in several films. He is a nationalist, struggler, aspirant, but sadly unhopeful. Although, in typical Bollywood style, he triumphs in the end, yet the feeling that the viewer is left with is defeatist. The good will inevitably suffer; in most cases, they will succumb to the bad.

In *Roti, Kapada aur Makaan (Food, Clothing and Housing;* this was also a political slogan of Prime Minister Indira Gandhi in the 1970s), he is an educated underemployed young man who becomes a low-paid singer. Somehow, he tries to take care of his family of two brothers, a sister and parents. With middle class fervor, he tries to educate the brothers so that they can lead a decent life. Finally, the "good" Bharat turns "evil" to ensure the wellbeing of his family. One of the brothers turns evil, and then good, and joins the army. Finally, it is all about the middle-class struggle for the three basic amenities: food, clothing, and shelter.

Bharat (and please do not miss the connection with India, which is *Bharat* in the Hindustani language) is the "nationalist" in *Upkaar (Kindness)* and *Purab aur Paschim (East and West);* the two movies, says www.imdb.com, contrast his "son-of-the-soil simplicity with western decadence." Although *Upkaar* is set in rural India and the other in the urban West, both denounce the Western influence on traditional Indian society. Saira Banu (the heroine in *Purab aur Paschim*), smokes, drinks, and wears short skirts, and Puran (Bharat's brother in *Upkaar*) is so influenced by Western materialism that money defines his life.

In both films, Bharat is the reformist, making all the sacrifices. Both characteristics are traditionally associated with the Indian middle class. The farmer Bharat in *Upkaar* gives away his property to his younger brother who has newly returned from

London, and then joins the Indian army. Again, the underlying nuance was the focus on two planks of the country's progress— agriculture and the defense forces—and Lal Bahadur Shastri's (India's former prime minister) slogan, *"Jai Jawan, Jai Kisan"* (Hail soldier, hail farmer). The educated, elitist Bharat in *Purab aur Paschim* reforms the members of the British–Indian society, especially his ultra-Westernized wife.

The moral degradation of the society due to its modern adherence to Western attitudes was shown in Dev Anand's *Hare Rama, Hare Krishna*. A bohemian life, drugs, open sex, and the so-called hippie culture gripped the urban youth, many of whom decided to drop out of society. At one level, it was the lack of hope that drove this trend. And on another, it was a fascination with the Westernized way of life.

Escapism, celebration of love, and an acceptance of the Westernized lifestyle also became a part of Bollywood during this era. This was adequately expressed by the romantic and melodramatic films starring Shammi Kapoor and Rajesh Khanna.

The carefree Shammi Kapoor, with his "drainpipes" and breakdance moves, was clearly the modern youth in *Junglee (Wild)*, *Kashmir Ki Kali (Bud of Kashmir)*, and *Bluff Master*. *Screen*, a renowned movie weekly, said this about him in 2006:

> He changed the very concept of the Hindi film hero from the over-chaste under-romantic to the ardor-filled lover who serenaded with passionate aggression without ... outraging the sensibilities of the audience of the late '50s, '60s and early '70s... [2]

And www.ultraindia.com felt that "exactly three decades have passed since his role as a hero came to an end, even then no other actor has been able to evoke the same impish charm and wanton spirit."

In comparison, Rajesh Khanna was the charming boy next door. Every middle-class man could identify with those looks. Every woman desired it in their man. Wikipedia, the online encyclopedia, says:

> He shot to fame with the 1969 film *Aradhana* which was his first major hit. From then on he was an extremely popular actor in the early 1970s, appearing in many romantic and melodrama films which were

hugely successful at the box office. ... During the peak of his career he would be mobbed during public appearances. Fans kissed his car, which would be covered with lipstick marks, and lined the road, cheering and chanting his name. Female fans sent him letters written in their own blood.[3]

But most of his movies were melodramatic, unreal, and an escape route for the audience. Watching a Rajesh Khanna film was like entering a nowhere world where you could only stay during the film's duration. In those three hours, it could make you laugh, cry, pity, care, love—in fact, it could make you live through hundreds of change-a-minute emotions.

At the same time, when romance and melodrama reached its zenith, directors such as Basu Bhattacharya, Basu Chatterjee, and Hrishikesh Mukherjee began their experiments with the personal and individual problems that beset the middle class. The most important strand was obviously marriage and relationships, and how they got stretched and reached breaking point because of middle-class aspirations and concerns.

Avishkaar (Discovery, starring Rajesh Khanna and Sharmila Tagore) and *Anubhav (Feeling*, starring Sanjeev Kumar and Tanuja), both directed by Bhattacharya, exposed the chinks that were fast developing in middle-class marriages due to work-related reasons. It explored the loneliness, fears, apprehensions, and jealousies of the wives and husbands.

Rajnigandha (Tuberose), *Abhimaan (Pride)*, and *Avishkaar* tell the audience about the fissures that are created in relationships if one of the partners does unbelievably well professionally, or is attracted to the glitz and glamour in certain professions. In *Avishkaar*, the wife feels neglected after the birth of her first child, when her husband starts working at an advertising agency, in constant touch with beautiful women. In India, as probably elsewhere, many married women feel less confident and uncared for after they become mothers.

By contrast, *Abhimaan* is about a successful singer, who is unable to accept his simple, village-bred wife becoming a more popular and successful singer than him. And *Rajnigandha* is about Deepa (actress Vidya Sinha), who has decided to marry Sanjay (Amol Palekar). The twist in their relationship comes when Deepa goes to Bombay for a job interview, meets her old flame Navin (Dinesh Thakur), and finds that she has to choose between the two men in her life.

In this movie, Deepa is the more ambitious person, whereas Sanjay is satisfied with the way things are. Deepa eventually returns to Delhi, and finds the familiar bunch of *rajnigandha* waiting for her from, obviously, her husband. Therefore, Deepa does what the middle class has traditionally done over the decades—she opts for comfort, the status quo, and an uncomplicated life, rather than excitement, adventure, and possible upheavals.

Yet again, we continue to find these characters in today's middle class. Many women are grappling with their loneliness as they are forced, or decide, to quit work after marriage. Some of them, who have children, are also aware that their husbands are probably involved in extramarital affairs.

The only difference today is that some of the urban women are not content to sit back and watch the breakdown of their relationship. Some split and separate. Others get into another relationship. A few begin working to keep themselves busy with their own professional work or problems. I know hundreds of people who have taken such decisions.

In the same vein, the middle-class man is trying to accept that his partner may do much better professionally. Wives may earn more, travel more, and get more recognition in their work sphere. And the spouses are dealing with it in their own way with the emotional, mental, and physical stress that this leads to. So there is a budding trend where the Neo Middle Class (NMC) man is willing to accept and share responsibilities in every way possible. He cooks, changes diapers, and takes paternity leave.

These concepts have now caught on, even if in a small way, which is visible from the portrayal of the man in ad films. Raymonds, a well-known garments brand, has a series with the punchline, "The Complete Man." In one, the man leads his wife to the upper deck of a ship, closes her eyes, and when he removes his hand, both see the spectacle of two dolphins jumping out of the sea. Talking about this ad, Shekar Swamy, president, R K Swamy BBDO, which created the ad, said:

> The creative idea is that "The Complete Man" will go to great lengths to arrange something really, really special for his spouse, and she is absolutely dazzled by his thoughtfulness and extravagance in thought.[4]

However, some experts feel that "The Complete Man" is merely a concept. In reality, the middle-class man or woman is changing in radically different and damaging ways. He or she is laying the foundations for an immoral, corrupt, and degraded society, which will self-destruct in the near future. Like other Western countries, India will become a nation devoid of a socio-cultural foundation, which is so important for the survival of a civilization. In the past, societies have fallen apart for the same reason. Many of the causes relating to the decline of the Mughal empire in India, moral corruption in the Elizabethan era, and the current state in Japan can be traced to this overriding facet.

Pavan K. Varma, sociologist and author of *The Great Indian Middle Class*, is probably the biggest and the most assertive critic of the modern middle class in India. In his book, and in subsequent columns, he has admonished this segment for neglecting its rightful duties, for abdicating its responsibilities and, indirectly, allowing the country to go to the dogs. With its individualistic, self-centered, and materialistic mindset, the middle class—or the change driver in any society—has created a social vacuum.

But even Varma has made nuanced changes in his theory. In a column he wrote for the *Outlook* in October 2006, he said that:

> ... undoubtedly, the middle class is still very insular, oblivious to any interests outside its turf. It remains, as in the past, socially insensitive to issues of poverty and deprivation. But, there is, however faint, the first glimmering of hope that educated Indians are willing to break from their individualistic insularity towards conscious and collective action in the public sphere.[5]

He concluded by saying that

> ... the question is whether this civic-consciousness, and the ability to follow up on it through concrete action, will strengthen or get submerged by cynicism. If it's the former, India will benefit; if it's the latter, middle-class Indians will continue to prosper, but remain poor citizens.[6]

Do such views and thoughts not remind you of the feelings of the nationalist Bharat (Manoj Kumar)?

Although Bharat is still alive in the hearts and minds of many middle-class people, it was as good as dead as a worthy

Bollywood plot by the mid-1970s. By then, Hindi movies became obsessed with Vijay (a character played by superstar Amitabh Bachchan in many films), the angry young man who refused to be cowed by the system, who became the new rebel without a cause (except his own) or a pause.

Vijay signaled a new trend in movies and in Indian society. It was the birth of the anti-hero, a character who became a part of the corrupt system and shaped it to himself, who bent all the rules, whose formula for success lay in the ability to become more corrupt, ambitious, aggressive, and powerful than others. It was the birth of the in-your-face, risk-taking, I-me-myself and forget-the-morals-and-values segment of the middle class.

Most importantly, the trend epitomized a period in which having these instincts and impulses was believed to be critical for survival. There was nothing wrong in becoming a part of the system, and it was not to be frowned upon. The anti-hero became the new hero of a violent society that rebelled to subserve self-interests.

It started with *Zanjeer (Chain,* 1973), in which one saw a mix of the old and the new. An honest cop (Vijay) fights dishonest smugglers and the underworld. He is trapped and spends time in jail. He comes out and becomes a vigilante whose only priority is revenge. He takes the law into his own hands, and, finally, kills the mafia kingpin who is also his father's killer. But this trend changed with *Deewar* (1975).

Within two years, Vijay was transformed from an essentially honest person who uses immoral means only for a justified social end, to one who deliberately chooses to become a smuggler when given the opportunity. The success and popularity of Amitabh Bachchan in *Deewar* proved that the Indian middle class did not mind smugglers and crooks, that this section of society was convinced that the so-called wrong is right today.

So it was in *Trishul (A Three-Edged Spear),* in which Bachchan bribes his way to success in the already corrupt real estate business. The only moral, but individual and not social, caveat in the movie was the cause; he did it to seek revenge on his illegitimate father.

While the violent anti-hero became the social star, there was a similar but divergent trend in Bollywood at the same time.

Taking off from *Rajnigandha, Anubhav,* and *Avishkaar,* several directors tried the ironical comedy plots to tell the story of the other middle class, which was getting snowed under but somehow trudged through life in a happy-go-lucky manner. Here too, the middle class realized it could not change things, so it used dishonest means to achieve its ends and play the system!

The only difference: the stories were treated differently— without violence and with dollops of black humor, and the ends that the characters sought were almost petty. It was as though the middle class was only using dishonest and unfair means to make its life a wee bit better, and it was not harming the larger society in any perceptible or impressionable way. It was a defense-cum-survival mechanism.

Hrishikesh Mukherjee was probably the most prominent master of this genre. His characters somehow seemed frivolous and fun loving, yet were grounded and serious. They were immoral, yet possessed values. They cut corners, but only for the so-called "right" issues. There was nothing wrong with their ends but the means were questionable.

Cut to *Golmaal (Hodge Podge)* starring Amol Palekar, who emerged as the nonglamorous, down-to-earth, but lovable hero of the late 1970s and 1980s. The urban, happy-go-lucky Lucky (or Lakshman Prasad) changes his looks and behavior to get a job. He fools his boss several times, and maintains a double identity as twins, one of whom does not exist. But this is not judged as wrong by the audience, because, at the end of the day, Lucky is a decent middle-class person who is just trying to get through his stressed modern-day life.

Another Mukherjee film, *Chupke Chupke (Stealthily)*, portrays a naughty prankster, Dharmendra, who makes a fool of his wife's sister's father-in-law. The moral decay in society is ironically shown through his friend's (Amitabh Bachchan) dilemma because he is impersonating Dharmendra, so he has a wife, but is in love with another woman.

In *Rang Birangi (Colorful)*, Nirmala (Parveen Babi) complains about the lost romance in her seven-year-old marriage to her brother, who encourages her husband Ajay (Amol Palekar) to have an affair to rekindle it. Soon Nirmala realizes that Ajay has become more attentive, loving and caring, because he is simply repeating what he is doing with his "girlfriend," Anita (Deepti Naval). To get the husband back to his sister, the brother concocts a story about Nirmala's affair. It is a movie with a happy ending, and one leaves the theatre with a feeling that post-marital relationships are not so bad after all if they are as innocent as Ajay's, who has a bit of "clean" fun only to put the zing back into his relationship with Nirmala.

Directors such as Saeed Mirza used the irony–comedy style to make a bigger comment on society's degeneration. In his movies *Albert Pinto Ko Gussa Kyon Aata Hai (Why Does Albert Pinto Get Angry?)*, *Arvind Desai Ki Ajeeb Dastaan (Arvind Desai's Weird Saga)*, *Mohan Joshi Hazir Ho (Enter the Courtroom, Mohan Joshi)*, and *Salim Langde Pe Mat Ro (Do Not Cry For Salim Langda)*, Mirza used micro-stories of ordinary middle-class people to sketch insightful macro-pictures that highlight urban socioeconomic problems.

In *Mohan Joshi Hazir Ho*, a middle-aged, middle-class couple in Mumbai fight with their landlord, who has failed to repair the house for years. Their endeavor yields no results, as their lawyers milk them, and the legal case is not decided for years. The underlying focus is on the sad state and shortage of urban housing and the helplessness of the tenants. It is also a comment on the judiciary, which is unable to administer justice to the powerless, un-networked middle class. After all, justice delayed is justice denied.

The auto mechanic in *Albert Pinto Ko Gussa Kyon Aata Hai* changes from a passive personality—which the middle class generally is—to an active resisting force—which the middle class can become—after being awakened by his family's suffering.

In the recent past, one has seen Albert Pinto-like middle-class activism, both in reel and real life. The movie that became a hit with urban youth was *Rang De Basanti (Color Me Yellow)*, which also gained global recognition. Juxtaposing the past with the present, the stories of freedom fighters in pre-independent India and those of yuppy college kids of today, it traced the transformation of the students and their passionate struggle for freedom from internal politico-socioeconomic shackles in independent India.

Five friends decide to take revenge when their sixth friend, a fighter jet pilot, dies in a crash that was caused by spare parts of questionable quality used in air force jet planes, bought at the behest of corrupt policymakers. In Bollywood style, they kill the middleman (the father of one of them) and the defence minister, but are shot dead by security forces after they have spread their nationalistic message over the state-owned radio station.

Almost a replay of this—minus the violence—happened in real life, after the accused in the Jessica Lal murder case was found "not guilty" by a lower Indian court. Jessica Lal, a model, was a typical middle-class girl, who was shot dead when she refused to serve a drink at an illegal Delhi pub run by a socialite family. The powerful families of the accused worked the system, and used money and other means to influence the legal case successfully. The police conducted a shoddy investigation, almost all prosecution witnesses turned hostile, and there were visible attempts to save the accused.

Unlike in other cases, this time middle-class India turned hostile and waged a technological war on the system and the powerful people involved. It used text messages and emails to petition the president and prime minister of India. TV and print journalists, who normally have middle-class roots, gave vent to their bottled-up feelings through this tussle. They highlighted the shortcomings of the case, and asked their viewers and readers to join the fight. Hundreds of thousands of people text messages or emailed their angry feelings. My friends told me that *Outlook* should do a cover story on Jessica Lal. I said it would be possible only if the readers wrote to the editor asking for it. And they did! My editor agreed to do the cover.

The fact is that the intelligentsia, even if it was biased towards the power centers, was forced to notice this movement that had no leaders or masterminds, was not backed by political parties, nor was spearheaded by any NGO. The rage gathered an unheard-of momentum of its own, as the middle class from across India joined in. Jessica Lal, a Delhi-based model, became a much-discussed name in cities and towns from Mumbai to Kochi, Coimbatore to Bhubaneswar, Bareilly to Kota.

Finally, India's apex court, the Supreme Court, intervened and ordered a retrial. After months of hearings, the main accused was convicted and sentenced to life imprisonment.

During the late-1980s, and up to the present time, violence mingled with comedy, and vice versa, as Bollywood tried to find that perfect recipe for a successful plot. It produced hundreds of banal and inane films that flopped at the box office. Nonetheless, it was affected by the strong winds of change: economic reforms, globalization, and corporatization, during a period that signified the triumph of the private sector and changing power equations in favor of the middle class, rather than the privileged segments.

India steadily became younger, and now more than 50 percent of its population is less than 25 years of age. Millions of people crashed into the so-called middle class. As we have seen in the first chapter, a proportion of them became the NMC or the Spenderati and introduced a new consumption-led subculture. Many of them, especially in the services sector, became CEOs and billionaires in a typical rants-to-riches way. The middle class that usually raved and ranted against the system but did little else began to take advantage of the new opportunities to get rich quickly. And there was a growing aspiring segment that wanted to ape the real middle class and become a part of it.

Given this scenario, it is clear that movie genres had to change as well.

One set of movies appealed to the north Indian middle class. *Hum Aapke Hain Kaun (Who Am I To You)*, which had the longest run in Bollywood's history, *Dilwale Dulhania Le Jayenge (Those With a Heart Will Take Away The Bride)*, and *Kuch Kuch Hota Hai (Something, Something Happens)*, belonged to this category. They showed conservative, extended, middle-class north Indian families caught in times of significant change. They celebrated all the traditions and rituals to comfort themselves, worried as they were about the increasing Westernization of the younger generation. So they showed Westernized youth retaining a strong attachment to their cultural and social roots.

A premarital affair flourished—and was even encouraged—in *Hum Aapke Hain Kaun*. In *Dilwale Dulhania Le Jayenge*, the hero tells his girlfriend that he will not marry her unless her conservative father gave his consent. This is despite having the option to run away with her, knowing that the father would never agree to the marriage. Interestingly, the hero's liberal-minded father cajoles his son to go from London to a Punjab village to woo his sweetheart. *Kuch Kuch Hota Hai* leaves one with the feeling that an Indian woman looks attractive only in Indian clothes (*sari* and *salwar-kameez*), yet easily accepts a widower with a child. Ironically, the child is instrumental in cajoling her father to remarry—to a college friend, who still secretly loves him from those days.

More changes were on the stocks. Lately, there have been movies that have accepted relationships between older men and much younger women, and vice versa, in *Nishabd (Without Words)*, *Cheeni Kum (Less Sugar)*, and *Ek Choti Si Love Story (A Small Love Story)*. Gay relationships, featuring both men and women, were explored in *Fire, Girlfriend,* and *My Brother Nikhil* (in which Nikhil dies of AIDS).

All these ideas had traditionally been looked down upon by the society and mainstream cinema (apart from a few bold, breakthrough movies). But that these movies were made—and accepted—clearly shows that the middle-class audience had come to accept new truths with some level of comfort.

As relations between India and Pakistan reached a low ebb and riots broke out frequently in urban India, as the Indian mafia expanded its rule all over India and abroad, as politics became the playground for crooks, these issues became the concern of the Indian middle class. It was desperately looking for possible solutions, so Hindi cinema dabbled with these themes in movies such as *Roza, Bombay, Ab Tak Chhappan (Till Now 56)*, *Shootout at Lokhandwala, Company,* and *Omkara.*

But what was interesting was the release of several movies that dealt with the mindset and attitude of the characters that formed an integral part of the NMC and the Spenderati, as well as those who aspire to assimilate with the NMC.

There was a spate of movies, for example, on teenage love, which was becoming a common phenomenon in colleges across cities and towns. Or, maybe, the trend gathered steam because of the movies! Anyway, among the first of this lot was *Qayamat Se Qayamat Tak (From Apocalypse to Apocalypse)*, starring the now-famous Aamir Khan. Such films firmly established "puppy" love and premarital sex in mainstream society.

Moreover, the characters of the heroes changed: now they were baby-faced, young, not too obsessed with education, street smart, quick on their feet and quick-minded, and confident. These seemed very much like the traits generally visible among the NMC. It marked the rise of the three Khans: Aamir, Shah

Rukh, and Salman. All of them started in these roles and only much later assumed different on-screen personalities.

The next big change in middle-class characterization happened when *Dil Chahta Hai (DCH, or Heart Wants It)*, a story of three friends, was released in 2001. As Santosh Desai, an advertising guru who writes on popular culture, pointed out:

> For the first time, it (*DCH*) allows PLU (people like us) audiences to peer into the mirror called Hindi films and not flinch. For one, their protagonists are more PLU than ever before. What makes *DCH* special is that it's a film about today with no reference to yesterday.[7]

When Desai talks about PLU, he is referring to the NMC.

DCH's protagonists, Akash, Sameer, and Sid, had different shades that were borrowed from different constituents of the NMC. They wore branded clothes, their hair was blow-dried and gelled, their looks made a fashion statement (such as Akash's "goatee," which became a rage), and they had a gait to match John Travolta's in the opening scene of *Saturday Night Fever*. To summarize, they looked like cool dudes.

More importantly, they had an attitude and a lifestyle. During their college days, they led a carefree life, partying into the night, holidaying in Goa, utterly sure they could hook any girl, or, if not, try their luck with any they met, having fun at other people's expense, even pulling one another's leg. They lived their lives together—which is so common among urban middle-class students.

The arrogance of youth (which is on the rise, especially among the NMC) is clear from the interaction between Akash and his father, who believes his son is not maturing fast enough to take any responsibility in his business.

> Dad: *"Yehi haal raha toh mere budaape tak ek aadh cheque to sign kar loge."* ("If the situation remains like this, you will just about learn to sign checks by the time I become old.")
>
> Akash: "Dad, *zindagi mein cheque sign karne ke ilaava bhi bahut kuch hai.*" ("Dad, there is much more to life than just signing checks.")
>
> Dad: *"Aur kya hai yeh bahut kuch?"* ("What are these many other things?")
>
> Akash: *"Abhi tak to nahin pata magar pata lagte hi sab se pehle aap ko bataunga."* ("I don't know yet, but when I do, you will be the first to find out.")

The trio reflect how, slowly but surely, friends are becoming the new family for many youngsters. This changing mindset among youth is reflected in *DCH* in a scene in which the three friends are talking about their future holidays together in Goa.

> Sid: *"Kiski zindagi kisko kahan le jaayegi, kya pata? Kabhi socha hai ki har saal yahan aana to ek taraf, shayad dus saal mein ek baar bhi milna mushkil ho."* ("Who knows where life will take us? Have you ever thought, forget about meeting here every year, we may find it difficult to do it once every ten years.")
>
> Akash: *"Hum dost they, hain, aur rehenge—hamesha ke liye."* ("We were friends, still are, and will remain so—forever.")

Their confidence emerges from the lyrics of the song they sing at a party.

> *"Koi kahe, kehta rahe kitna bhi humko deewana. Hum logon ki thokar mein hai yeh zamaana ... Hum hain naye, andaaz kyoon ho puraana?"* ("Let whoever, how many times whatsoever, call us wild. The world is at our feet ... We are the new, so why should our attitudes and mindset be old?")

The brashness of the urban youth comes across in the scene in which Akash meets Shalini for the first time at the graduation party, goes down on his knees, and proposes to her. Obviously, she refuses, dismissing it as a joke. Which it was!

But more than anything else, *DCH* is about the changing dynamics of social relationships in middle-class India. There are two trends that are emerging among this segment. The first is that parents have realized the consequences of the inevitable generation gap and, hence, try to become friends with their kids. The second is that because of many socioeconomic factors, friends are becoming family for many. Scared that their child may self-destruct due to drugs, crime, and immature love decisions, middle-class parents are consciously taking steps to bridge the generation gap. To make that connection, parents high-five with the kids, drink with them, discuss women and other topics such as the latest music and movies, and try to think like them. They put themselves in their children's shoes.

Because modern times may compel parents and children to stay in different cities because of education or work, the kids are forming their own social circles to cater to their emotional and other needs. In the case of unmarried people, friends logically become the family. So it is with divorcees and separated couples, whose numbers are increasing. Married couples, too, sometimes feel more free and comfortable discussing their problems with close friends.

One of the worst fears of this confident, ambitious creed is to be "judged" by others in their times of weakness (emotional, professional, or other). Parents and partners instinctively do that, but most friends do not. (One of the reasons for broken relationships today is the lack of communication between partners.) *DCH* elaborated and highlighted the "parents as friends" and "friends as family" trends.

Post-*DCH*, one saw movie characters who borrowed liberally from Akash, Sameer, and Sid. Friends take care of each other's problems in *Pyaar Ke Side Effects (Love's Side Effects)*; the movie was also about a live-in relationship that, finally, is consummated. *Rang De Basanti* was about slick 'n' suave young urbanites, who share things in their lives, and endure their sorrow and happiness together in a platonic–intimate manner.

Issues and themes that caused conflict for, and confronted and troubled, the nonresident Indian (NRI) community also caught on with Bollywood during this period. As more Indians flew to the United States, Europe, and Africa to study or work, the number of lonely families back home grew. So directors and producers made films for both the families at home and those living abroad. Many of these films did well at the international box office.

Since India became a global leader in software, the scramble for the American visa by techies and other lighter and darker shades of a software engineer's life have been portrayed in movies such as *Hyderabad Blues* (with a bad sequel too).

The latest in this saga of projecting the middle class in Hindi cinema is *Guru* (supposedly based on the life and times of India's most successful business group, the Reliance group of industries owned by the House of Ambani, which has now been split between the two sons of the patriarch). The story of the late patriarch, Dhirubhai Ambani, is a typical rags-to-riches one. He built India's largest private sector organization within three decades. And the germ of the idea to make a movie about him must have been born when the scriptwriter, a shareholder of the Ambani-owned group, attended Reliance Industries' annual general meeting at Mumbai's Brabourne Cricket Stadium, where thousands gathered to listen to Dhirubhai.

I can imagine this: *"Aap sab ko Gurubhai ka salaam,"* says Gurubhai (the reel-life Dhirubhai) as he raises his hands in front of the 50,000 present at a huge sports stadium. "Twenty-five years ago, we took a pledge to build India's largest company. We've done it. Now, it's time to chase a new dream. Do you want to become the world's largest?" asks a smiling Gurubhai. The crowd screams "yes, yes." Among the thousands of Gurubhai's shareholders sit three movie buffs in the 30–35 age group, seated hundreds of feet from each other.

All three harbor the same Bollywood dream. They want to be involved in the making of a movie on the changing middle class in India. Their inspiration is their business hero, who has helped them become millionaires in a few years, enabled them to buy an apartment and flashy car, and live a lifestyle where they could pub and eat out every day. Gurubhai has turned them into a captive consumer of Western ideals, and they have become an integral part of a class that is brand conscious and risktaking.

Through Gurubhai, and other characters, they wish to celebrate the emergence and success of a confident and ambitious entrepreneurial class. Through them, the trio hope to portray the growing middle class, which is successful, materialistic, consumption-oriented, global, yet rooted in Indian values. This is what they were thinking of as they heard Gurubhai's voice declare: "If India has to emerge as a superpower, it needs change-drivers like us, and not those karmic-believers who blame everything on destiny."

Well, one has to admit that the subplot about Gurubhai was this author's feeble attempt at scriptwriting. But the fact remains that Dhirubhai, or Gurubhai, has become the new icon of the Great Indian Middle Class today.

Endnotes

1. http://www.upperstall.com/films/jagteraho.html
2. *Screen* "Flashback: Serenading Forever?," October 31, 2006, http://www.indiafm.com/ features/2006/10/31/1766/index.html

3. http://en.wikipedia.org/wiki/Rajesh_Khanna

4. As quoted in http://www.indiantelevision.com/mam/headlines/y2k6/apr/aprmam63.htm

5. Pavan K. Varma, "Living Statues of Liberty," *Outlook*, October 16, 2006, http://www.outlookindia.com/fullprint.asp?choice=1&fodname=20061016&fname=CNew+Middle+Class+%28F%29&sid=1

6. ibid.

7. Santosh Desai, "Aamir as a PLU Sign," *Outlook*, September 17, 2001, http://www.outlookindia.com/full.asp?fodname=20010917&fname=Column+Dil+Chahta+Hai+%28F%29&sid=1

Chapter 5

Retail's Short Tail

The tail is important. It is critical in the context of modern retailing. The 20–80 theory—according to which 20 percent of brands in any category account for 80 percent of sales and almost 100 percent of profits—is being turned upside down. Niche and invisible customers are becoming as important as mainstream customers. Chris Anderson writes in his famous book, *The Long Tail: Why the Future of Business is Selling Less of More*, "The era of one-size fits all is ending, and in its place is something new, a market of multitudes ... Increasingly, the mass market is turning into a mass of niches."[1]

What Anderson is saying is that the advent of new low-cost distribution channels (especially the Internet) has enabled marketers to sell a cumulative amount of products (running into the millions) in a specific category, even if the market for them is fragmented globally. So the market for niche products is becoming as big as the market for the more popular brands. For example, if a company sells, say, only five copies of a particular music album every day in 50 countries, the market for the album would amount to 450,000 copies in five years, which is a huge number.

Even in the physical retail store models (malls, superstores, and hypermarkets), the long tail is growing in importance. These outlets stock dozens of brands in each product category because they have realized that while the few mainstream brands do sell a lot, the combined sales of the huge number of lesser-known "other" brands can be significant too. A well-known Unilever brand, Surf, may sell in thousands every day. But the cumulative sales of 50 lesser-known detergent brands, which sell 20 packs each a day, can also account for one thousand.

Anderson traces this new trend to the fact that "the ants have megaphones," or to the reality that the view of the customer regarded hitherto as unknown and inconsequential is "now a public conversation, carried in blog comments and customer reviews," and as someone who now influences large-scale purchases. Such sales can be in several million dollars.[2]

As India witnesses a revolution in organized retail, the bigger players are becoming aware of the tail, apart from the profitable head and body. This is prompting them to think of size. Some of them are talking of retail stores spread over 1,860–2,320 sq m. For instance, the Mumbai-based Raheja Group plans hyper cities, each with a floor space of 7,430 sq m. This will enable it to stock more brands in product clusters.

The same thing is happening with small retail stores, albeit in a different manner because they do not have the financial resources to get into the floor-space race. A Delhi-based bookshop is always keen on procuring titles that it does not already stock. The management makes sure of informing customers about the availability of the new titles. One of the store owners told me that he sells many books to order. The idea, once again, is to take care of the tail, as it can be as lucrative as the head, that is, the more popular, fast-moving books.

The outward appearance of the head and the rest of the body is epitomized by the glass-and-concrete structures that dot the Indian urban skyline. Hundreds of malls, superstores, and hypermarkets are being constructed; there are some whose foundations are still being dug, and others whose metallic spines are standing. But there are many, which are complete and are ready to provide a completely different shopping experience to customers.

As one drives down the highway from Delhi to Gurgaon, a burgeoning information technology (IT) and corporate hub to the south of the city, one sees the glass-and-steel exteriors of hundreds of new office buildings of modernist design that reflect the exterior environment in various shades and hues, dozens of larger-than-life-sized billboards, and giant LCD screens (each 6 meters) flashing news and advertising images. In Gurgaon, nearly a dozen malls line both sides of a 0.8 km stretch; another three or four malls are under construction.

This is the general trend in most Indian cities, and even in some of the larger towns. As middle-class Indians become mall rats, realty companies are scrambling to build more malls to woo them. According to many experts, organized retail will be among the fastest-growing sectors over the next few years. That is why it is attracting some of the best-known names in Indian business—Tatas, Birlas, Ambanis, Biyanis, Goenkas, and Rahejas. Even global giants like Wal-Mart, Tesco, and Metro are eager to enter the front-end retail market in India.

No one is talking about setting up a dozen new outlets in the near future. Instead they are talking about constructing thousands of outlets covering hundreds of thousands of square meters of space. Reliance Retail aims to have a presence in nearly 800 urban towns and more than 6,000 rural towns, with a total floor space of 9.3 million sq. m. Subiksha, a chain that operates on a low-cost, low-capital model, and offers huge discounts, plans to expand its current tally of 100-plus outlets to 750. The Bharti–Wal-Mart tie-up plans to set up hundreds of outlets over the next five years.

All are convinced that the changes in the buying habits of Indian consumers will now be accelerated. First, they will move from the neighborhood store to the retail outlet. Then they will buy branded products. Next, they will shop in a place that is pleasurable, comfortable, and offers good prices. Then they will want a wide array of choices. Finally, they will prefer single-point shopping.

Kishore Biyani, the owner of one of the largest Indian retail chain, Pantaloon Retail, describes the changing needs and attitudes of Indian consumers. He cites the example of a family in Sangli, a trading town in Maharashtra, a state in western India; rich sugarcane farmers live in the areas around Sangli.

Mohan Jadhav is one such sugarcane farmer who lives in Walwa, another 40 kms from Sangli. Forty-five years old, Jadhav lives in a joint family that has 127 members. He also happens to be our biggest customer till date. On a sunny Tuesday morning in March 2006, he drove down to Sangli in his Bajaj Trax pickup van along with his wife, sister-in-law and nephews. The six of them visited our Big Bazaar outlet ... and indulged in some frenzied shopping activity—buying grocery, utensils, shirts, dhotis, saris, shoes, toys and much more. At the cash-counter his bill turned out to be fourteen feet long. The total amount he had shopped for, on a single day at this Big Bazaar outlet, was Rs 1,37,367 (almost US$3,500).[3]

Take another example when my friend, Kavita, helped me set up a house. We decided to do the shopping in phases—basic necessities first, kitchenware next, and expensive items last— buying these from organized retail outlets such as Lifestyle in Gurgaon, Home Town in Noida, and Fabindia in South Delhi. We found that the goods at these malls or big outlets were as cheap, or even cheaper in some cases, than at the smaller shops. Similarly, another friend, Bonita, a young single working woman buys bread, milk, and vegetables from the local grocery every second day or so, and does all her other household shopping weekly at a large retail store in South Delhi's Vasant Vihar. Urban India has thousands of customers like these people. Their numbers are growing every day.

Kishore describes his Big Bazaar experiences:

It was a Thursday morning that started like no other. At 7.30 in the morning, I received a call from Sadashiv Nayak, head of our operations in the western region, informing me that there was a long queue of customers waiting outside the Big Bazaar in Lower Parel, Mumbai... Similar calls from Bangalore, Gurgaon, and Kolkata informed me of long queues of customers waiting outside Big Bazaar stores at those places as well ... In Kolkata, where one of our stores is located on the V.I.P. Road that connects the city to the airport, eager customers had spilled on to the streets and [had] blocked the airport traffic. Our second outlet in Kolkata is located within a residential compound called Hiland Park. There our managers had started to pull down the shutters after residents of the locality complained that they couldn't get in or out of the compound due to the large crowds blocking the entrance. A similar step was being taken at the V.I.P. Road as well, but Kolkata being Kolkata, customers had started banging on the shutters and heckling the staff. The police, who had earlier insisted that the store be shut down, were now unable to control the situation and told our staff to reopen the store ...

At almost all locations, the police came in to control the crowds waiting outside the stores. And within a couple of hours of business, most stores had to be closed down so that the situation didn't go completely out of hand. At Koramangala in Bangalore, attempts at shutting down the store failed. This prompted the local police official to unilaterally announce on the public address system that the sale had been extended by another day. Each one of us in the organization was surprised by the response from customers. High-ticket items like televisions, mobile phones, and DVD players flew off the shelves like vegetables ... The Sabse Sasta Din [Least Expensive Day] had turned into a topic of national importance covered by the media almost to the fervour of a one-day cricket match.[4]

Kishore is describing the highly publicized discount sale on January 26, 2006. The most surprising feature of the day was neither the crowd nor the confusion. It was a day that convinced marketers that the "aspirant" class, which usually avoids malls because it lacks the confidence to shop at big outlets, can be wooed to do precisely this. It was probably the first time that the middle class and the aspirant class had shopped together at the same store.

But the Pantaloon owner looks at this from a different perspective. He divides the country's consumers into three categories: India 1, India 2, and India 3. India 1, or the consuming class, constitutes only 14 percent (180 million) of the population. According to Kishore, modern retail formats mostly attract customers from this segment. India 2, or the serving class, includes people like household help, office peons, drivers, and washermen. This group makes the life of India 1 easier and comfortable; it accounts for more than 40 percent of the population. India 3 is the struggling class, the poor who barely get two meals a day. They comprise the "other" India.

India 1 does not want India 2 to progress, either socially or economically. Subconsciously or otherwise, India 1 tries to keep India 2 at the same level at which it is now. India 1 also does not care to pay India 2 enough to enable the latter to have more disposable income and thus become a part of the consuming class. But India 2 has aspirations and wants to join India 1. Kishore says that on January 26, 2006, India 1 and India 2 shopped together at the Big Bazaar outlets.

Given these numbers and trends, it is not surprising that retailers are excited about the Indian market. Their hopes are backed up by statistics collated in the *India Retail Report, 2007*[5]:

❏ Of the annual private consumption expenditure of US$480 billion, less than 3 percent is through organized retail. However, organized retail is growing at over 36 percent every year and will cross the Rs 1,000,000 crore (US$25 billion) annual sales mark before 2010. By

2007–08, India is likely to have 100 million sq. ft. of shopping center space generating annual sales of Rs 50,000 crore (US$12.5 billion).

❑ More than 200 malls with a combined space of 25 million sq. ft. are sprouting across the country. They will require an investment of Rs 12,500 crore (US$3.12 billion), or eight times the Rs 1,500 crore (US$0.38 billion) invested until 2006. The total investment in organized retail is expected to be Rs 20,000 crore (US$5 billion) by 2010. An ICICI study estimates that the annual revenues earned by the various malls will be more than US$9 billion by 2010.

The report also describes the various macro and micro socioeconomic trends that will lead to the escalation of the retail boom in the near future.

First, and we have discussed this in earlier chapters, the booming and fast-growing economy is enabling more people to join the middle-class bandwagon and, simultaneously, is increasing the disposable incomes of these households. This is why several think-tank experts and marketers are optimistic about the fate of their brands.

Second, the current demographic pattern is favoring consumption. The report states:

> The Indian consumer is among the youngest in the world as compared to the ageing population of the US, China, Japan, the UK, etc. Over 65 per cent of the (Indian) population is below 35 years old; 54 per cent of the population is below 25 years of age.[6]

One of the reasons for the large-scale outsourcing by Western companies to India is this age factor. In India, younger people work harder, can be hired at lower wages compared with people in Western nations, and are more willing to make quick work-related changes in response to the ever-changing global scenario.

Although labor costs in the business process outsourcing (BPO) sector in India are much lower than, say, those in the United States, Indian salaries are still many times higher than those in the traditional areas. For instance, the starting salary at a call center can be at least Rs 10,000 (US$250) a month for a graduate, compared to half of that in the traditional sectors. So India is lucky to have younger consumers, but with larger disposable incomes.

The report concludes:

> Young consumer also means that he or she will be quicker at experimentation ... These young consumers are socially aware and are making purchase decisions that they believe can make a difference. Expect more of them to embrace the concept of style and sustainability.[7]

Add to this the fact that younger consumers are generally more brand conscious, are keen to shop in a Westernized environment, and are eager to adopt the latest styles and fashions. More importantly, as we saw in the first chapter, some of the Indian consumers are changing in terms of their thinking and mindset. As the nuclear family becomes more and more common in urban India, experts point out that "time poverty is setting in" and claim that the consumer "is willing to pay more if it ensures freedom from hassles." As the report puts it, "The DINK segment has now begun to make its presence felt in the market."

A deeper analysis of two formats in the retail segment reveals the changes in the preferences of Indian consumers that have occurred in the recent past.

The first is about the trends in food and grocery (F&G) retailing. The organized subset of the segment is a Rs 5,000 crore (US$1.25 billion) industry, and the domination by regional players is changing into a pan-India presence. Newer players such as Reliance Fresh have entered the market, and regional chains such as Subiksha are expanding across India. These retailers covered 73 percent more cities in 2006, compared with 18 percent growth in the previous year. In terms of the total number of outlets in various cities, the number doubled in 2005, and it recorded a healthy growth of 65 percent the next year. In the near future, hypermarkets (the latest marketing innovation) will fuel this growth even further.

Another factor that will contribute to the F&G boom is the shift in consumer preference toward branded packaged food and the demand for a wide array of products under a single roof. The gradual globalization of the Indian palate is leading to increased sales of different kinds of food products. Due to time constraints, many people (especially working couples) are forced to shop at outlets that sell almost everything. Indian consumers are now demanding a "shopping experience" even when purchasing basic items like rice and *dal* (lentils).

Another area that has seen a remarkable change in attitude and buying patterns is the luxury segment. Devyani Raman, CEO, Luxury Marketing Council Worldwide, India, observes, "India, India, India—the new mantra on the global luxury marketer's tongue." She adds that although luxury has been associated traditionally with kings, princes, and feudal lords in India, the situation has now changed. "India today is demographically younger, geographically dispersed, and psychologically trans-formed into another type of target audience," says Ms. Raman. "It now comprises consumers who want to own the best that is available globally. For the affluent buyer, simple living is passé as everything has to be 'nothing but the best'. He/she is 'value-driven' and believes in the new maxim that 'wealth [is] to be enjoyed rather than displayed.'"[8]

Let us look at some numbers to gain an idea about the size of this affluent class in India. NCAER predicts that the number of households with an annual income of more than Rs 1 crore (US$250,000) will multiply seven times to 140,000 between 2001–02 and 2009–10. The *Asia-Pacific Wealth Report* by DSP Merrill Lynch and CapGemini India states that India had 83,000 high net-worth individuals (HNWIs) in 2005, an increase of over 19 percent from the previous year. These HNWIs together held US$290 billion in assets, or 3.8 percent of the total Asia-Pacific HNWI wealth. The *World Wealth Report, 2005* states that HNWI growth in India was 14.6 percent, or double the global rate. A report by the Knowledge Company says that India had 1.6 million luxury households, and predicts that the figure would cross 3 million by 2010. The new affluent customers are mostly CEOs, senior executives in their thirties and forties, returning nonresident Indians (NRIs), entrepreneurs in sunrise sectors like telecoms, and modern retailers.

Many of these new consumers are on a shopping binge. Raman points to the indicators of high-end growth in the US$444 million luxury market[9]:

❏ Luxury watch market is growing at 40 percent.
❏ Branded jewelry at 40 percent.
❏ Luxury cars at 50 percent.

❏ Wine at 30 percent.
❏ Global travel at 35 percent.

The next step is to define luxury, as the concept can be quite confusing for marketers and consumers. For example, some Indian consumers feel that a car that costs Rs 15 lakh (US$37,500) (Skoda) is a luxury; others think that a car priced at Rs 1.5 crore (US$375,000) (Bentley) denotes luxury. Some regard a watch costing Rs 70,000 (US$1,750) as a symbol of luxury; others put the figure at Rs 15 lakh.

The Luxury Marketing Council Worldwide defines luxury as

> ... things so distinguished by the quality of the art and science lavished onto and poured into them that they command a premium value. Premium value is one reflection of and emotional acknowledgement by the consumer of superior value; that value not necessarily being self-evident but evident to those with the knowledge and education necessary for appreciation.[10]

Raman elaborates this definition further:

> ... these products and services give the consumers the satisfaction of not only owning expensive items or being serviced by the best of breed, but the extra added psychological benefits like esteem, prestige and a sense of high status that reminds them and others that they belong to an exclusive group of only a select few, who can afford these high-priced items.[11]

The number of the "select few" is burgeoning. Many experts are convinced that younger Indians from wealthy families have more purchasing power than their American and European counterparts. Most of the disposable income, in some cases the entire income, goes toward buying branded luxury products.

The mania for luxury goods has spread to the not-so-wealthy sections too. Nibha, who works for a Delhi-based public relations firm and earns about Rs 10 lakh (US$25,000) a year, owns over a dozen watches, ranging from FCUK, Tag Heuer, Esprit, and Pierre Cardin. And she loves expensive jewelry. She does not blink when buying a watch for Rs 70,000 (US$1,750) or a necklace for Rs 1.5 lakh (US$3,750).

How can someone who earns this kind of a salary spend so lavishly? Does Nibha's consumer behavior contradict the arguments made in Chapter 3, where it was said that even individuals who earn such salaries may not completely be part of the consuming class? People like Nibha are still a minority, although their numbers are growing. Her example is meant to illustrate how the market for luxury products is expanding for totally unrelated reasons.

In Nibha's case, the reason for her lavish spending is that her entire salary is disposable. "My in-laws own the house where I stay, and my husband earns enough to take care of all our regular monthly expenses. Thus, my salary is entirely mine. I can spend it the way I like—to buy clothes, accessories, luxury products," she explains. More importantly, Nibha does not buy these items to show them off; she buys them because they make her happy. The Indian Nibhas are driven by an internal desire as opposed to external social pressure.

Although marketers love to think of all Indian luxury consumers as being "driven by value" and that they "hate to display" their expensive possessions, this is not entirely true. There is a subset that does think like this. There is another subset consisting of people, like Nibha who are not wealthy by any definition, but who still manage to shop for luxury products because of fortunate circumstances.

There is another, much larger segment that is totally driven by the need to ape others. This segment mostly does what others are doing, both in India and globally. There are two simple ways to know and understand this class. The first is to take a look at the expanding page 3 culture in Indian metropolises, and the other is to examine the "big fat Indian wedding."

Page 3 is a term that evolved from changes in the manner in which newspapers have covered local news over the past two decades. In the 1980s, this page of the paper was reserved for local news. So in the specific cities where editions of the paper were printed, it was widely read by the local populace. The page told readers about what was happening around them (social calendar, daily events), and what problems (such as traffic jams) they might face on any given day.

Slowly, as India began to open up its economy, and as the Indian middle class grew in size, and as urban society changed from a closed-door society to a glamorous glitterati-driven one, the contents of page 3 changed dramatically. Indeed, some newspaper barons took the page out of the main newspaper, converted it into a pullout supplement, and started covering the activities and lifestyles of the rich and famous. Over the years, the supplement became a platform for covering the parties thrown by the city's movers and shakers. With the advent of satellite or cable technology, TV channels increasingly used prime time slots to do the same. Page 3 soon became a recognized subculture within Indian urban society. It had somehow become page 1 for the middle class.

As Ashis Nandy, a social commentator, notes, "In a mass society, there is a thirst for a false sense of distinctiveness. People hate the fact that they are part of a mass culture and seek out those who are projected as not being part of the mass."[12] It becomes important for the upper-middle class and the nouveau riche to find any excuse and grab every opportunity to rub shoulders with the wealthy class. People find these opportunities in socialite party circuits. They sometimes use every trick in the book—bribing, using their connections, networking, pleading, even gatecrashing—to attend these parties. In 2000, *Outlook* magazine observed that "the metropolitan party is the new symbol of hyper-consumption. It is a shrine where a new aspirational middle class pays homage to the new ideals of success."[13]

The "wannabe wealthy," the "wannabe classy," and the become-rich-quickly are the largest contingent of the page 3 circuit. They are young politicians, middlemen, designers, models, culture icons, senior managers and CEOs, and senior journalists.

At these parties, Rahul Gandhi, son of the Congress party president, Sonia Gandhi, whispers to fashion designer Raghavendra Rathore, business tycoon Vijay Mallya hugs model Nina Manuel, former journalist and now consultant Dilip Cherian sends a flying kiss to politician Renuka Chowdhury, and editor Vir Sanghvi has a tête-à-tête with Ranjan Bhattacharjee, the foster son of a former prime minister, Atal Behari Vajpayee.

One of the most distinctive traits of these urban wannabes is their belief that to look their best, one has to simply mimic the lifestyles of the wealthy. So they will dress the same way, eat the same food, holiday in the same exotic places, own similar cars, and even talk and behave in the same way. If Anil Ambani owns a BMW, they will buy a Mercedes. If Vijay Mallya drinks Macallan (aged for 40 years), they will opt for normal Laphroaig. If Rahul Gandhi wears an Armani, they will go for a cheaper version by Rohit Bal. If French food is in, they will go to the best restaurant in town so that they can describe their dining experience to their friends.

The idea is to make the rich and famous feel that the wannabes and the nouveau riche are in the same class. It is for this reason that the latter try to outdo the former when it comes to organizing big events like weddings. They go all out to prove they can outspend, out-think, out-organize, outguest the really rich.

There is another category of "small-town wannabes," who also are pushing and shoving to get into page 3. But their origins are a bit different. They are generally from the nonmetros, even smaller towns and cities. Many of them were farmers, who owned large tracts of land and took advantage of the rising real estate prices to sell them at huge prices, and became instant millionaires. Others also made money from real estate—some started as property agents and became land brokers. There are cases of businessmen and traders, who earned a lot of money through unaccounted and irregular means, but have become part of the nouveau riche.

One of the best ways these small-towners-turned-rich get onto page 3 is by organizing lavish events and paying Rs 2 lakh each to the newspapers to carry the news. And the one event where such families love to spend money is marriage. That's the genesis of the new "big fat Indian weddings." Neeta Raheja, a Delhi-based wedding planner, who has organized several such weddings, gives an idea of what can happen at such events.

> It starts with the invitation cards. Most invites include either huge amounts of cash, or a mish-mash of gifts. In one instance, the bride's family, which usually invites all the guests as it invariably spends the most on Indian marriages, sent Rs 31,000 with each invite to the 140 general guests, and Rs 51,000 each to 50 families comprising the groom's family and their relatives. Others send a combination that can consist of designer chocolates, dates and sweets imported from Dubai and Kuwait, gift hampers filled with (foreign) branded products, exotic fruits like kiwi, foreign canned food, and silver glass sets. There's no limit to the number of the types of gifts. Still, some of these nouveau

riche look for bargains; one of the family that sent cash asked me to reduce the price of the pouch (that carried the cash) from Rs 25 each to Rs 22. In many cases, the gifts are packed in bags tied with silver/gold flowers, each costing Rs 5,000. Or they could be sent in boxes shaped like huge sea shells, or with marble-inlaid tops made by workers in Agra and Jaipur.

But nothing can surpass the bizarre and gaudy stuff that happens at the weddings (usually comprising several events spread over four or five days). One family hired the statue builders of Kolkata, known for their life-size statues of Goddess Durga during the festival of Bengali Durga Puja, to recreate the "White House" at their daughter's marriage. Another one hired Nitin Desai, who designed the sets for a famous Hindi movie, *Devdas* (starring superstar Shah Rukh Khan), and asked him to recreate one of the sets for a marriage—and that too, centrally air-conditioned and on a barren piece of land. A third imported roulettes and black jacks from Kathmandu (Nepal) as the theme for their wedding was "Las Vegas." Bridegroom arriving in a chopper, or bride dropping from the sky through a crane-controlled operation, and huge ramps built in the middle of the ocean have now become quite common at these flashy and glitzy marriages. On the whole, a marriage such as these can cost between Rs 50 lakh and Rs 10 crore each. And this expenditure includes the gifts given by both sides—like Armani suits, expensive cars, diamond-studded *sherwanis* (a kind of a long, Chinese-collar, flowing shirt), handycams, laptops, iPods, and clothes full of Swarovski crystals.[14]

In effect, the wannabes and the nouveau riche buy the same luxury brands as the truly wealthy. This is a major reason for the boom in luxury products.

Clearly, modern retail is booming in India. More importantly, there is a perceptible shift among Indian consumers—from shopping at local stores to shopping at malls, supermarkets, and hypermarkets. The footprint of modern retail is expanding at a rapid pace, and it is spreading to smaller towns, even villages.

However, it would be wise not to believe such sweeping generalizations about the booming Indian market. This is because the Indian market is like no other, but some comparisons can still be made with other South Asian, South-east Asian, and East Asian markets like Sri Lanka, Vietnam, and South Korea. As noted in the above paragraph, the operative word is "shift."

Overall, the Indian retail mart, including the organized and unorganized sectors, is growing at 6–7 percent every year. On a base of US$425 billion, this growth implies an additional annual spending of US$25–30 billion. This is no small change by any standard.

Looked at from another perspective, however, the growth figures do look like small change. The average annual wholesale inflation rate in India in the past few years has been 5–6 percent. So the increase in private spending, or the retail market, is just about ahead of the increase in the wholesale prices of various products.

The conclusions are even more dramatic if one takes into account the consumer price index (CPI), which is based on retail prices, rather than the wholesale price index (WPI). India's CPI has been growing at 7–8 percent in the recent past. That is, it is higher than the rise in consumer spending.

If the annual population growth in the past few years is included, we see that per capita consumer spending has declined by a few percentage points.

Similarly, the total food and grocery (F&G) segment, which constitutes the bulk of consumer spending in India, grew by a mere 2.2 percent in 2005–06. Given the fact that the price rise in food and basic items has been one of the highest among all product categories, the total F&G retail is growing less rapidly than the inflation rate. Hence there has been a net decline in consumer spending in this crucial retail area.

This conclusion may not make much sense to readers. We have been led to believe that the Indian middle class is growing, although it is still fragmented along the lines of class, caste, religion, and geography. We have also said that some subsets of this middle class are spending more than ever before. We have also maintained that the attitude of some of these consumers is changing—from an emphasis on saving to an emphasis on spending, from an emphasis on simple living to an emphasis on pursuing individual dreams and desires. We have claimed that the middle class, despite its small size, is exercising choices available in the marketplace, be these in terms of jobs, products, or lifestyles.

If all this is true, how can spending decline in real terms?

This is another aspect of the middle class—and the other India—that has largely been ignored by experts, economists, marketers, and policymakers.

In the new, reforms-oriented, globalized world, there is growing insecurity among many sections of the Indian middle class. As stated earlier, this development goes hand-in-hand with the trend in other sections, which are becoming more confident and ambitious and less averse to risk. This anxiety is witnessed more among those employed by the central and state governments, public sector units (both state and central), the defence forces, and even private sector factories.

Employment in the manufacturing sector has shrunk over the past few years. Studies have shown that there has been a 3 percent loss in manufacturing jobs in the past decade or so. This despite the fact that both domestic and foreign investments have grown manifold in the past few years, as India continues to achieve robust grass domestic product (GDP) growth.

The problem is that although investment per manufacturing unit has gone up as private promoters chase global scale and size, the number of people employed in these units has declined rapidly. Thanks to technology, a 1,000-MW power plant requires only 80–100 people. Recently, I was taken on a tour of a township built by the Mumbai-based Essar Group, which included a port and a steel plant. Surprisingly, there were few human beings to be seen in the workplace. Blast furnaces churning out molten metal in millions of tons every year were being manned by a handful of employees working on computerized controls. The port, said the Essar Group spokesperson proudly, employs less than 100 people. Indeed, the private sector hires more people at their headquarters than at the factory sites.

In the case of the public sector, both the central and the state governments have mustered the courage to close down inefficient, bleeding units. While the decision makes immense sense economically, it has led to the loss of thousands of jobs. It is important to remember that the public sector in India was (and still is to some extent) used as a means to provide employment, and was (and still is) used by various interest groups and powerful individuals to further their own sociopolitical ambitions and to woo their own constituents. As a result, these units became overstaffed and inefficient over the years.

Many public sector undertakings (PSUs) have been sold to the private sector, which, to bring about increased efficiency and productivity, has rid itself of the human flab. Some of the PSUs have even offered voluntary retirement schemes to reduce the size of their workforce. The result, according to the *Economic Survey, 2006–07*, is that total employment in the public sector (including quasi-government and local bodies) has declined from more than 19.5 million in 1997 to about 18.3 million in 2004. Compare this with the fact that during the period 1981–97, the number of public sector employees increased from about 15.5 million to more than 19.5 million. In the case of the private sector, the decline has been from about 8.7 million to 8.25 million in the period 1997–2004.

Per capita emoluments have grown in both the private and public sectors. The figure is an astounding 1,300 percent hike over 1971–72 emoluments after accounting for the rise in CPI. Nevertheless, employees are still worried about retaining their jobs. They don't know when their positions might be axed; they live in constant fear of becoming unemployed.

The situation is worse in agriculture. Thanks to low productivity, high inefficiency, and inconsistent growth due to excessive dependence on the monsoon rains, agriculture in India is unable to provide a viable livelihood for the rural population. Villagers move to the cities in search of better-paid jobs, only to find that they are not required in manufacturing, nor can they be employed in the services sector since they do not have the required skill sets. As a result, they have to settle for low-paid, low-skilled jobs. Many of these migrants belong to the rural middle class; they own land and lived a comfortable and self-contained life in the villages until such time that agriculture became an unviable and unreliable source of livelihood. Discussing the crisis in agriculture, an economist, B.B. Bhattacharya, noted in 2007 that "in agriculture, where productivity is extremely low, wages have hit rock bottom. This is discouraging rural laborers from staying in agriculture."[15] Y.K. Alagh, a former cabinet minister, said that "there is a crisis that is emerging at the village level."[16]

But the typical response of think-tank personnel and policymakers is that the booming services sector is making up for the fall in employment in manufacturing and agriculture. Telecoms, modern retail, IT/BPO/KPO and financial services are adding millions of new jobs, they claim.

These are the sectors that are creating the consumption-driven new middle class; the jobs in these sectors pay handsomely, providing their employees with huge disposable incomes; they help their employees connect with the global village and to mimic Western consumers. They are the future of the consumer revolution in India.

Unfortunately, the services sector, which accounts for 55 percent of India's GDP, employs only 2 million people, or less than 0.5 percent of the country's labor force of 400 million.

It is true that there are 190 million self-employed people, primarily in the services sector. But not all of them have the spending power. Many of them lead a hand-to-mouth existence. They cannot be called the middle class, or even an aspiring class.

We need to accept this bitter fact: India is currently not able to create enough jobs for all its citizens, thus leaving millions unemployed. Most of these people are educated, come from middle-class families, and possess the traits necessary for becoming real consumers. But they will not become real consumers, because they simply cannot do so. Even if they could afford to become real consumers in the near future, they are likely to look at the past and turn into savers.

In April 2007, *Outlook* magazine had this to say about India's future:

> It's a paradox that has baffled everyone. In the near future, it is likely to assume ominous proportions. India is one of the few countries that is staring at the unenviable prospect of jobless growth—a sizzling economic spiral, which is, ironically, leading to higher unemployment. If the trend continues, it can blow up in the policymakers' faces. If hundreds of millions are left out of the prosperity cycle, and similar numbers are added to the job queues, the combustible mix may lead to a social implosion.
>
> Do not laugh off the idea yet, because it is in the realm of possibility. Picture this: by 2020, India's unemployment rate is estimated at 30 per cent, or over 200 million. This implies a fifteen-fold-rise from the existing level of just over 13 million people. Ninety per cent of the unemployed in 2020 will be in the 15–29 age group. Imagine, if this group of frustrated and angry men and women decides to react against the state in the next decade. The reason why TeamLease Services, which arrived at the above figure, thinks India has the potential to experience an "unemployment explosion".[17]

This is one part of middle-class India. The other part, which is the overwhelming majority, is driven by the value-for-money mindset. This VFM-conscious middle class does not go on buying binges. Instead, it seeks bargains and good deals, shops where prices are the best, and will not buy a product (even if it is branded) without looking at the price tag first.

Kishore Biyani, who is considered one of the pioneers in India's modern retailing revolution, agrees completely with this logic, and also agrees partly with the contention that consumer spends are not rising in any dramatic fashion. According to him, the Indian retail model has to be different than those found in other countries in terms of pricing, look-and-feel, and shopping experience.

For one, the Indian retail model has to be a model that offers the best prices, even when compared with the neighborhood stores (F&G) or with the smaller markets (for other products). Kishore's Big Bazaar realized this truth on one particular day, January 26, 2006. The truth was that attractive and discounted prices are probably the single most important factor in attracting Indian consumers to malls, supermarkets, and hypermarkets. Indian consumers will come only if the prices are lower than those they have to pay at competing retail outlets.

Invariably, almost all customers in modern retail outlets behave in exactly the same manner. They all follow the same buying routine, which differs only slightly from the routine they follow when they shop at the local store. Customers will approach a rack displaying the products that they like, need, or desire. They will pick the item that they think is the best and study it. But even before they lift the product from the rack to take a closer look, they will instinctively look at the price tag. And if the price is seemingly high and not what they consider VFM, they will immediately shift their attention to another product. They do this always, without fail.

Only if they are convinced that the price is good will the following sequence of events take place: they will take the product off the shelf, look more closely at it, and then try it (if it is a garment, shoe, bag, watch, perfume, or some other accessory).

Similarly, most people when eating out will first look at the price, rather than at the food or drink item listed on the menu.

People in the 35-years-plus generation still tend to order the lowest-priced items. Perhaps this caution stems from the age-old habit of bargaining with everyone, whether it is the grocer, the vegetable seller, or the tailor. In places where they cannot bargain, or where they hesitate or are reluctant to do so, they opt for the lowest-priced goods.

When I was shopping with Kavita to buy products for my house, we too consistently rejected items that we liked merely because of the price factor. Sometimes I would say that the item "was too expensive." Mostly, she would respond that she can pick up a similar item "at a much lower price from another outlet." And, remember, most experts would categorize the two of us as part of the consuming NMC.

According to a study on the behavior of Indian consumers:

> While languages, religions and consumer preferences may differ from one Indian region to the next, the "desire to milk the most out of the last rupee spent" is one of the unifiers of this diverse nation[,] cutting across income levels, cultures and genders. India has over 12 million retail outlets—more than the rest of the world combined—for 200 million households. The Organized Retail sector is in its infancy—while consumers continue to throng the highly fragmented "traditional" retailers and road side hawkers, in search of variety, customized service and rapport, and in haggling over the items individually purchased that is more for the pleasure of bargaining than [for] the best price. The psychological satisfaction is in having got the better of the "other"—the retailer, the neighbour who can be boasted to, about the bargain obtained, the mother-in-law, who is traditionally a rival to her son's affections, the other consumers ahead and behind you.
>
> In the West, Paco Underhill has spoken of the "Butt Brush Factor" (shoppers are spooked by too-close quarters, and don't like being brushed from behind), but Indians subconsciously gravitate towards the most crowded parts of a bazaar in the belief of the best bargain being available [here]. With the spatial accommodation [that] a billion Indians constantly participate in, the small joys are gained in the fiercely guarded "elbow room" made for oneself, in day to day transactions.[18]

This phenomenon explains in part why real consumer spends are actually down despite the retail revolution. Modern and organized retail has been forced to offer price options that are lower than others'. It has been pressured to offer discounts to woo customers.

In addition, due to economies of scale and competitive pressure, manufacturers have slashed prices in many key consumer-related areas such as IT, telecoms, consumer electronics, white goods, consumer nondurables, garments, and kitchenware. Logically, consumers have to spend less for the same, and most do not desire more. Some sections have deliberately reduced spends because of economic anxieties, financial worries, and other pressures. The two factors have contributed to lower growth in consumer spending.

So the so-called retail revolution is mostly the result of the "substitution" effect. Consumers have "shifted" from unorganized to organized retail. Instead of shopping at traditional outlets, they are thronging malls and supermarkets. While that is true, it does not mean that overall spends in real terms have gone up.

The retail revolution does not imply unbridled consumption-led consumerism.

Some other hard truths about modern retailing in India should be mentioned here, to inform readers that Indian consumers are radically different from their counterparts in other markets. No country can claim to have so many varying sets of consumers.

The best way to understand this comparison is by pointing out the differences in the physical structure and design of malls in the United States and India. This analysis will reveal what retailers think of the customers' behaviors in their respective geographies.

In the United States, the birth of the mall culture began with the Southdale Mall, built in 1956, which still exists. It was designed by Victor Green. A 2004 article in the *New Yorker* describes what Green did:

> Until then, most shopping centers had been what architects like to call "extroverted," meaning that store windows and entrances faced both the parking area and the interior pedestrian walkways. Southdale was introverted: the exterior walls were blank, and all the activity was focussed on the inside. Suburban shopping centers had always been in the open, with stores connected by outdoor passageways.
>
> Green had the idea of putting the whole complex under one roof.... . Green put stores on two-levels, connected by escalators and fed by

two-tiered parking. In the middle, he put a kind of town square, a 'garden court' under a skylight, with a fishpond, enormous sculpted trees, a twenty-one-feet cage filled with bright-colored birds, balconies with hanging plants, and a café. The result ... was a sensation.[19]

The article continues:

... today virtually every other regional shopping center in America is a fully enclosed, introverted, multi-tiered, double-anchor-tenant shopping complex with a garden court under a skylight. Victor Green didn't design a building, he designed an archetype. ... He invented the mall.[20]

After Green, A. Alfred Taubman, the legendary mall designer, describes his concept of a modern mall. The New Yorker said that:

... he likes the main corridors of his shopping malls to be no more than a thousand feet long—the equivalent of about three city blocks—because he believes that three blocks is about as far as peak shopping interest can be sustained, and as he walked he explained the logic behind what retailers like to call "adjacencies."[21]

This means that the locations of the stores selling related products are, in some sense, interconnected. For example, shoppers looking for electronic items in one shop will be just a few feet away from two other shops selling similar products, thus enabling them to compare features and prices. Similarly, all the shops selling high-end brands would be placed in a cluster for the convenience of consumers with expensive tastes and deep pockets.

Taubman says that "lots of developers just rent out their space like you'd cut a salami. They rent the space based on whether it fits, not necessarily on whether it makes any sense." In the mall that Taubman showed to the New Yorker writer, the Legal Sea Foods restaurant was "off the main mall, at the far end of a short entry hallway, and it was down there for a reason." Taubman explains:

A woman about to spend five thousand dollars at Versace does not want to catch a whiff of sautéed grouper as she tries on an evening gown. More to the point, people eat at Legal Sea Foods only during the lunch and dining hours—which means that if you put the restaurant in the thick of things, you'd have a dead spot in the middle of your mall for most of the day.[22]

Similarly, there is a logic to why so many malls in the United States are two-storied. Taubman sketched out a rough design to explain why this is so:

"You have two levels, all right? You have an escalator here and an escalator here." He drew escalators at both ends of the floors. "The customer comes into the mall, walks down the hall, gets on the escalator up to the second level, goes back along the second floor, down the escalator, and now she's back where she started from. She's seen every store in the center, right? Now you put a third level. Is there any reason to go up there? No."

... Taubman was the first to put a ring road around the mall—which he did at his mall in Hayward—for the same reason: if you want to get shoppers into every part of the building, they should be distributed to as many different entry points as possible. At Short Hills—and at most Taubman malls—the ring road rises gently as you drive around the building, so at least half the mall entrances are on the second floor. "We put fifteen percent more parking on the upper level than on the first level, because people flow like water... . They go down much easier than they go up. And we put our vertical transportation—the escalators—on the ends, so shoppers have to make the full loop."[23]

A blogger, Douglas Rushkoff, has this to say about the science of modern retail design:

The first tactic is to keep people inside the mall—the longer they stay, the more they buy. Early malls were sealed from daylight, like casinos designed to keep gamblers from realizing how long they've been playing. But more recent testing showed shoppers felt claustrophobic—and stay inside longer if they are allowed to catch just a glimpse of sky. Careful lighting still keeps them from perceiving the passage of time. As the sun goes down, these lightbulbs slowly fade up. Complex floor plans help keep patrons from knowing exactly where they are. They're not supposed to.

Once disorientation is achieved, the retailers begin their attack on the senses:

Start with Sight: Because they're lost, patrons use the only images they recognize as anchors: the big-name department stores. You don't go "north"—you move towards Macy's. These "Anchor" stores are always placed at angles to each other, so that you can't see one from the entrance of another. Each anchor presides over its own section of the mall, like a reigning emperor—and a visual landmark.

... Then there is the sense of Touch: Designers often use hard floor surfaces in the halls and softer ones inside the store—gently coaxing customers to come inside if they want their feet to feel good. Other studies show that women feel more powerful— and buy more—if they can feel and hear their heels clicking on polished hard wood.

Which brings us to Sound: We all joke about "elevator" Muzak—but it works. Dozens of different soundtracks scientifically engineered to increase the rate at which we purchase products at any moment of the day—is pumped into the mall and the stores. There is a special and tested melody, rhythm and sequence to maximize the efficiency of any shopping behavior you can imagine.

Do not forget Taste: Free food lures strollers into shops. It is always visible from the corridor. Eating food turns customers, quite literally, into consumers.

They even use Smell: Cookie shops spread scents throughout the mall, attracting customers from hundreds of feet away. One study showed that people act nicer—and buy more—when they can smell baking cookies. More advanced scientists, like those in the "chemo-reception industry," test flowers, spices, and synthetics for their effects on human behavior. Williams Sonoma uses a special holiday scent. Vanilla helps make people feel sexy— perfect to lower inhibitions in the lingerie store. But even beyond the five senses, the most advanced attacks are on the emotions—and the subconscious.

Each store has its own carefully researched theme. They are total environments—stage sets where the brand values become OUR values. It is a self-contained world, where retail psychologists can overwhelm us with the culture of their products. The only way to fit in, is to buy. The stores also hire their own battalions of behavioral researchers— many of whom use the security cameras to study consumer behaviors, like an anthropologist studying a tribe in its native habitat.

Ever wonder why certain store aisles are so wide? Chalk it up to the butt-brush. If a woman is brushed up against while she inspects a product, she'll get up and move. Items that require close inspection by women ... are put in wider aisles.[24]

In comparison, Indian malls are guided by the three Cs: chaos, crowds, and concealment. Each of these factors has its advantages.

Chaos is forced. It starts right from the time customers try to enter the mall in their cars. Invariably, there is a queue of cars that extends to the main road. Whether this is because of bad planning, narrow entrance roads, or a conscious effort to make shoppers remain in their cars for several minutes before they can reach the parking lot, it helps to push customers into spending more time in the mall.

By the time the customers have negotiated their way into the mall parking lot, they are harrowed and irritated. Hence when they enter the building, they respond positively to the air-conditioned comfort and cleanliness of the mall. After having "sweated it out" earlier, they are likely to want to spend more time in this pleasant environment than they might have originally intended. And, in my case, I would love to hit the first pub for a glass of cold beer. Studies on the behavior patterns of Indian consumer have shown that hassled and worried people are likely to shop more to make themselves feel better. Indian shoppers gain this satisfaction from their shopping experience, and it is enhanced if they are troubled or frustrated when they enter an outlet.

We all know people who shop when they are depressed or sad. Shopping changes their mood, if only for a few hours. Some psychiatrists see this as a disease, but most Indian shoppers, especially women, suffer from it. However, most customers regard "retail therapy" as an easy way to feel happy.

As a design element, the chaos factor is extended to the interior of the mall. There is no apparent reason for placing some shops near each other. Unlike Taubman's logic as seen in the design of American malls, the food court in an Indian mall may be located right in the middle of the building. In a Delhi mall, as soon as people enter the building from the main entrance, they encounter small food counters in the aisle.

Directions to shops in the outlet are few and far between. The only way to know the location of a store is through the signboards near the elevators; if customers are anywhere else, they will have difficulty in finding the shops they are looking for. Nothing is scientifically or logically designed; the mall design seems to have no discernible purpose. The stores are not uniform in look or size; this adds to the element of chaos and randomness.

Kishore Biyani writes that the interiors of Big Bazaar outlets are meant to evoke an impression of chaos. Instead of long neat aisles and shelves designed to help customers spot the products easily, Indian malls seek to create an ambience of a bazaar or local marketplace. As at a local *mandi* or small market, everything appears to be chaotic, crowded, poorly designed, and unplanned. Each of the U-shaped substructures in a Big Bazaar store acts like a mini-marketplace. This gives consumers a sense of visiting several mini-markets under the same roof, yet in a clean, comfortable, air-conditioned environment. Customers feel as though they are shopping at Delhi's Sarojini Nagar or Lajpat Nagar markets, or at Mumbai's Crawford Market. This is one of the reasons Delhi's malls have open shops in the aisle, much like those of street sellers of jewelry and trinkets commonly found in local markets.

While the "butt-brush" factor may be important in the United States, it does not make much sense in India. Shoppers here are more comfortable with a sea of people around them. In India, people feel a sense of safety and security in crowded places; no one is looking at what you are doing, so you need not be self-conscious because this is your first visit to a mall.

Let me give you a few personal experiences to illustrate the shopping habits of many middle-class Indians. My friend Nidhi and I went shopping during a visit to Jaipur, and we went to a market we had never been to before. So we didn't know which shops were better, where we could get good bargains, and which ones to trust for quality. Nidhi, who was an experienced shopper, unlike me, took a whirlwind tour of the entire market (with a few dozen shops) and, suddenly, without warning, started shopping at a few specific ones. I was curious why she was only going to those shops to buy.

When I asked her, her reply was: "When we went window-shopping, I spotted the ones that seemed busy and were crowded. For me, crowds imply that the shops are known among consumers and there's a word-of-mouth appreciation by consumers for those shops. In addition, the shops are doing better business than others."

I have seen this mindset in many customers. While commuting long distance, they will stop for a meal at a *dhaba* (roadside eatery) that is already packed with people, mostly truck drivers taking a break and other locals. If truck drivers (who are presumably discerning clients because they travel a great deal and rely on these eateries for almost all their meals) eat at a particular *dhaba*, the customers reason, then the place must serve delicious, and healthy food. Similarly, when they visit new towns, they gravitate toward shops with the biggest crowds.

Many of us, when we are alone and in search of food or entertainment, tend to frequent crowded places where we are unlikely to be noticed or be bothered by acquaintances. We welcome the anonymity of being a part of a large crowd. For most middle-class Indians, the razzmatazz and dazzle of multi-theater complexes, pubs and restaurants, and malls are new. They tend to feel somewhat self-conscious and awkward in such places, so it is not surprising that they find it reassuring to be part of a crowd.

Retailers have realized this and hence design their malls to give the impression of being crowded even if they are not. Narrow aisles, packed outlet spaces, and open counters on the walkways are all design features meant to enhance this feeling. Even individual outlets look crowded because the provision of less space for customers is a deliberate design decision.

Luckily, Indian malls tend to be crowded for another reason. Young Indians (like young people all over the world) love hanging out at "happening" places with their friends. Earlier, local markets or cinema complexes were popular hangout spots. Today, malls have become the new hangouts. Nearly half the people in malls may simply be hanging out with no intention of doing any shopping.

Given the Indian consumer's fascination with, and preference for, chaos and crowds, architects can afford to design multi-storied malls, while rejecting Taubman's logic of a two-storied mall. Indian shoppers love to get lost; they like the concept of irregular entrances and exit escalators. Finding their way around a mall is a process of discovery, a game, which is where the concealment factor comes in.

Consumers in India and in other emerging markets in South America and in South and Southeast Asia derive considerable satisfaction when they discover a new shop or a fantastic deal that not many others know about. So they seem to be shopping aimlessly in a chaotic manner but this is actually a search for something new and unexpected, something hitherto unknown. They are convinced there is an exciting surprise in every market, that there is one place, one counter, one outlet that is better than every other.

Scientifically designed markets aimed at providing a comfortable experience for shoppers do not work for Indian consumers. Most successful retailers design their malls and supermarkets to give this "discovery" experience to customers.

In many malls, the bargain shops are tucked away in corners, hidden in basements, or otherwise concealed from public view. This, too, is mostly by design.

This characteristic of consumer behavior helps explain why multistoried malls work and why there is enough public flow toward the higher floors despite the belief that people flow like water, that is, downward. In India, they flow upward, and sideways too. They move in a Brownian fashion, that is, all the molecules in a fluid move in an entirely chaotic fashion with no scientific principles guiding them, in the hope that they will accidentally find a clearance sale or discover an incredible deal.

After examining the "retail" behavior of Indian consumers, it is now time to study their attitudes in terms of brand consciousness and brand acquisition.

Endnotes

1. Chris Anderson, *The Long Tail: Why the Future of Business is Selling Less of More*, Hyperion, 2006, Introduction.
2. ibid.
3. Kishore Biyani and Dipyan Baishya, *It Happened in India*, (Rupa & Company, 2007), p. 110.
4. ibid., pp. 2, 4, 5.
5. *India Retail Report*, Images F&R Research, 2007.
6. ibid.
7. ibid.
8. ibid.
9. ibid.
10. ibid.
11. ibid.
12. Sagarika Ghose, "Celebrity Times," *Outlook*, April 17, 2000, http://www.outlookindia.com/fullprint.asp?choice=1&fodname=2000041 7&fname=cover_story&sid=1
13. ibid.
14. Neeta Raheja, interview with the author, 2008.
15. Saikat Datta, Anuradha Raman et al., "A Ten Foot Trench, Rs 14.50," *Outlook*, April 9, 2007, http://www.outlookindia.com/full.asp?fodname= 20070409&fname=KJobless&sid=1
16. ibid.
17. ibid.
18. Piyul Mukherjee & Damodar Mal, *Haggling, Bargaining and Fixed Price Policies: The Changing Face of Indian Retail*, abstract, http://www.esomar. org/index.php/haggling-bargaining-and-fixed-price-policies.html

19. Malcolm Gladwell, "The Terrazzo Jungle," *New Yorker*, March 16, 2004, http://www.newyorker.com/archive/2004/03/15/040315fa_fact1?printable =true

20. ibid.

21. ibid.

22. ibid.

23. ibid.

24. Douglas Rushkoff, CBS script, posted December 19, 2002, http://rushkoff.com/index.php?s=muzak&x=39&y=9

The Brand Bandwagon

In the 1980s, two high-profile corporate wars were fought in India.

One was the famous Ambani versus Wadia battle, which led indirectly to the fall of at least two central (federal) governments and nearly claimed a president. It was a fight between two textile tycoons, Dhirubhai Ambani (whose two sons, who have split, now together control one of the largest private sector business group in the country), and Nusli Wadia, the grandson of Pakistan's founder, Mohammad Ali Jinnah.

The other battle, however, was more interesting from a consumer's perspective. The outcome of this battle unleashed an unprecedented consumerist hunger among the Indian middle class. This was Ramesh versus Ramesh, or PepsiCo versus Parle. It opened the floodgates for the entry of foreign brands into the Indian market, and resulted in one of the most successful conquests by a foreign consumer brand in the country.

Pepsi's Ramesh Vangal was a typical multinational corporation (MNC) manager. He was well educated, smart, suave, and articulate. He could engage policymakers and media persons for hours in intellectual discussions. He was a globetrotter, who could bring in an international perspective to every debate. He took up the fight for Pepsi's entry into India with determination.

Pitched against Vangal was Parle's Ramesh Chauhan, a typical patriarch of an Indian business family. He was rustic and street-smart, believed everything was fair in love and business, and was willing to go to any extent to protect his near-monopolistic turf in the organized cola market. In the mid-1980s, he had only a one-point agenda: to stop the entry of Pepsi into India. The reason: after Coca-Cola had been ordered to quit India in 1977 by the then Janata regime, Parle's Thums Up was the only national brand in the Indian cola market.

The two men were a study in contrast. Chauhan favored white safari suits and white shoes (or even sandals). Vangal was always impeccably dressed in a black or striped dark suit during business hours; outside the office, he could be seen zipping around town in a bright red refurbished Willy's jeep, and dressed in a T-shirt and denims.

The story begins in 1977 when the Janata Party came to power after Indira Gandhi's stint as prime minister. The new union minister for industry, George Fernandes, a socialist who had spearheaded a countrywide railways strike in the early 1970s, threw American brand icons IBM and Coca-Cola out of the country. He asked all MNCs to reduce their stake in their Indian subsidiaries to 40 percent or below, and, when these two firms refused to do so, they were politely asked to leave.

Over the next few years, Chauhan's Parle became a market leader in the cola and fizzy soft-drink segment. In 1977, he and his brother launched brands like Thums Up, Gold Spot, and Limca, and captured the lion's share in the organized sector.

The situation changed in 1984 when Rajiv Gandhi, a young pilot and the older son of Indira Gandhi, who had recently been assassinated, won a clear electoral mandate, and decided to steer the economy in a different direction. He favored opening up the Indian economy, and felt that encouraging the private sector was as important as expanding the public sector. He also believed that India should become a truly mixed economy, and give up its socialist stance. Over the next two years, Rajiv Gandhi liberalized imports, encouraged foreign direct investment, and laid the foundation for a revolution in information technology (IT) and telecommunication. Today, India is a leader in both these sectors.

One of the decisions that Rajiv Gandhi took was to de-license the soft-drink sector in 1985. This paved the way for the re-entry of the American cola companies, and this time it was Pepsi that took the initiative in wooing Rajiv Gandhi. An apocryphal story goes that one hot afternoon, Rajiv Gandhi took a sip from his Pepsi can and said, "Let's allow Pepsi to enter the Indian market."

But the reality was quite different.

As soon as Pepsi decided to take the plunge, Parle was ready to slug it out. By the time Pepsi submitted its first proposal, Chauhan was ready to strike. He used politicians, policy influencers, the media, and civil society to launch an all-India protest against the entry of the MNC. Nothing was unfair in this unique cola war between an American and an Indian. Ironically, it turned out to be a fight between two Indians, Ramesh and Ramesh.

In 1986, the Indian government rejected Pepsi's first proposal, but the U.S. giant was not prepared to give up. It persisted and initiated talks with the government on a reworked proposal. By this time, the unusual cola wars in India became as dirty and murky as the one in the United States (between Coca-Cola and Pepsi).

Invoking the nationalist argument, critics said that it was "shameful" for India to be importing soft-drinks concentrate. After nearly four decades of independence, could not India with its present level of industrialization make a domestic soft drink? Were we economically as weak as our neighbor, Pakistan, which even imported needles? If we wanted foreign brands, why not allow them in more critical areas and not in consumer goods?

Taking such arguments further, Parle's supporters alleged that Pepsi had links with the Central Intelligence Agency (CIA), and charged the company with aiding the overthrow of Chile's head of state, Salvador Allende.

At the strategy level, the critics tried to prove that Pepsi was only interested in soft drinks, and declared that its projected profits from the venture were amazingly high. Documents, scraps of paper, and rumors damaging to Pepsi floated around freely. Anyone, anywhere had only to make a few phone calls to get this information.

Initially, Pepsi's Ramesh Vangal used MNC tactics: counter so-called misinformation with information, face allegations with so-called truths, and woo critics with the power of logic and reasoning. He invited journalists and discussed the issues with them for hours, even days. He met policymakers for the same purpose. He talked 24/7 to whoever was willing to listen. It was a desperate act to get people to support Pepsi's cause.

Vangal would invariably begin by saying that Pepsi was not a foreign company, but one that was as nationalist as, if not more so than, any Indian firm. He would then quote from various committee reports that concluded that India needed to invest in agriculture infrastructure to stop the rotting of fruits and vegetables; India needed to graduate to value-added food products to increase farmers' remuneration; and India also needed to get rid of agricultural middlemen who exploited farmers.

Pepsi intended to work in all the three areas mentioned above by manufacturing agro-based products (potato wafers), going in for contract farming to procure the agriculture raw materials, and establishing an agricultural research institute.

More importantly, Pepsi would be setting up its agro-products unit in Punjab, thereby generating employment in a state that was then plagued by terrorist violence; in the 1980s, it was argued by some that young people in Punjab were joining terrorist outfits because of lack of employment opportunities and unviable farming.

Moreover, Pepsi had agreed to export agro-based products that would help put India on the global map. Vangal never missed a chance to point out what Pepsi had done for Stolichnaya, the Russian vodka brand. In 1972, Pepsi brokered a deal with the Soviet Union whereby the then USSR allowed the American cola maker to sell its products in the country, and in return Pepsi offered to market Stolichnaya in the United States. Within a few years, Stolichnaya became a popular brand in America, and continues to be one of the few Russian brands to have a decent market share in the country. Pepsi promised to do the same with Indian agro-based food products.

The cola was only an incidental business in India to ensure the viability of the entire "nationalist" project. It constituted only a quarter of the proposed investments.

After an intense battle, Pepsi was given the green light in 1988, along with clearance for additional clauses relating to food products, agriculture-related research, and exports. Although Pepsi was not able to do much on the agricultural product front, over the years its colas gained considerable market share.

In the 1990s, Coca-Cola too entered the Indian market. Ironically, Chauhan finally sold out to Coca-Cola. The Pepsi–Coca-Cola combine soon garnered an impressive two-thirds share of the cola business. Today, Pepsi and Coca-Cola together have a 95 percent share of the organized Indian cola market.

This is a remarkable story of total domination by foreign companies of an Indian market segment.

While asserting their domination, Pepsi and Coca-Cola changed the tastes of Indian consumers. Young people did not merely drink an American beverage, but they also adopted Western attitudes, including the consumer mindset. Cola consumption was merely the external face of much deeper social changes, most of which took place in the minds of India's new middle class. Soft-drink consumption per person in India went up from three bottles in the late-1980s to eight bottles in 2007.

In addition, the success of Pepsi and Coca-Cola made other foreign companies sit up and seriously think about the potential of the Indian market. Pepsi and Coca-Cola paved the way for the entry of Levi's and McDonald's (and perhaps even Wal-Mart).

Something similar happened in the consumer electronics and white-goods segments in the 1990s. In the color TV segment, the two late entrants, South Korea's LG and Samsung, have more than one-third of the market share; only Onida, an Indian brand, continues to compete with them. In the premium and more expensive liquid crystal display (LCD) segment, Samsung, LG, and Japan's Sony together have a sizeable 80 percent market share.

When it comes to refrigerators and washing machines, Samsung and Whirlpool control over half the market. The only Indian brand giving competition to the foreign companies in white goods is Godrej.

In the four-wheeler segment, except for a dozen-odd models rolled out by Tata Motors, Mahindra & Mahindra, and Hindustan Motors, all the others are foreign makes. India now has over 100 models manufactured by a range of international companies.

Apart from Pepsi, Coca-Cola, LG, Samsung, and Suzuki, the most recognized foreign brand in India is McDonald's, the American fast-food chain. It, too, "Westernized" the Indian middle class, and today epitomizes the consumption mindset of this class.

An analysis of McDonald's' triumph offers lessons on both how to succeed in India and the pitfalls that foreign companies can face here. It is a tale of positives and negatives, reality and myth, and what should and should not be done. McDonald's' experience in India (which is more than a decade old) needs to be examined in greater detail.

McDonald's opened its first outlet in a market complex in Vasant Vihar, in South Delhi, a posh locality popular with young people who just want to hang out there in the evenings. Today, the company has nearly 90 outlets, two-thirds of them in cities and towns in north India. More importantly, McDonald's has become a place for family outings, a must for children in specific segments of middle-class households. Children force their parents to host their birthday parties at McDonald's. Families regard visits to McDonald's as a picnic, which offers more of an entertainment than a gustatory experience. Going to McDonald's is like going out for a drink or a movie. McDonald's is equivalent to a "fun" and "happy" experience. It is more than a brand in India, so its experience here can tell readers about the elements that are essential for success in this country.

A detailed case study on McDonald's had this to say about its strategy in India:

> In India, McDonald's has positioned itself as a family restaurant ... McDonald's has become an attractive place for working and busy young parents on weekdays. On weekends, residents of Delhi and Mumbai bring their children to McDonald's so that they can relax, while their children play in McDonald's hugely popular play places.[1]

It added that it has done everything to woo children:

> When one of its outlets was opened in South Mumbai, a children's parade was organized all along the popular Marine Drive, led by McDonald's mascot, Ronald, who was accompanied by a 40-feet-long float depicting the various tourist destinations in Mumbai. Its "Happy Meals" and the accompanying Lego toys are a great attraction for children. Kids like McDonald's outlets because they are brightly lit and full of young people. During their visits, kids are showered with knick-knacks. The Noida outlet near Delhi even has a low-height order counter for children. McDonald's outlets provide the kids with a hassle-free experience where no one tells them "sit down," "don't move," or "keep out of my way."
>
> McDonald's also promotes birthday parties complete with cake, candles, and toys in a television advertisement aimed directly at kids. In some Indian cities like Mumbai, Delhi, and Bangalore, birthday parties are all the rage for upwardly mobile youngsters. Given that most young people in these cities live in small, overcrowded flats, McDonald's has become a convenient and welcoming place for birthday celebrations.

McDonald's has become a popular place for many jean-clad teenagers, who use the outlets as a venue to meet their boyfriends/girlfriends, still a tricky issue among Indian middle-class families. McDonald's appeals to India's new westernized elites because its food is clean, safe, and reliable. India's ... families show considerable interest in enjoying what is often described as the "McDonald's experience."[2]

How did McDonald's do this? What "magic" strategy did it use? The case study provides answers to these questions.

To begin with, the fast-food giant knew that it would face strong opposition at the political, religious, and health-related levels, and that was only during the clearance stage. It had seen the problems faced by another fast-food chain, Kentucky Fried Chicken (KFC).

KFC opened its first outlet in Bangalore in July 1995. The city was then being hailed as the "electronics city," and was on its way to becoming a global software and business process outsourcing (BPO) hub. Techies from across the country—young, educated, Westernized, and middle class—were settling in the city in large numbers, making Bangalore a major melting pot of India. Just over a month later, the city's municipal inspectors knocked at KFC's door to sample its chicken. In August 1995, the authorities announced that one of KFC's secret ingredients was monosodium glutamate (MSG) and claimed that the chicken they had sampled contained 2.8 percent MSG. Unfortunately, the percentage was much more than the 1 percent stipulated under India's Prevention of Food Adulteration (PFA) Act. Since MSG is harmful, the Bangalore inspectors revoked KFC's license, and ordered that the city's outlet be closed down.

Just over a fortnight after KFC opened an outlet in Delhi, on November 6, 1995, the city authorities canceled its license, alleging that the chicken contained sodium aluminum phosphate, another harmful chemical.

KFC consistently maintained that its products did not contain any harmful chemicals, and that the use of all chemicals was within the permissible limits. It claimed that Indian laboratories were not equipped adequately to measure the quantities of MSG accurately.

But critics contended that fast food was essentially junk food, and consequently unhealthy. M.D. Nanjundaswamy, who heads the Karnataka State Farmers Association (KRRS), said that KFC chicken was "full of chemicals [meant] to fatten them quickly." Traditional Indian dishes like tandoori chicken were more nutritious and healthy, he claimed. Politician–activist Maneka Gandhi, daughter-in-law of the late Indira Gandhi, joined the attack. She got 20 members of parliament, including two former prime ministers, to protest against KFC. Both Maneka Gandhi and Nanjundaswamy alleged that the fast-food invasion would encourage farmers to shift from basic food crops to poultry, thus turning India into a country of food shortages. In January 1996, farmers, led by the KRRS, ransacked KFC's Bangalore outlet. This was nearly ten months before McDonald's opened its first outlet.

To prevent similar criticism against it, McDonald's took several pre-emptive steps. It lobbied policymakers even before it got the permission to set up outlets in India. In deference to local tastes and religious and cultural proscriptions, it decided not to serve beef or pork, as the cow is sacred to Hindus and pork is forbidden to Muslims, who constitute the largest minority in India. The fast-food chain announced that it would not serve its most famous product, the beef-based Big Mac. McDonald's thus indicated its willingness to compromise on its core products to appease the majority population (Hindus and Muslims) in India.

Over the years, McDonald's has tinkered with its menu and Indianized it. The company claims that nearly three-quarters of the products it offers in India cater to the taste buds of locals. One of its most popular burgers is McAloo Tikki, an Indian-style potato cutlet in a bun, which caters to the bulk of Indians who do not eat meat.

Several foreign food giants and other consumer goods manufacturers have successfully given an Indian flavor to their products. For instance, sales of Domino's and Pizza Hut products shot up after they introduced Indian-style vegetarian and "tikka" (slices of roasted chicken or lamb) pizzas.

Chinese food has always been popular with middle-class Indians, mainly because local restaurants and outlets have Indianized it. Over the years, the south Indian *dosa* (a griddle-cooked crepe or pancake made of fermented rice paste) took on various forms, including those stuffed with *keema* (minced meat) and *paneer* (cottage cheese), as opposed to the traditional filling of potatoes (north Indians love *keema* and *paneer*). Even *sambar*, the curry served with *dosa*, has been changed to satisfy the preferences of north Indians.

The firms that thought they could bring in products developed elsewhere and sell them to Indians without understanding their needs suffered. Consider, for example, Kellogg's initial failure with its breakfast cereals. The products were made with the Western consumer in mind; most people in the United States and Europe eat their cereals with cold milk. But in India, cold milk is believed to be unhealthy, and most people prefer it hot. But Kellogg's cereals could not be had with hot milk because they became soggy. It was only when the products were changed that it garnered a decent market share.

The makers of Tang, the orange drink, failed to read the breakfast habits of Indians. If Indians do have juice, which is consumed only by a few, they prefer freshly squeezed juice. Most Indians do not like concentrate-based fruit drinks. Even today, most Indians will consume only those packed juices (in Tetra Pak cartons) that are considered "fresh."

Daewoo's Cielo model flopped mainly for one simple reason— a car design that did not take into account the poor conditions of Indian roads. Unlike the smooth American freeways and German *autobahns*, Indian roads are uneven and bumpy, full of potholes and other unseen dangers; their condition deteriorates during the monsoons. The Cielo's base was very low, and its floor would hit the road every now and then, especially on the many speed-breakers on Indian roads.

A recent study by the Boston Consulting Group (BCG) states that:

> ... the most successful (foreign) companies have developed products specifically for India's huge mass market. General Electric, for example, created an inexpensive portable ultrasound scanner that has given it a 35 percent share of the market for these devices—one and a half times that of its closest competitor. Nokia, which has more than 60 percent share of the mobile phone market, offers a vast range of products priced under US$150. Market leader LG customized the audio system in its televisions—they feature oversize speakers with a booming bass—while retaining the regular picture tubes. Ford

developed its Ikon model specifically for India and claims a 20 percent market share. Honda offers low-frills versions of its models, with modifications to horn settings, suspension height, and other features. It boasts a 16 percent share of India's automobile segment.[3]

As is evident from the BCG paper, pricing is extremely important in the Indian market. No brand will command a mass middle-class customer base if it is priced above a certain value-for-money benchmark. The buyer has to be convinced that the price she is paying represents value for money.

McDonald's got this right too. As in many other emerging markets, the pricing of its products in India was a critical element in McDonald's success in the country. It played the volumes game as it slashed prices. In 1997, it cut the prices of its vegetable nuggets from Rs 29 to Rs 19 (from 73 cents to 48 cents) and that of its ice-cream cone from Rs 15 to Rs 7 (from 38 cents to 18 cents). Four years later, McDonald's introduced a pure vegetarian burger for Rs 17. The earlier-mentioned case study on McDonald's also stated that "McDonald's was able to sell the veggie burger 40 percent more (in volume terms) than what it expected within a month."[4]

Vikram Bakshi, who is the McDonald's franchisee for north India, and is responsible for two-thirds of Indian outlets, told the author of the case study:

> Our clear strategy is to bring the customers in initially and provide a range of entry-level products so that they can try new items and graduate to the higher groups. Thus, if a customer starts with a McAloo Tikki Burger, what he graduates to finally is a vegetarian burger. Or, if a customer starts with a Chicken Kebab Burger, what he graduates finally to is the McChicken.[5]

Interestingly, in India and elsewhere, McDonald's strategy has focused on the customer's purchasing power, or ability to pay. The McDonald's case study took the example of Big Mac prices in various countries and compared these to the price in the United States. It found that the Indian price was less than the U.S. price by 74 percent. The underpricing in other emerging markets was much lower than in India: Argentina (-49 percent), Brazil (-41 percent), China (-57 percent), Egypt (-44 percent),

Malaysia (-34 percent), Philippines (-57 percent), and Thailand (-50 percent).

That the Indian market is generally price sensitive in most sectors is best illustrated by the automobile sector. Price has played a key role in the success of models across segments, from small to big cars, from inexpensive to expensive models, from sedans to sports utility vehicles (SUVs). In each subcategory, price has been an important factor in defining and determining buyers' preferences and purchasing decisions.

Two examples from the small-car segment will prove the point. For years, the Maruti 800 model was the prince of the Indian road in terms of sales. As noted, it was once a status symbol, representing an attitude and symbolizing a mass consumer movement. Every middle-class family wanted—and most owned—a Maruti 800, but this was only until the launch of the Alto by the same company.

As the Maruti 800 was overtaken by newer models, it lost its sheen. By now, consumers could choose from a range of small-car models with the latest technology and better looks. In addition, these other models were priced only slightly higher than the Maruti 800. Daewoo's Matiz and Hyundai's Santro soon became the entry-level cars for many consumers. Maruti–Suzuki knew it had to do something drastic to combat competition and retain its market share.

Surprisingly, it launched the Alto, which was priced almost the same as the Maruti 800, but with a new-generation engine and more advanced technology. The Alto dented the growth of the Matiz and the Santro. Importantly, it also cut into the sales of the flagship Maruti 800. Today, the Alto has upstaged the Maruti 800 to become Maruti's largest-selling model. Maruti managed to ease out the Maruti 800 without losing much market share. (The Maruti 800 still sells but experts contend that it is only a matter of time before it is totally phased out. The Maruti strategy seems to be, however, to continue with the Maruti 800 as long as it sells.)

Compare this with the pricing strategy of Tata Motors. Known for its trucks and buses, the company got into the car business only because of the passion of its promoter, Ratan Tata, probably India's most respected businessman. Ratan Tata wanted to prove that an Indian company could design and launch a car model successfully; this was not just the preserve of the foreigners. And he wanted to launch a people's car.

Enter the Indica. Although the Indica did not turn out to be the people's car as Ratan Tata had envisaged, it was priced aggressively against the Maruti 800 and the Santro. Moreover, its diesel version soon became a hit because of its low operational cost; in India, diesel costs almost 30 percent less than the retail price of petrol. This variant has become the preferred model for private taxi services. Even the Indica's petrol version sells quite well.

Now Ratan Tata has showcased the "real" people's car priced at Rs 1 lakh (US$2,500), the cheapest car in the world. In 2004, *Business 2.0* reported on the possibility of a small-car revolution in India:

> Tata Motors, India's second-largest automaker, is expected to be first off the drawing boards with its entry. The company should finalize plans … for a four-seat hatchback powered by a 600cc two-cylinder engine. To hit its target price, Tata's as-yet-unnamed vehicle will be homegrown and made mostly of low-cost local materials. To pare manufacturing costs, the vehicles will probably come off the line in kit form to be assembled in rural factories. Other cost-cutting options under consideration include using thermoplastics for certain parts that are usually made of metal and replacing nuts and bolts with adhesives wherever possible.
>
> One thing is sure: The US$2,200 car would not be confused with a luxury model. Forget amenities and good looks; Tata admits that passengers may find the car's ride noisy and its appearance ungainly.
>
> Competitors are already lining up to take on Tata's ultra cheap vehicles. General Motors's Indian subsidiary is considering a move into the market, perhaps by buying assets of bankrupt Daewoo Motors India and adapting Daewoo's Matiz mini car platform. India's Kirloskar Motors, allied with Toyota, is also said to be interested but has been tight-lipped about its plans. Conspicuously, however, Maruti Udyog, India's largest auto maker, has no plans for a bargain automobile of its own.[6]

After Ratan Tata showcased his small car, *Newsweek Asia* had this to say about the "Nano Revolution."

> But the car generating the most buzz hasn't even hit the road: the $2,500 Nano. A car for the price of a laptop PC is transformational. Before it even goes on sale in India later this year (2008), the Nano is

changing the rules of the road for the auto industry and society itself. Millions of emerging-market commuters can now own four-wheel transportation, creating unheard-of-mobility for the masses ... "The Nano is the 21st century equivalent of the Model T," says Global Insight analyst John Wolkonowicz. "The Nano will put the Third World on wheels, and that will have far-reaching implications."

It's already shaking up the industry. All the major car companies dispatched teams to New Delhi Motor Show in January (2008) to snap photos and build a dossier on the new Nano. The little car from India could lead to an overhaul in the global auto industry, which was always geared to earn big profits from big cars. Now the car czars will have to learn to make a business out of selling lots of little cars that make less money.[7]

Now other companies such as Bajaj Auto and Mahindra & Mahindra are talking about launching a low-priced small car that can help double annual sales.

In the more expensive, bigger-car segments, the Honda Civic rattled the Rs 8–12 lakh (US$20,000–30,000) segment with its aggressive pricing and improved features. Honda City did the same in the slightly cheaper segment. Renault's Logan, the first French model and the first wide-bodied automobile in the country, is already a huge favorite. It provides all the features of a luxury car and starts at just around Rs 5 lakh (US$12,500). It has received a huge response even in the face of other new launches like the Suzuki SX-4, the Chevy UV-A and Aveo, and the Fiat Palio Stile.

Once a company has got the price right for its model or brand, it needs to be at the right location to deliver its product efficiently and effectively to the consumer. As the BCG study puts it:

Getting products to market is another considerable challenge in India. Faced with [a] dispersed population, some 12 million retail outlets, and an underdeveloped transportation infrastructure, the most successful MNCs have introduced innovative strategies to handle distribution complexity. Many companies work with more than 500 distributors, in addition to wholesalers and franchised outlets, to cover the market. LG, for instance, parks its own vans next to general retail kiosks— called *haat*s—in semi-urban and rural areas, and then mounts product demonstrations and picks up orders. Similarly, HLL (now Hindustan Unilever) uses vans to convey its products to some 15 million rural consumers.

Innovation in logistics is also required when MNCs source products from India for the Indian market. Companies such as Nestle and PepsiCo have integrated their sourcing networks all the way back to the villages. They provide farming assistance to villagers and buy products directly from the villages to avoid the middleman.[8]

When McDonald's decided to expand rapidly in India, it was a question of "location, location, location." The company realized that the location of its outlets and getting the logistics right would be critical to delivering products of uniform quality to consumers who had to be wooed to come to the outlets. Fortunately, McDonald's has been able to find the best locations in almost all the countries it operates in. India is no exception. It was rumored that each time McDonald's chose a location in India, real estate prices in that area would shoot up immediately by 100–200 percent.

Here is what the McDonald's case study says about the company's location-driven strategy:

> Logistics plays a critical role in McDonald's location strategy. As a part of its quick service restaurant (QSR) business, McDonald's had initially decided to open its outlets only within a 500 km radius of its main distribution centers in Delhi and Mumbai. This is the reason why McDonald's has not opened a single outlet in metropolitan cities like Kolkata in the eastern part of India, despite the city's huge urban and cosmopolitan character.[9]

The fast-food giant instead focused on opening its outlets in metropolises such as Delhi and Mumbai, and also in the satellite towns of Delhi (Noida and Gurgaon) and Mumbai (Pune).

> McDonald's has partnered with the state-owned oil company, Bharat Petroleum Corporation Ltd (BPCL), to set up restaurants in the latter's petrol stations in and around Delhi to make it more convenient for automobile-driving consumers. BPCL is the leading petroleum retailer in India and has the largest number of petrol stations in and around Delhi ... Keeping an eye on the huge potential for eating out venues for the lower middle class Indians, McDonald's has partnered with a railway station and a bus station in Delhi to open outlets ... to tap the automobile-driving consumers, business travelers and tourists, McDonald's has set up drive-through outlets in Delhi and along the national highways ... to tap into the business of shopping mall and film-going consumers, McDonald's has set up outlets in shopping malls and new multiplexes in metros ...[10]

In comparison, Domino's initially made a mess of its location strategy. It decided to expand too fast, too soon. It opened outlets in smaller towns and cities in a bid to reach the target of establishing more than 100 outlets in India as soon as possible. But soon it realized that customers in smaller towns were not keen on digging into its pizza slices. Daily sales at some of these outlets were pathetic. Finally, Domino's decided to close down many of these outlets, and instead focus on those that were doing well.

However, it must be added that Domino's did choose some of its locations wisely. For instance, its outlet within the Infosys campus in Bangalore generates the highest sales volumes in the country. It is no surprise that the young, educated, and Westernized Infosys techies would enjoy their pizza slices whether at lunch or while working late at night.

For any company, the key to financial success is to have a controlled rollout plan that is flexible enough to adjust to changing customer preferences. Foreign automobile majors in India consistently bring out variants of existing models, and introduce new models, either to cater to changing tastes or to meet the needs of different sets of consumers within the so-called overriding consuming class. So do the white goods and consumer electronics companies.

In the fast-food business, the trick lies in realizing which items on the menu will move quickly on a particular day or during a particular period. Fast-food firms conduct exhaustive analyses to track this flow based on time slots (day, afternoon, evening), or days (weekdays and weekends), or season (summer, winter, festivals).

This factor becomes critical for a firm like McDonald's, which claims that its products are thrown into the trash if they remain on the shelf for more than a few minutes. Its philosophy is to maintain consistency in quality.

Atul Punj, a franchisee for TGIF (Thank God It's Friday), recounts an interesting anecdote. He said that his colleagues had tried everything they could think of to get a sense of daily sales. But there seemed to be no correlation between daily sales and any given variable. Each day would be different, so would each week. It seemed that it was God who was deciding the daily sales on a totally arbitrary basis.

Until one day someone got this weird and wild idea to plot daily sales from our outlets with the Sensex [Bombay Stock Exchange Index] for the day. Lo and behold! He found that the resultant graph followed the same trend. On days when the Sensex was up, TGIF's sales were up. When the Sensex was down, the outlets did badly. Obviously, we could not use these data as a part of our sales strategy, but it did seem to be an interesting correlation, especially in the case of the metros. Maybe Indians want to enjoy themselves when they find out that their paper profits have gone up.[11]

McDonald's took into account scientific and sociocultural factors in predicting sales trends. This is crucial because sociocultural factors tend to become important in influencing short-term (daily and weekly) sales. For example, even nonvegetarians in India avoid meat on Tuesdays for religious reasons. There are periods in the Hindu calendar, such as the *Navratras*, when they do not eat meat for nine days. Similarly, marketers need to take into account the Ramadan period in the case of Muslims, especially in Muslim-dominated areas.

The case study pointed out that:

Indians, typically, spend more money on eating out and purchasing new products during festival seasons (as Americans and Europeans do during [the] Christmas season). To capitalize on the spending habits of Indian consumers, McDonald's has often sought to launch new products, the so-called 'fourth flavor[,]' during India's festival season, which falls between September and November.[12]

Cultural sensitivities are also important when it comes to advertising or marketing a brand. A draft dissertation by a management student at the Xavier Labor Relations Institute (XLRI), Jamshedpur, in the late 1990s listed some of the blunders made by foreign companies in various markets. The student gave a few examples:

Scandinavian vacuum manufacturer Electrolux used the following in an American ad campaign: "Nothing sucks like an Electrolux."

The name Coca-Cola in China was first rendered as ke-kou-ke-la. Unfortunately, the Coke company did not discover until after thousands of signs had been printed that the phrase means "bite the wax tadpole" or "female horse stuffed with wax" depending on the dialect. Coke then researched 40,000 Chinese characters and found a close phonetic equivalent, ko-kou-ko-le, which can be loosely translated as "happiness in the mouth."

In Taiwan, the translation of the Pepsi slogan "Come alive with the Pepsi generation" came out as "Pepsi will bring your ancestors back from the dead."

Also, in Chinese, the Kentucky Fried Chicken slogan "Finger-lickin' good" came out as "Eat your fingers off."

The American slogan for Salem cigarettes, "Salem—feeling free," got translated in the Japanese market into "When smoking Salem, you feel so refreshed that your mind seems to be free and empty."

When General Motors introduced the Chevy Nova in South America, it was apparently unaware that "no va" means "it won't go." After the company figured out why it was not selling any cars, it renamed the car in its Spanish markets to [sic] the Caribe.

Ford had a similar problem in Brazil when the Pinto flopped. The company found out that Pinto was Brazilian slang for "tiny male genitals." Ford pried all the nameplates off and substituted Corcel, which means horse.

When Parker pen [sic] marketed a ballpoint pen in Mexico, its ads were supposed to say "It won't leak in your pocket and embarrass you." However, the company mistakenly thought the Spanish word "embarazar" meant embarrass. Instead, the ads said that "It won't leak in your pocket and make you pregnant."

An American T-shirt maker in Miami printed shirts for the Spanish market which promoted the Pope's visit. Instead of [the] desired "I saw the Pope" in Spanish, the shirts proclaimed "I saw the potato."

Chicken-Man Frank Perdue's slogan, "It takes a tough man to make a tender chicken," got terribly mangled in another Spanish translation. A photo of Perdue with one of his birds appeared on billboards all over Mexico with a caption that explained, "It takes a hard man to get a chicken aroused."

Hunt-Wesson introduced its Big John products in French Canada as Gros Jos before finding out that the phrase means "big breasts." In this case, however, the name problem did not have a noticeable effect on sales.

Colgate introduced a toothpaste in France called Cue, the name of a notorious porno magazine.

In Italy, a campaign for Schweppes tonic water translated the name into Schweppes toilet water.

Japan's second largest tourist agency was mystified when it entered English-speaking markets and received requests for unusual sex tours. Upon finding out why, the owners of Kinki Nippon Tourist Company changed its name.[13]

The draft dissertation went on to give other examples of brand failures resulting from a lack of understanding of different cultures:

Multinational companies sometimes fail to read the cultural foundations as they move from country to country selling their products. They feel that the strategy which had delivered them success in other countries and [in] their home turf would [could] be replicated in most of the countries. But sadly this is not so. Procter & Gamble blundered while trying to sell Camay in Japan. It aired a popular European advertisement showing a woman bathing. In the ad, the husband entered the bathroom and touched her approvingly. The Japanese however considered such behavior to be very inappropriate and in poor taste for TV.

Again, Revlon tried to launch a perfume in Brazil that smelt of camellia flowers. It overlooked the fact that in Brazil, camellia flowers are funeral flowers. Predictably, the brand failed.

Procter & Gamble, when it launched the "Cheer" laundry detergent in Japan, overlooked the fact that [the] Japanese wash their clothes in cold water[,] and the advertising campaign [showing] that Cheer washed clothes at all temperatures seemed rather meaningless.

IFB Bosch decided to go ahead with its front[-]loading washing machines[,] ignoring the fact that in India, most of the washing is done in buckets and [that] using the top[-]loading machines resembled the act of putting clothes in a bucket ...

The ignoring of racial and religious sentiments can also backfire badly for companies. Muslims in Dhaka, Bangladesh, went on a rampage, ransacking shoe stores[,] because they mistook the Thom McAn logo on some sandals as the Arab characters for "Allah." They thought that the western company was denigrating the religion. Police were called in to stop the rioting and at least one person was killed and fifty injured.

When Pepsodent was launched in south-east Asian countries, its teeth[-]whitening property was positioned as "wonder where the yellow went." It was taken as a racial slur.

In India, the program "Nikki Tonight" tried to experiment [sic] as a wacky, irreverent show but certain comments on Mahatma Gandhi that were aired earned extremely bad publicity for Star Plus (an entertainment channel) and the show was taken off the air.

Till recently, the widely publicized plans of Cadbury Schweppes to open a huge champagne[-]shaped bottle of Canada Dry on the midnight Parliament session commemorating 50 years of Indian Independence backfired and earned the company rather negative publicity. The statements made by Rebecca Mark, the CEO of Enron India[,] that she had spent money for educating Indians earned negative publicity for it.[14]

Even if a company manages to get all the above-mentioned factors right, it can still fail. This is because most companies, both Indian and foreign, have exaggerated, or otherwise misread, the potential base of consumers—not earlier, not now, but consistently in the past two decades. Let us examine a few cases to see why and how this has happened.

In 2003, Indraprastha Gas Ltd. (IGL), which supplies compressed natural gas (CNG) for vehicles and piped natural gas (PNG) to households and large retail users, described the potential market in both these segments in its public issue prospectus:

> The consumption pattern of Natural Gas in NCT (National Capital Territory, including Delhi and satellite towns) of Delhi, where we operate, provides us significant growth opportunities in the CNG production and marketing business. Delhi has a large number of private vehicles, almost all of which run on petrol and diesel. We believe that these vehicles can be targeted for conversion to CNG due to its lower cost and its contribution to lower pollution levels in ambient air.
>
> Similarly, the consumption of PNG is expected to grow as it is perceived by the commercial and domestic users to be an economic[al], safe and convenient fuel. As on 1 April 2003, there are 3.435 million LPG connections in [the] NCT of Delhi. . . . As we currently supply PNG to only approximately 1,000 users of CNG in this area, we believe that there is significant potential to gain additional users for PNG.[15]

What has been the experience of IGL in the subsequent four years?

It had 154 CNG stations in 2007, compared to 115 in August 2003, or an increase of less than 10 percent annually.

Its CNG was being used by 77,482 vehicles on August 31, 2003, a whopping 197 percent increase between March 2001 and August 2003, because the Delhi government forced public transport vehicles to switch to CNG. In mid-2007, IGL was fuelling 128,000 vehicles, or an increase of less than 15 percent annually.

The number of buses using CNG increased from 9,394 to 11,535, or about 5 percent a year. The number of auto rickshaws using the fuel went up from 53,197 to 70,159, or less than 10 percent annually. And what happened to private cars?

The number of private cars using CNG showed an almost dramatic sevenfold increase, from 5,263 to 35,229, or an increase of over 100 percent annually. But check out these numbers against the population of private cars in Delhi. The figure stood around 1 million in 2003, and has now gone way past 1.5 million vehicles. The conversion rate from petrol to CNG has gone up from 0.005 percent to 0.02. Now that's an achievement!

For IGL, capturing a larger market share, or wooing more customers for CNG and PNG, should have been much easier than it has been for companies in other sectors, considering that IGL is a monopoly player and could have pushed itself to achieve this objective. However, it did not—or could not—do so for several reasons.

Price obviously played an important role. A CNG converter costs around Rs 35,000–40,000 (US$875). In a country where even the rich try to bargain for a discount of Rs 10,000–30,000 (US$250–750), or try to get the best deal on car purchases, not many consumers wanted to spend this extra cash.

In addition, the average car user spends about Rs 1,000 (US$25) on petrol each month. Even if car owners save, say, 40 percent on fuel costs by switching to CNG, it would take over eight years to recover the cost of the initial investment on the CNG converter. Most owners are not willing to wait that long to recover their capital. If one adds the interest and opportunity cost of the money, the period may well be closer to 15 years. If owners do want to save money on fuel, they are likely to reduce driving time and use the public transport system for part of the month. As we have seen in an earlier chapter, many car owners use their vehicles only on weekends. In the case of many other car owners, the fuel bill is financed by their employer. So, who cares about savings?

No one took note of the problems associated with buying CNG. A total of about 150 CNG stations in a city of 20 million people and 1.5 million cars is a very small number. In the early years of this decade, it was almost impossible to get CNG; buses and auto rickshaws had to stand in a queue for hours for refueling. No car owner would want to spend that kind of time to refuel. Petrol, although expensive, was simpler to get. Even now, finding a CNG station in this vast city of Delhi is difficult.

Let us not forget that a car is a lifestyle statement. It is meant to convey an attitude. Few consumers want a car that slows down, or whose acceleration comes down, because it is running on CNG. They want their car to zip through the city traffic. They want their car to touch 80 km per hour on the Noida toll road, not crawl at 65 kms per hour.

Compared with CNG, surely, the situation has to be different when it comes to the "real" consumption items, such as cars, motorcycles, color TVs, refrigerators, washing machines, even air travel.

In 2003, Japan's Hitachi claimed that there was a huge potential waiting to be tapped in the air-conditioner segment. The reason: the penetration level per household was a mere 1 percent, and, with the middle class exploding, demand was certain to go up several times. The truth: in 2005, the penetration level remained at 1 percent. Even worse, all the growth that did take place was in urban areas. The penetration level among rural households remained almost zero.

The next year, Electrolux of Sweden told its investors that the refrigerator market was bound to explode. Most refrigerator purchases were taking place in the subeconomy (under Rs 8,000 or US$200) and the economy (Rs 8,000–10,000 or US$200–250) categories. Since these prices were affordable for rural households, the market was certain to grow by leaps and bounds. The truth: sales did go up by 2.5 million in 2003 to 4 million in 2006–07. But the penetration levels remained low, at 8 percent in rural India and at 20 percent for the entire country. More importantly, industry analysts believe that the annual sales growth in refrigerators, which has been in the single digits for the past few years, may slow down further. The reason: penetration in urban areas has reached 60 percent, and is unlikely to rise really fast. And rural families continue to shy away from buying a refrigerator because of frequent and long power shortages. Only companies that have taken innovative steps to woo rural consumers (like LG Electronics) have had some success in this segment.

Did the predictions made for other consumer categories by market experts in the early years of the twenty-first century materialize? Overall, car (including jeep and van) penetration was 3 percent in 2000–02; it stood at 4 percent in 2005, and has not really increased much. Two-wheeler (motorcycles and scooters) penetration, which was 20 percent in 2000–02 (according to NCAER), remained the same in 2005. The penetration of color TVs and refrigerators did go up, but the growth is now slowing down considerably after the initial hectic growth phase.

The XLRI draft dissertation cites many such examples from the 1990s, when MNCs went totally wrong in assessing the size of the Indian middle class, which at that time was estimated at 200 million. According to the author:

> One segment that was expected to do well was that of the foreign liquor (FL) segment. Thus, we saw a spate of entrants into the FL segment like Hiram Walker, IDL, Seagram, and W.D. Gilbey. However, they had no idea of the tremendous competitiveness of the IMFL (Indian-made foreign liquor) segment, supplied primarily by bootleggers. Hiram Walker had estimated that out of the 1.5 million cases of Scotch that was [sic] sold in India, 182,000 was [sic] officially imported, [and] the rest was spurious Scotch supplied by bootleggers. So, Hiram Walker had conjured up a picture of selling 2 million cases per year; however, the company fell so hard that after one and a half years of operations, it has only been able to garner a 4.5 percent of the market from the bootleggers. The other companies share another 4.5 percent among themselves.
>
> So, what went wrong for these companies? Initially, they had assumed that any Scotch label would do well in India as long as it was foreign. What they mistook here is that Indians buy Scotch more to flaunt [the brand name] rather than to consume [it]. What excited him [sic] was more elite brands like Johnnie Walker Black Label, Chivas Regal, and Royal Salute. Rather than getting these, he got lesser brands like Highland Queen and Spey Royal. Thus, he found no compelling reason to discontinue [relations with] the bootlegger. Besides, most of the people believe that the quality that is being offered is far lesser [sic] than the actual quality because most of these brands have been blended with Indian whisky.[16]

Let us further examine this sector to understand Indian consumer behavior. The fact is that most Indians do not really recognize or appreciate the taste of good Scotch. When they flaunt a Black Label or a Red Label, their guests have no idea whether it is the real Scotch or whether it is a spurious bottle purchased from a bootlegger. I know of several people who blend local whisky in a Black Label bottle and serve it to their unsuspecting guests. The guests are happy believing that they are drinking a good, expensive Scotch, and the hosts can serve another bottle of blended whisky at another party (and save money).

Similarly, it is surprising that most pubs and five-star hotel bars in the Indian metros price Chivas Regal and Black Label at almost twice the price of single malts, which are more exotic whiskeys. This differential pricing is indeed surprising (although many approve of it because they can get their Macallan and Laphroaig quite cheaply). But as an hotelier once observed, people in India perceive Black Label and Chivas Regal, and now Jack Daniels, to be premium brands as most have not heard of single malts.

In addition to the manufacturers of Scotch, other foreign companies also did not assess the Indian market intelligently. In the 1990s, for example, Reebok, the footwear giant,

> launched its products with much fanfare, with swank outlets that were called Infinity and with outrageously priced shoes that were locally sourced from Phoenix International. Everything was Indian except for the brand name. However, it had overlooked the fact that Indians are not so fitness conscious and [that] sports shoes are a fashion accessory in India, and worn primarily by young people. By pricing it [sic] outrageously high, it had shut out the bulk of the middle class consumers who had rather cheaper choices from Liberty, Lakhani and Action shoes. Coupled with it, the average number of shoes that an Indian owns is not more than one [pair]. Thus, it [Reebok] was saddled with rising inventory and sagging sales[,] which worsened as the economy hit a recession. Reebok was forced to do a seconds sale in Bangalore. Having burnt its fingers, the company is re-doing its strategy, lowering prices and trying to deliver value for money.[17]

It is only now—in the second half of the first decade of the twenty-first century—that foreign shoe companies have managed to make inroads into the upper and middle middle-class households. As Indians become younger and wealthier, they want to wear sports shoes. And as consumerism sweeps the country, they want to own several pairs. Still, the sales at Nike, Adidas, and Reebok outlets are nothing to write home about.

Even in the case of sectors where the expected boom has been realized, it has not helped the manufacturers or the service providers.

Take the example of air travel. When Jet Airways came out with its public issue, it estimated a manifold increase in the number of domestic passengers. Some of the reasons cited for this optimism by the private airline are given below:

> Despite recent growth in air passenger traffic, India continues to have gross under penetration of air services[,] with an average air travel of 0.014 trips per person per year as compared to an average of 2.02 trips per person per year in the United States. This signals the level of potential demand which may be generated as the economy grows and air travel becomes more affordable for a large population, which otherwise uses road or rail transport.
>
> The aviation market in India consists of two principal groups, leisure travelers and business travelers. Leisure traffic tends to be more price elastic. While historically, business travelers have formed the majority of the domestic air travel[ers] in India, with increasing income levels and the emergence of flexible fare schemes, a shift is likely in the travel habit of middle to high income groups[,] from premium class travel in train to air traffic. In contrast to 15.25 million airline passengers in fiscal 2004, the Indian Railways carried approximately 52 million passengers in its premium class products, i.e., air-conditioned and first class coaches.[18]

Thanks to cheap tickets, some priced as low as Rs 1, the boom did materialize. Domestic air traffic zoomed to 30 million within a couple of years. Thousands of people are now traveling for the first time because the price of their air ticket is less than the fare for a bus ride or a train reservation. Indeed, in some cases, the cost of air travel is less than the cost of a car ride from their home to their office in the same city.

Captain Gopinath of Air Deccan, a low-cost, no-frills airline in which Kingfisher has recently purchased a 26 percent stake, revolutionized air travel in India. As he has said repeatedly, Captain Gopinath's dream was to build a people's airline, not unlike Ratan Tata's passion to build a people's car. Captain Gopinath succeeded to a large extent in realizing his goal as increasing numbers of Indians from lower-middle-class homes in *mofussil* (peripheral) towns (and even villages) have begun flying.

The cost of a Delhi–Mumbai–Delhi ticket is now cheaper than ever. A Delhi–Kochi ticket sometimes costs less than a Delhi–Mumbai ticket, although the former flight covers a distance that is more than twice the distance covered by the latter. No one could have imagined that a Delhi–Kochi air ticket would be cheaper than a train ticket from Delhi to Chandigarh, which is a fraction of the distance.

Given this price-cut madness, the Indian aviation minister, Praful Patel, predicts that there will be more than 180 million domestic passengers by 2010.

But the flip side of the coin is that all the private airlines in India, without any exception, are incurring huge losses. Clearly, the cheap air travel scenario cannot be sustained for a long time. Things have already begun to change. Consolidation moves, with several mergers and acquisitions, have taken place. Jet Airways has taken over Air Sahara, while Kingfisher has bought into Air Deccan. It looks like another low-cost airline, SpiceJet, is looking for a suitor. The immediate impact of such consolidation has been a hike in air fares. Jet has decided to transform Sahara into a value-service airline, under a new brand name, JetLite, with ticket prices positioned between the low-cost airlines (Air Deccan) and the full-service airlines. Kingfisher has decided that Air Deccan cannot survive with such cheap fares, and the latter has decided that its lowest fare will be Rs 650 (not Rs 1) on some routes. As Captain Gopinath stated even before the alliance with Kingfisher, he had realized that such low fares could not go on forever. Air Deccan had to increase fares at some stage.

If fares increase, the passenger growth rate will almost certainly decline. It is likely that the prediction of domestic traffic increasing to 180 million will not happen for a long time. It is possible that the 52 million premium rail travelers may not switch to air travel, as was previously envisaged. The truth is that either the airlines will have to increase passenger traffic and incur losses, or they will have to improve their margins at the cost of possible growth in volumes.

As we have seen repeatedly, pricing is critical in India. Indians are still not consumers in the Westernized way. They can shun certain brands and shut out the organized sector if the price is too high or if the perceived value for money does not materialize as expected. In other words, marketers selling to the Indian middle class should pay serious attention to what C.K. Prahalad and Stuart Hart have to say.

The *bottom of the pyramid* theory, proposed by Prahalad and Hart, is quite simple. MNCs should now look at not the traditional principle of selling more to the same set of customers but rather to selling to a new set—the poor who constitute a sizeable 4 billion-strong consumer base globally. Companies need to rethink everything from scratch in order to make products that they can sell to this class. Prahalad and Hart argue that not only can this goal be achieved but also that it can be hugely profitable. They write:

> The real source of market promise is not the wealthy few in the developing world, or even the emerging middle-income consumers. It is the billions of aspiring poor who are joining the market economy for the first time . . . Doing business with the world's 4 billion poorest people— two thirds of [the] world's population—will require radical innovation in technology and business models. It will require MNCs to re-evaluate price–performance relationships for products and services. It will demand a new level of capital efficiency and new ways of measuring financial success. Companies will be forced to transform their understanding of scale, from a "bigger is better" ideal to an ideal of highly distributed small-scale operations married to world-class capabilities.[19]

Both Indian and foreign firms have to do something similar in India, and should aim to sell their products only to the bottom of the middle-class pyramid.

In India, companies have to face another major hurdle—understanding the differing needs and requirements of the highly fragmented subsets of the Indian middle class. Not only has this to be done in terms of low prices but companies in India also have to carefully think about product variants and the logistics or distribution system to reach middle-class consumers. Only then can they reach the class referred to by Prahalad and Hart—the aspirants.

As we have seen in this and the earlier chapters, success has come in those areas and sectors where prices have been slashed considerably (telecoms, computers, airlines, food and grocery retail) or where value for money is perceptible (cars and financial services) or where newer operations have been implemented successfully.

To conclude, let us cite one of Prahalad and Hart's favorite examples in their own words:

> In the 1990s, a local firm, Nirma Ltd, began offering detergent products for poor consumers, mostly in rural areas. In fact, Nirma created a new business system that included a new product formulation, low-cost manufacturing process, wide distribution network, special packaging, and value pricing.

HLL (Hindustan Lever Ltd. and now Hindustan Unilever Ltd.), in a typically MNC fashion, initially dismissed Nirma's strategy. However, as Nirma grew rapidly, HLL could see its local competitor was winning in a market it had disregarded. Ultimately, HLL saw its vulnerability and its opportunity. In 1995, the company responded with its own offering for this market, drastically altering its traditional business model.

HLL's new detergent, called Wheel, was formulated to substantially reduce the ratio of oil to water in the product, responding to the fact that the poor often wash their clothes in rivers and other public water systems. HLL decentralized the production, marketing and distribution of the product to leverage the abundant labour pool in rural India, quickly creating sales channels through the thousands of small outlets where people at the bottom of the pyramid shop. HLL also changed the cost structure of its detergent business so it could introduce Wheel at a low price point.[20]

What HLL found was that selling Wheel added to the company's bottom line. In 1999, Wheel's annual sales in value terms were half of those of HLL's high-end products; Wheel's margins were 18 percent, or less than those of the high-end products (25 percent). But the return on capital employed (ROCE) in the case of Wheel was 93 percent, or more than four times that of the high-end products (22 percent). It is a different story that Nirma's ROCE was 121 percent.

Postscript: Prahalad and Hart forgot to include a crucial part of the Nirma–Wheel saga in their analysis. Both Nirma and Wheel are still consumed largely by lower-middle-class households, or by aspirant households, which are expected to be part of the middle class within a few years. They have only begun to climb into the ranks of the lower middle class. So the bottom of the pyramid in the case of the Indian market now is the middle class. Marketers have to think long and hard about how to sell to the middle class rather than to the poor.

Note

The weekly news magazine, *The Economist*, introduced its Big Mac Index in 1986 to explain the subtle nuances in purchasing power parity in different countries. It is based on the concept of equal pricing of the Big Mac burger in all countries. If this were true, the ratio of the burger price in China divided by the burger price in the

United States would have yielded the exchange rate ratio between the two currencies. For example, the price is Rs 34 in India and US$2.90 in the United States. On the basis of *The Economist*'s calculations, the exchange rate between the two currencies should be 34/2.90, or Rs 12/US$1. However, the Big Mac Index fails to take into account the disparity between per capita incomes. If the Indian income is five times less than that of the United States, this would mean that the price of the Big Mac is five times more as a percentage of the average income of the Indian consumer. Or else, the exchange rate has to be skewed in favor of the rupee. At the time of writing this book, the dollar is worth just under Rs 40, or 3.3 times the Big Mac Index-based rate.

Endnotes

1. Kishore Dash, "Integrating Case Study 2: McDonald's in India," *Thunderbird*, The Gavin School of International Management, 2005, p. 164.
2. ibid.
3. Vikram Bhalla and Janmejaya Sinha, *India: The Next Frontier for Consumer Companies*, Boston Consulting Group, 2006, p. 5.
4. Dash, op. cit., p. 158.
5. ibid.
6. Alam Srinivas, "Driving Towards the $2,200 Car," *Business 2.0*, August 1, 2004, http://money.cnn.com/magazines/business2/business2_archive/2004/08/01/377368/index.htm
7. Keith Naughton, "Small: It's the New Big," *Newsweek*, February 16, 2008, http://www.newsweek.com/id/112729/output/print
8. Bhalla and Sinha, op. cit., p. 6.
9. Dash, op. cit., p. 161.
10. ibid.
11. Atul Punj, A talk with journalists from *Business Today* magazine, 1997.
12. Dash, op. cit., p. 163.
13. Sudipta Roy, *Brand Failures: A Consumer Perspective to Formulate a MNC Entry Strategy* (a draft report), January 1998, pp. 4–5.
14. ibid., pp. 6-8.
15. Indraprastha Gas Limited, *Draft Red Herring Prospectus*, pp. 50–1, http://www.sebi.gov.in/dp/igl.pdf?uc_dept_id=1
16. Roy, op.cit., p. 9.
17. ibid., pp. 9–10.
18. Jet Airways, *Draft Red Herring Prospectus*, pp. 34–5, http://www.sebi.gov.in/dp/jetair.pdf
19. C.K. Prahalad and Stuart L. and Hart, "The Fortune at the Bottom of the Pyramid," *Strategy+Business*, Issue 26, First Quarter 2002, pp. 1–2.
20. ibid., p. 5.

Chapter

7

Brahmin Businessmen

Hundreds of years ago, there were several similarities between the Boston Brahmins and Indian Chitrapur Saraswat Brahmins. Both had migrated from other places. They were powerful and wealthy and owned large tracts of land. They believed in education and were, therefore, well educated. They set the benchmarks for moral and ethical values in their respective societies. Both sets influenced local issues, policies, and administration. They were the elitists in their respective geographies. But then, none of the sects' members would have met each other in those days.

The origins of both these castes, and subcastes, are fascinating. More important, it is critical to understanding the growing influence of the middle class in modern India.

Since the beginning of the sixteenth century, after Martin Luther nailed his 95 theological theses (declarations) to the castle church door in Wittenberg, Germany, the Reformation movement among the Christians in England went through several ups and downs. The reign of Henry VIII spelled good news, but the subsequent one of Mary I (or Bloody Mary) turned out to be a disaster. It was during Mary's time that one witnessed the first wave of emigration by Protestants, opposed to traditional Catholics, to settlement pockets in other parts of Europe: Geneva and Frankfurt.

But the situation became more unbearable by the beginning of the seventeenth century, when James I came to power. Brandon Gary Lovested, writing for www.iboston.org, feels that this was one of the major turning points in the history of nonconformist Christians.

> In 1607, a group of reformers—the ones that had had enough of the Church, the King, and the warm beer—put enough shillings together to hop on a ship from Boston, England, to [the] Netherlands ... He (the Captain of the ship) turned them in to the local authorities, and they

were thrown in jail. After a brief stay, they tried again in 1608, and this time succeeded. That is to say, they reached the Netherlands. After 12 years, they decided the Dutch people were not the right kind of people, and split for the New World.[1]

Around this time, the reformist nonconformists in England were clearly divided into two categories. There were the Pilgrims (including the ones who reached the United States in 1620), who were in no mood to wait. "They wanted to attain 'reformation without tarrying (delay)', even if it meant separating from the Church and their nation."[2] It was the Pilgrims who sailed the *Mayflower* to land at Plymouth, Massachusetts, in 1620. They who inspired the now-famous prose

> April showers bring Mayflowers
> What do Mayflowers bring?
> Pilgrims?

On the same side, but with a slightly different mindset, were the Puritans. They were the ones who

> wanted to remain a part of the English establishment, working for biblical reform from within. To them, the purpose of their new colony (in New England or the US) was to be a biblical witness, "a city on a hill," which would set an example of biblical righteousness in Church and State for Old England and the entire world to see.[3]

The Puritans emigrated to Boston, Massachusetts, beginning in the 1630s. Ironically, none other than Charles I, who pushed England more toward Catholicism and hated the Puritans, helped them. What turned the tide toward this nonconformist sect was the growing and bitter tension between the king and parliament. Between 1625 and 1629, parliament was summoned and dissolved thrice. Subsequently, Charles I did not even bother to summon it. In revenge, the legislative body refused to relinquish its hold over the privy purse. As Lovested puts it:

> He (Charles) financed his reign by selling commercial monopolies; today, we call them "franchises," and extracting ship money—a fee demanded from towns for building naval warships; today, we call that "extortion." One such commercial monopoly was the Massachusetts Bay Colony.[4]

This is how Charles helped the Puritans, yet again in Lovested's words,

> On March 4th, 1629, the Massachusetts Bay Company was given its charter ... Although it was a commercial company interested in culti-vating trade in the new colony, the leading promoters of it were Puritans intent on creating a church free from outside interference. Apparently, they did not write that down on their application to the King. When King Charles granted a colonial charter ... the document failed to specify that the governor and officers of the company had to remain in England.
>
> ... The Puritan stockholders took advantage of this omission, and moved the whole company and its colonial government flock, stock, and barrel to America. They would then establish a Biblical commu-nity—"a holy commonwealth"—as an example to England and the world. The Puritans would finally get to leave England, under the nose of the King, all because of a legal loophole. The Massachusetts Bay Company would ferry thousands of Puritans to America over the next few years.[5]

Both the Plymouth and Boston colonies in America—the Pilgrim and Puritan communities—remained separate and dif-ferent politico-religious entities, until they were merged or com-bined by England in the late 1680s.

While the New Englanders sailed the seven seas (philosophi-cally and literally), the Chitrapur Saraswats, considered a Puritan Brahmin caste in India, traveled thousands of kilometers over land. But their initial journey began much earlier.

Their original home was in Kashmir, and they were generally considered a part of the Gaud Brahmins, who lived north of the Vindhya Mountains, and more specifically, an integral con-stituent of the Saraswat Brahmins, who lived to the west of the mythical Saraswati River. For several social, political, and reli-gious reasons, the Saraswats migrated to various parts of India and are today found in several southern and western states such as Goa, Maharashtra, Gujarat, and Karnataka.

Mythology details how they got to Goa (west India) thou-sands of years ago. Lord Parashurama was a Brahmin reincarna-tion of Lord Vishnu, one of the three central Hindu gods. To avenge his father's death, Parashurama killed all the warriors and kings on earth, and then, in a bout of shame, decided to cleanse himself by retiring to a land of peace. The Sea granted him a boon that it would recede as far back (on the Western Ghats mountain range along India's west coast) as Parashurama could throw his axe (his favorite weapon).

Land was available between the Gulf of Cambay and Cape Comorin, which included Goa, and the Brahmins who were settled there by Parashurama came to be called the Gaud Saraswat Brahmins.

In the fourteenth and fifteenth centuries, the Saraswats were forced to move further south of Goa. Yet again, as in the case of the Boston Brahmins, religious persecution, in this case by Muslim rulers, was the main reason for this exodus. "In 1328, the army of Delhi Sultans (Tughlaqs) captured Kadamba's capital, Chandrapur ... and ransacked it," said a website on Chitrapur Saraswats. From 1352 to 1366, the area remained under the Muslim conquerors.

> Then in 1472, the Bahamani Muslims attacked. They destroyed many temples and forced the Hindus to get converted to Islam. To avoid these insults and religious persecution, several Saraswat families moved to the neighborhood kingdom of Sonde, more to Kanara (Karnataka), and a few to even far-off Kochi (Kerala) in Malabar Coast. Then came another exodus from Goa in the early part of the 16th century.
>
> In 1510, Panaji (Goa's capital) was captured by the Portuguese general Alfonso Albuquerque from the Adil Shah dynasty of Bijapur ... At first, the Portuguese did not interfere with the locals, although they banned the Sati rite (the burning of widows). They employed Hindus and engaged them in their armies, and they maintained good trade relations with the Hindu empire of Hampi (in the south). When different Christian missionaries arrived in Goa, the question of religious tolerance began ... In 1559, King Joao III of Portugal issued a decree threatening expulsion ... of non-believers.[6]

While the Saraswats succumbed to the desires and wishes of the new rulers, the rich and powerful had enough clout to resist the social changes. Those who comprised the middle class simply decided to flee to adjoining states—to interior Maharashtra and coastal Karnataka. Many fled by ship to even more distant places in Kerala. The last of those expelled by the Portuguese landed at the port of Calicut in Kerala, but were driven out again and settled in two other ports in the state, Cochin and Travancore.

Slowly, the links that these emigrants had with Goa's Gaud Saraswats loosened. But a catalytic change for the Brahmins who went to Karnataka (Kanara) came during the reign of Basavappa Nayaka I (1696–1714) when the people of Kanara accused the Gaud Saraswats of not being true Brahmins. The reason: unlike other Brahmin sects, the Saraswats did not have a guru, or spiritual leader. They worshipped their two deities and, thanks to their prayers, a *sanyaasin* (female ascetic) of north Indian Gaud Saraswat origin arrived in their area. At the request of the local Saraswats, she agreed to guide and represent the community in 1708. This marked the beginning of a new Brahmin caste, the Chitrapur Saraswats.

Over the decades and centuries, both Boston Brahmins and Chitrapur Saraswats (or, as I call them, the Bangalore Brahmins, since many of them had shifted to Karnataka's capital) amassed huge wealth in terms of real estate and other assets.

Here is the story of the economic rise of the Boston Brahmins and Bangalore Brahmins.

Acquiring real estate was never an issue for either of the two communities because they moved into new geographies where land was plentiful, and available. Talking about the origins of the now-renowned Boston Brahmin families, the Appletons and Lawrences, Anthony Mann wrote in an article in the *History Journal of Massachusetts* that "neither family can be labeled unambiguously poor." Both these families, unsurprisingly, had decent estates by the eighteenth and nineteenth centuries.

First, there is Winfred Rothenberg's sample of 512 estates probated between 1720 and 1838 in Middlesex County, home to the Lawrences, just across the state line from the Appletons. Adjusted to 1800 dollars, the mean net worth of the sample amounts to $3,600. Second, there is the figure of $80,000, the sum of the estate, probated in 1802, of John Lowell, a lawyer/jurist/financier, which can be seen as representative of a family comfortably established within Boston's post-revolutionary economic elite.

Samuel Lawrence, the father of Amos and Abbott, was a farmer. In 1807, when Amos began his career as a Boston shopkeeper, he estimated his father's estate to have been worth $4,000. Isaac Appleton, father of Samuel and Nathan, was also a farmer. He died in 1806 ... leaving an estate of $7,500 ... Samuel Lawrence was in a position to mortgage part of his farm to supply Amos with the $1,000 he desired to commence his business life. Yet, the sons still had much to do ... [7]

And this is what one of the Internet sources said about Saraswat Brahmins.

> Once the migrants arrived in Goa, they occupied various plots of land and organized their community ... These founders produced magnificent fields of rice on their new land. However, the cultivation of land was probably forced upon the lower caste natives of Goa, who were traditionally given a percentage of the crops.[8]

Future generations in both these "Brahmin" communities ventured into business, and multiplied their wealth. Boston families have somehow perpetuated the myth that they started from absolute scratch, and represent a typical rags-to-riches story. But the evidence, as we have seen in the earlier paragraphs, suggests that they were already quite well-off before their transition from farmers to entrepreneurs.

Let us first look at some of the legends surrounding Boston Brahmin families such as the Appletons and Lawrences. According to Mann, both were

> held up as archetypes of success in the 19th century. Real-life versions of Horatio Alger heroes, they began their lives in small rural communities ... From such obscure beginnings, contemporaries described the way they came to Boston, like Amos Lawrence "with nothing but himself"; or as Abbott "a poor, unknown and friendless boy" with three dollars in his pocket, beginning in business like a third brother, William "with no capital, but his own energies and talents." The Appletons were pictured in a similar fashion ... it was to the credit of Samuel Appleton, that he commenced life with a single four-pence half-penny, paid to him by a drover who passed his father's house, for assistance in driving (cattle).[9]

The key characters in the two families have only added to these stories. In his diary, Amos Lawrence says that he arrived in Boston with "no other possessions than a common country education, a sincere love for his family, and habits of industry, economy, and sobriety." Other writers agreed. Theodore Parker, one of them, said that the merchant prince's success was due to "honest industry, forecast, prudence, thrift."

In his journal, Nathan Appleton expanded on these themes. It is only in America

where the poorest of your sons—knows that by industry and economy—
he can acquire property and respectability—and has ambition enough to
make the attempt—which seldom indeed fails of success.[10]

Later, he wrote:

The eloquent advocate, the learned divine, the able writer, the successful merchant, manufacturer, or agriculturist are allotted the highest
places in society. These places are only obtained through an active and
successful industry.[11]

His father, Amos, wrote to Nathan that "we are literally all
working-men."

As we have seen earlier, the truth lay elsewhere. Both these
families were not rich, but were certainly well-to-do before they
ventured into business. Also, the earlier generations had a repu-
tation within their respective communities. As Mann puts it:

They (the two families) did, however, enjoy a degree of status within
their respective towns. William Appleton's father was pastor to his
community. Samuel Lawrence's family had been resident in Groton
since 1660. Lawrence had represented the town in the General Court
in the mid-eighteenth century, and Samuel himself was a major in the
Continental Army and later a justice of the peace. He also served in a
number of local offices, including some forty years as church deacon,
and was elected for shorter terms as a selectman, town clerk, assessor
and moderator.

Living in many ways a parallel life, Isaac Appleton, whose family
was among the first settlers in New Ipswich in 1750, between 1751
and 1790 served fifteen terms as town moderator, twelve times as
selectman, and five terms as town clerk ... Appleton was an active
organizer of the town's Patriot movement, and like Samuel Lawrence,
he held the office of deacon in the New Ipswich church for thirty
years.[12]

The decision by a few members of the two families to pursue
new economic activities was forced upon them. It was driven by
the declining opportunities in native towns. Mann says that by
the 1790s, agrarian prospects had stagnated in both Ipswich and
Groton. This is reflected from the demographics of the two
towns. The population of Ipswich rose sharply from 350 in 1760
to 1,241 in 1790, but thereafter stabilized around that figure,

reaching 1,278 in 1820. In identical fashion, the population of Groton rose from 1,400 in 1764 to 1,840 in 1790. Thirty years later, the town's populace stood at 1,897.

Mann is convinced that it was the shortage of farmland, which kept getting divided among generations that changed the outlook of these agrarian families.

> Increasingly, as the land resources of a family reached their last point of distribution, families sought to diversify their economic activities, innovating in terms of market production, capital investment, and child vocation ... The strategies of the Appletons and Lawrences in the late nineteenth century need to be viewed through such a prism of declining traditional opportunity; as families holding insufficient resources to be complacent about structural changes, yet possessing sufficient wealth to be able to become engaged in alternative means of wealth production and enabling their children to pursue new vocations, securing their independence without threatening the family estate.[13]

Finally, there is fresh evidence to indicate that honest and ethical practices took a back seat in many of the ventures pursued by the merchant princes. A biography of Thomas Handasyd Perkins (1764–1854), a renowned Boston businessman, by Carl Seaburg and Stanley Paterson details the way business was generally conducted in those days.

An Internet review of this book says that Thomas and his brother, James, set up a commission business in 1783,

> in which slaves were a major commodity, along with dried fish (slave food), flour and horses ... When the China trade opened in 1789, Thomas went as supercargo of the Astrea on a slow and unhealthy trip from Boston to Canton via Batavia.[14]

While he was at Canton, he observed the trade in sea otter skins, which were smuggled into China from America and sold for US$70 each. He decided to get into it and organized two ships, *Hope* and *Margaret*. Although the *Hope* expedition did not succeed, *Margaret* did. At the same time, the Perkins brothers were selling food in revolutionary France in a sellers' market. The Perkins, made ten trips to Europe, and their ships even went to Africa, Russia, the West Indies, and China.

During the Napoleonic wars and the War of 1812, Perkins' ships were given safe passage by all sides. The Internet review says that Perkins paid for this, and

> ... bribery, smuggling and hard-ball politics were standard at all locations.
>
> The Perkins' *Jacob Jones* captured two British merchant ships while on its way to China in 1814. Both carried opium, and this changed the Perkins, business model dramatically when they realized the profits involved.[15]

China had deemed the opium trade illegal in 1800.

> The fact that they were entering a trade forbidden by China was known to all the merchants involved. Nor was the fact that many considered it immoral to use opium any deterrent to the traders. They cheerfully rationalized that the opium habit was not nearly as debilitating as the habit of drink.[16]

Everything was fair in business and war.

Like many of the Boston Brahmin families, the Indian Saraswats (especially the Chitrapurs or Bangalore Brahmins) started off by becoming prominent members in their new, local communities. The families that moved to Karnataka in the 1400s and 1500s were largely educators and administrators. Such professions were logical for any Brahmin community in India since they were the only ones who had easy access to education. Being the highest caste in India, the Brahmins controlled the education system and, for several thousands of years, were the only ones who could teach and learn.

Using their intelligence and experience in public service, the Chitrapur Saraswats secured positions as accountants in the courts of Hindu rulers. One of the kings, stated a website dedicated to this community, was

> so impressed by the diligence and skills of the Saraswat accountant that he decreed that each village in the kingdom be administered by a Saraswat. Eventually, these Saraswats took on the name of the village as their last name.[17]

Circumstances pushed some of them to become traders and entrepreneurs.

According to a website:

In 1627, Vira Kerala Karma Raja of Cochin gave the Konkanis (Saraswats) certain rights and privileges such as exemption from payment of Purushantharam or succession fee, permission to construct houses with brick mortar and also to conduct business from Cochin with foreign countries. This is considered the Magna Carta of the Konkani community in Kerala.

Again in 1648, the Raja of Cochin ... gave the community the civil and criminal powers to be exercised by them within the well-defined boundary of their settlement called "Sanketam." The Saraswats could secure all these privileges in Cochin because of their skill and ability as overseas traders.

... the Dutch company had secured in 1663 the privilege of extraterritoriality for the Konkanis and Christians in the Cochin kingdom. The privilege permitted the Konkanis and the local Christian subjects of the Cochin prince for trial of all suits filed by these people or against these people, in the Courts of the Dutch Company. They secured this privilege (for the Konkanis) because they were the people whose help the Dutch needed the most for their commercial transactions ...

The Saraswats competed with the Jaina traders and the Muslim traders on the west coast in their overseas trade. The Europeans ... who disliked the local Muslims for their close alliance with the Arabs who were the rivals of these Europeans in oceanic trade, maintained special relations with the Saraswats in their commercial transactions. The Dutch, who founded their factory at Cochin and monopolized the trade of the port, relied on the Saraswats for securing goods like pepper, rice, forest products, etc.

The Dutch had settled in Cochin at the full tide of Konkani predominance. The Dutch had given them the right to collect income from Mattancherry and Cherlai and of Konkani temples. In the agreement made in 1772 with the Raja of Cochin, the Dutch had also stipulated that the Raja shall impose no new demand on the Konkanis, who shall have full liberty to complain to the Dutch Governor, if aggrieved, and the Raja shall not interfere in any matters of the temple without the ... consent of the Company.[18]

Francesca Trivellato of Yale University has traced some of the business correspondence between Chitrapur Saraswats and foreign traders and businessmen:

Leghorn was then (in the seventeenth and eighteenth centuries) the most thriving Mediterranean port after Marseille and the largest Sephardic settlement in Europe along with Amsterdam. Ergas &

Silvera was a prominent merchant house, with a branch in Tuscany and one in Aleppo (Syria).

The additional specialty of the Sephardim of Leghorn was the exchange of Mediterranean coral and Indian diamonds. From the 1660s, this lucrative and risky barter came increasingly under the aegis of the English East India Company, and London became the world market for rough diamonds ... However, throughout the eighteenth century, and especially until the 1730s ... the Sephardim of Leghorn continued to carry out the exchange of coral and diamonds relying on a Portuguese connection centered on Lisbon and Goa. Indeed the latter remained the center of diamond trade until 1730.

Of the 13,659 surviving letters of Ergas & Silvera, 242 were addressed to Christian (mostly Italian) merchants in Lisbon, and 86 to Hindu merchants in Goa. They all concern the coral and diamond trade. In light of the diversity of these intermediaries and the lack of an over-reaching legal authority to which any parties could bring their complaints, it is natural to wonder how it was possible for trust to be built across such geographical and cultural distances. The answer, I believe, lies primarily in the intense and widespread circulation of business letters among these merchants, which created and nourished mechanisms of mutual obligations and reciprocal control that worked even in the absence of formal enforcing institutions.

... Ergas & Silvera invested in the Portuguese branch of the exchange of coral and diamonds for a period of over thirty years, between 1710 and 1741 (when they preferred London and Madras to their previous destinations). They opted for the Portuguese connection because they could count on merchant letters to help them create a niche in a pre-existing network of correspondents in Lisbon and Goa, who also served other Sephardim of Leghorn and their co-religionists in Amsterdam and London ...

Most of Ergas & Silvera's letters sent to Goa were addressed to the Camotim family (Portuguese for Kamath, a common surname among Saraswat Brahmins) who, like all their other agents, belonged to the Saraswat caste, which was the leading native elite throughout the four-and-a-half centuries when the city was under Portuguese rule. In the 1730s, the Camotims were probably the richest family in Goa. And from Ergas & Silvera's correspondence we learn that they operated as a united clan, concerned for the good standing of their members and the continued delivery of new orders from Leghorn.[19]

Business can rarely be an absolutely clean affair. So, it is not surprising that there were many stories about the lack of trust and faith among Chitrapur Brahmins, as was the case with the Boston merchant princes. The following story is enough to highlight how far Indian Brahmin traders were willing to go to make that extra buck.

In the eighteenth century, Baba Prabhu, a prominent Saraswat trader of Cochin had close links with a Jewish businessman, David Rahabi. In the 1750s, the two families entered into a trading partnership, but, unfortunately, Prabhu ran up a debt to his partner, who, in turn, took over a warehouse owned by the Prabhus. The Prabhus approached the governor, who asked the Rahabis to return the keys of the warehouse.

Almost a year later, the two partnering families went to court to resolve their dispute. To humiliate the Jewish traders and also the raja of Cochin, the Prabhus established contacts with the generals in Hyder Ali's (a neighboring ruler) army. The correspondence was detected in time, and the Prabhus were exiled to the Cape of Good Hope. (Interestingly, this was probably the first Indian family to settle in South Africa.)

The intertwining of politics, religion, and business can be gauged from yet another incident involving Saraswat traders, the raja of Cochin and the Dutch Company.

In 1791, the raja of Cochin imposed several restrictions on the Saraswats, as an indirect tax. He demanded a contribution of the jaggery they produced, and refused the gathering of crops from their temple land. When the merchants refused to comply, the king arrested them and also asked them to pay custom duty in violation of the kingdom's 1772 agreement with the Dutch Company. The Dutch intervened, but the relations between the Saraswats and the king further deteriorated.

On October 12, 1791, several leading Saraswat traders were massacred; the Dutch attacked the king's palace, but were repulsed. The raja's army went berserk and looted the wealth of the merchants and their temple.

The persecuted Saraswats went to the king of Travancore and pleaded for help. The enraged ruler urged the Dutch to take action, but was finally forced to retreat from the dispute at the behest of the English Company's agent at Travancore.

Despite such problems, the Brahmin traders survived in Boston as well as in Bangalore. However, successive and more recent generations of these two communities seemed more interested in education, culture, and upholding of moral values within their respective societies.

Going back to the Appletons and Lawrences, let us once again refer to Mann's short study on the two families. According to it, both Samuel Lawrence and Isaac Appleton gave undue attention to the education of their children:

> In 1787, Isaac Appleton was one of the thirty-two local men who combined their efforts and resources to establish the New Ipswich Academy. Two years later, Samuel Lawrence was one of the forty-three men who subscribed to the establishment of [the] Groton Academy. Both institutions represented a sharp break with the type of local education which had previously been offered. Both were fee paying institutions, Groton charging one shilling a week, New Ipswich twelve shillings a quarter in advance. Both were to be run by educated men; the first preceptor of the New Ipswich Academy was Dartmouth graduate John Hubbard; Groton first hiring Samuel Holyoke, a recent Harvard graduate.
>
> Both institutions offered a classical curriculum, aimed at providing an education sufficient to pass college entrance exams. Such schooling allowed children to diversify careers, whilst retaining or increasing status. Two of Isaac's sons, Joseph and Moses Appleton, went on to graduate from Dartmouth College ... Moses went on to enjoy a-medical career, studying first with Governor Brooks of Medford, gaining a diploma from Massachusetts Medical Society in 1796 ... In a similar fashion, the oldest of the Lawrence boys attended Harvard, graduating in the class of 1801 and studying law with a locally eminent lawyer before establishing a successful practice in Groton.
>
> More than providing vocational and academic training, the academies provided a web of valuable future contacts. The oldest of the Lawrence boys, the Harvard graduate Luther, gained much from his early training. One of some fifty students in his year, his social acceptability is demonstrated in membership of the exclusive Hasty Pudding Club and selection as club orator of the 1801 semi-annual public exhibition.
>
> When Luther returned to Groton, he entered the highly successful legal practice of the Honorable Timothy Bigelow, a Harvard graduate himself who sat in the General Court for more than thirty years, before and after his move to Boston in 1806. In 1805, having established an independent legal practice, Luther married Lucy Bigelow, sister of his old employer and grand daughter of the Honorable Oliver Prescott, MD of Groton, also a Harvard graduate, thirty two years a selectman, major-general, judge of probate and, like Bigelow, local gentry with ties to men of wealth and status in Boston.[20]

While education has been the focus of Indian Brahmins, the Chitrapur Saraswats were among the few sects who took it to another level. It was around the end of the nineteenth century that many of the Bangalore Brahmins started migrating to key cities like Bombay, Calcutta, and Madras. The only reason for this movement was the thirst for modern education. In those days, students could complete their schooling only upon successfully passing an entrance examination conducted by the universities in these three cities. The Chitrapur Saraswats invariably chose Bombay or Madras because of its proximity.

However, one of the first to migrate to Bombay sought employment, and not education. Shamrao Vithal Kaikini (1841–1905) learnt English from a tutor during his teens in Kanara, and in 1859 he passed an examination that enabled him to join the public services. Initially, he worked with Kanara's revenue department but later, when he was 20 years old, decided to go to Bombay to become a lawyer.

He returned soon after, and in 1867 he went with his brother to handle a case in Bombay. His talent was recognized there, and soon after, he was appointed as the second Kannada translator in the Bombay High Court. In 1871, he cleared the Bombay High Court Pleaders' Exam, which allowed him to start his legal practice.

Over time, Shamrao formed his own caste-driven network, which flowered over the next few decades. At first, he helped his family members, including his nephew Narayanrao Ganesh Chandavarkar, who became the first person from his community to receive a BA degree from Bombay University. He then helped other caste members to come to study in Bombay.

One of the websites on Saraswat Brahmins states:

> The first group ... that came to Bombay for their education established a room club, or a hostel, in an apartment near Shamrao's residence in Khandewadi ...
>
> The first ... to matriculate from the University of Madras was Ullal Baburao in 1869, when he received his Bachelor's degree in law ... Madras had earned an excellent reputation in terms of its educational prospective and employment opportunities in the field of administration. However, the weak point ... was that it was not very technologically advanced and, thus, did not offer many ... opportunities for fresh graduates ... Madras did not become as popular ... as did Bombay, which was a more modern city.[21]

For obvious reasons, the lethal combination of real estate, business wealth, modern education, elitist social networking, and access to rulers and policymakers due to the nature of their employment transformed the Boston and Bangalore Brahmins into a kind of new aristocracy. They had become a class apart from the others.

Oliver Wendell Holmes, who first coined the phrase Boston Brahmins in an 1860 article he wrote for the *Atlantic Monthly*, described them in this manner:

> There is, however, in New England, an aristocracy, if you choose to call it so, which has a far greater character of permanence. It has grown to be a caste—not in any odious sense—but, by the reputation of the same influences, generation after generation, it has acquired a distinct organization and physiognomy, which not to recognize is mere stupidity, and not to be willing to describe would show a distrust of the good nature and intelligence of our readers, who like to have us see all we can see and tell all we see.[22]

Holmes was of the view that individuals who belonged to this caste, or these families, could be easily identifiable by their looks, behavior, attitude, character, or just their family surnames.

> In a large city, this class of citizens are familiar to us in the streets. They are very courteous in their adulations; they have time enough to bow and take their hats off—which, of course, no businessman can afford to do. Their beavers are mostly brushed, and their boots well polished; all their appointments are tidy; they look the respectable walking gentleman to perfection. They are prone to habits—to frequent reading rooms, insurance offices—to walk the same streets at the same hours— so that one becomes familiar with their faces and persons, as a part of the street furniture.[23]

But those who managed their lives and became successful slowly became an integral and critical part of the economic, social, cultural, and political elite.

Let us see what Mann says about the Appletons and Lawrences:

> In addition to sheer wealth, they occupied positions of central economic importance in the rapidly developing New England economy. Appletons and Lawrences sat on the boards of a clutch of Boston-based financial institutions, including the Suffolk Bank, which from 1818 played a dominant role in providing New England traders with a stable regional currency. Moreover, from its founding in 1823, Amos

and Abbott Lawrence, alongside Nathan, Samuel and William Appleton held high office in the Massachusetts Hospital Life Insurance Company, the single most important supplier of investment capital in pre-Civil War New England. Both institutions were a part of the economic infrastructure established and run by Boston Associates, a close-knit group of businessmen who established the Waltham-Lowell textile mill system within which the two families were heavily represented, both as investors and as directors. It is no exaggeration to state, as the business historian Frances Gregory has, that from 1811 hardly any successful venture in New England was begun without the support of the Appletons, the Lawrences and Thomas Wren Ward, agent of the British bankers, the Baring Brothers.

Not only were the two families represented at the heart of the ante-bellum economic culture, they were also frequently selected and elected as political representatives of federalists and then Whig conservatism. Nathan Appleton, active in the federalist movement from 1808, first represented Boston in the Massachusetts legislature in 1815, serving five further terms before 1828, when his elder brother Samuel began the first of his three terms. In 1830, Nathan gained election to Congress, winning a pivotal contest as the candidate of protection over free trade; four years later, his seat in Washington was filled by Abbott Lawrence, a man described by John Quincy Adams in 1838, as "perhaps, the most leading man of Whig politics in Boston." In 1848, Abbott missed his party's vice-presidential nomination by six votes, and, ... effectively missed the presidency too.

... Further signs of communal approbation can be traced in the election of Appletons and Lawrences to distinguished positions within the voluntary institutions which also characterized the Brahmin elite. Members of the two families were chosen by their social peers to serve on the boards of the Massachusetts general Hospital and Boston Attenaeum, as well as gaining membership to exclusive social institutions such as the Massachusetts Historical Society and the Humane Society ... Evidence of social acceptability is also seen in second generation marriages, uniting Appletons with Coolidges and Lymans, and Lawrences with Prescotts and Lowells.[24]

During the nineteenth century, the Chitrapur Saraswats also gained immense socioeconomic and political clout. Since they were among the first to adapt to English education, and since the British rulers were looking for Indians to administer the vast country, the Bangalore Brahmins were quickly absorbed in key positions in the various district and collectors' offices across the country. They became key advisors to the British, as well as in independent India's first government in 1947.

Sir Benegal Narasing Rao, a Chitrapur Brahmin, was among the framers of the Indian Constitution. Some experts believe that, contrary to common perception that B.R. Ambedkar was the main writer of the Constitution, it was Rao who played the major role and wrote most parts of it. Rao later served as a minister in the Central Cabinet, and occupied senior positions in several banks that were later nationalized. He also represented India at the United Nations. Before independence, he was the prime minister of the state of Jammu and Kashmir and a renowned jurist.

By the early part of the twentieth century, the Chitrapur Saraswats had become a thriving community. When it came to business, its members made huge profits during and after World War I, taking advantage of the shortages of several commodities. They realized the importance of modern education, and ensured that each generation was well educated. With an excellent grasp of mathematics and commerce, they also indirectly controlled the banking sector and financial institutions. The Saraswats founded two of India's major banks, Canara Bank (1910) and Syndicate Bank (1925), and continued to control them until the government nationalized them in 1969.

Thanks to the economic prosperity of its members and the largesse from princely states and the British, the community's temples and mutts became richer and owned vast tracts of land. The money was partly used for providing modern amenities to the community in the form of schools and health centers. During this period, most of the Chitrapur Saraswats belonged to the middle class, mainly upper-middle class, and upper class.

After independence, their fortunes witnessed dramatic changes. Land reforms initiated by various state and the central governments fixed ceilings on land holdings. The temples and mutts were forced to give away much of their real estate to the government. The policymakers' insistence that the cultivating tenants, who were hired by the temples and landlords, own the land meant that huge agricultural incomes vanished instantly. Suddenly, the landlords and religious institutions lost their power base.

The nationalization of banks ensured that employment opportunities for community members reduced drastically. More important, Saraswat businessmen who depended on help and largesse from Canara Bank and Syndicate Bank had to compete with other traders for access to finance. The close linkages that the traditional trading caste, the Vaishyas or the Banias, developed and honed with independent India's political class implied that new opportunities were grabbed by them, rather than the Chitrapur Brahmins.

(In the Indian caste system, Brahmins constituted the uppermost caste with their education and religious clout; they were the upholders of morals and values in the society. Then came the Kshatriyas, the warriors, followed by the Vaishyas, or traders. At the bottom were the Untouchables, Dalits or Shudras.)

Even the middle-class Chitrapurs were affected by the growing wave of reservations, either directly or indirectly, in both jobs and educational institutions. This was especially true in the southern states, where regional political parties, headed by those from the lower castes, shifted the axis of power from the Brahmins toward their own communities. The swing of the political power pendulum forced employers such as the public sector units and government to provide more jobs to the lower and backward castes.

Each and every segment of the Chitrapur Saraswat community, therefore, was adversely affected by the socioeconomic–political changes in independent India. Other Brahmin clans, too, felt a similar impact.

Ironically, the Boston Brahmins also went through a period of declining influence in the twentieth century. Alexandra Hall, writing for www.bostonmagazine.com, had this to say about the current state of the city's original first families:

> Rumors about the Brahmins' influence in old and modern Boston are as plentiful as they are contradictory. Without a doubt, the Brahmins were (and, some believe, still are) the shadowy cabal that pulled the city's strings from on high. Others say their wealth and power have dried up, that all they have left are their names and what's left in the trust funds. Admirers retort that the Brahmins are this city's caregivers, lovers of culture and education; detractors claim that they are elitist and provincial Boston royalty.
>
> ... "The Brahmins?" asks Eleanor Spaak, sounding surprised to even hear the term. "The Brahmins are nowhere right now." Socialite and society columnist for the *Newbury Street and Back Bay Guide*, she's watched the last vestiges of Brahmin clout shift to new families and new groups—Irish, Jewish, Italian. "They don't have the power they once did, and they simply aren't giving money like they used to because they don't have it.

She's not the only one who thinks so. "Certainly there are still Honeywells and Cabots, but by and large most of the money that's being donated in town is coming from newly rich Irish, Jews and Italians," says Soroff. "Look at the board of the Symphony—that was once a Brahmin haven. Now Peter Brooke is the chairman. Tom Stemberg from Staples, George Krupp, Chad Gifford, Nancy Fitzpatrick: These are not Brahmin names. So, yes the Brahmins are the social history of Boston, and there's still a strong thread of that tradition, but they are not what they once were."[25]

However, during the last few decades of the twentieth century, the histories of the Boston Brahmins and Bangalore Brahmins have diverged visibly. In the past 20–30 years, there has been a sort of resurgence among the Indian community, even as the one in Boston continues to struggle and largely revels in the glory days of the past.

Surprisingly, the new generation of Chitrapur Saraswats is again becoming founders and financiers. Other Brahmins in India are fast emulating what it is doing. More importantly, there is an ambitious surge among the middle class—cutting across caste, class, religion, and any other socioeconomic segregation—to become owners. This points at the slow, but distinct, transformation in India's business environment. It epitomizes the second coming of the Brahmin Businessmen, and the unexpected upsurge in the number of educated entrepreneurs and professional promoters.

For many analysts and observers who have witnessed the steady fall in the stature of the Brahmins and the middle class' almost-religious attraction to the materialistic in independent India, the new trend seems shocking, to say the least.

Post-independence, most Indian businessmen came from the trading families. They comprised the Marwaris in the north and east, Gujarati Jains in the west, and the Nadars in the south. The familiar names that rang a bell in the 1960s and 1970s were the Birlas, Bajajs, Dalmias, Goenkas, and Modis. They were also a few well-known Parsis such as the Tatas and Wadias. Even the few who represented the typical rags-to-riches stories, such as the Nandas and Ambanis, had some sort of family legacy in business.

Most of these families thrived in modern India because of the networks they assiduously built with Indian leaders during the freedom struggle. J.R.D. Tata, G.D. Birla and Jamnalal Bajaj were among the few who closely interacted with, advised, and helped Mahatma Gandhi, Jawaharlal Nehru, and Sardar Vallabhai Patel. And in some ways they shaped the country's economic and business vision.

This may sound contradictory because the private sector cannot survive when pitted against public sector, which is essentially what Nehru did with his economic policies. Indeed, this is what the Tata Group's official website has to say about the relationship between the two:

> Nehru and JRD shared an unusual relationship. They had been friends for long and there was plenty of mutual respect, but they differed significantly on the economic policies India needed to follow. JRD was not a political animal and he never could come to terms with the nature of the socialistic beast then ruling the roost (he once joked, many years after Nehru's passing, that the Chinese steward the Taj Group of Hotels had brought in from abroad earned more money than him). JRD was an articulate and persistent votary of economic liberalization long before it was finally implemented in India.[26]

Despite Nehru's focus on public investments and high-handed government controls over the private sector, these business icons thrived. The reasons: because of the first-mover advantage in several sectors, they retained their edge over public sector units which became inefficient, less productive and costly; the license-permit raj (in which business and commerce were regulated through the granting of licenses, permits, and quotas by the central and state governments) ensured that the near-monopoly of the existing business houses continued, at least in the private arena; and only the Birlas or Tatas had the deep pockets to buy out firms that the British promoters decided to sell when they left the country.

In addition, the existing businessmen used their political proximity and financial clout to gobble up the new licenses that were issued by the government in sectors that they operated in or the ones that were opened up for private investment. In a sense, it was mostly these powerful business groups who could increase capacity.

Using education as their only asset, the Brahmins restricted their presence and influence to backroom power centers. Initially, they became bureaucrats, public and private sector employees, and agents of intellectual change. Slowly, as the middle class grew within other socioeconomic groups, the Brahmins lost this edge too. For most of the Neo Middle Class, (NMC) getting into the Indian Administrative Service (IAS) or a job with a multinational corporation (MNC) was the ideal professional strategy. So, like the Brahmins earlier, they became public servants, engineers, doctors, chartered accountants, and lawyers.

This is what the abstract of a 2005 paper by Vaishali Honawar said about this phenomenon:

> Though middle-class families in India have long steered their children into professions like engineering and medicine, the trend has taken off over the past decade. It's been spurred by the demand in the 1990s for software workers in the United States and other Western countries, and more recently by the phenomenon of outsourcing by Western multinationals to Indian shores.[27]

An almost karmic belief in the virtues of education forced middle class and Brahmin parents to send their children to Europe or the United States for higher studies in engineering, medicine, management, and such professions. Those who had the money because they managed to retain a part of their land holdings, or were excellent savers, had no problems in achieving this objective. Those who were not wealthy enough pressurized their sons and daughters to study hard to attain foreign scholarships.

Tens of thousands of Indians flooded foreign colleges during the 1970s and 1980s. After their graduation or post graduation, most of them settled abroad. In time, there were thousands of Indian doctors, engineers, and MBAs working in the United States and Europe (mainly in the United Kingdom). Simultaneously, graduates from premier Indian institutes like the IITs and IIMs were aggressively wooed by global MNCs. This resulted in a parallel wave in which Indians crossed the seven seas for attractive jobs. The number of Indian professionals abroad shot up. Over decades, by the 1990s, many of them had successfully climbed up the corporate hierarchies to get into decision-making positions.

This was dubbed the "brain drain" phenomenon, which led to an intense debate about its impact on the Indian society.

An inconclusive article in *OECD Observer* said:

> Mostly, the problems caused by the brain drain in poorer sending countries are great. Migrants from developing countries are generally more likely to stay in the host country than migrants from advanced countries. Survey evidence on the share of foreign Ph.D. graduates in science and technology who stay abroad show that 79 per cent of 1990–91 doctoral recipients from India and 88 per cent of those from China were still working in the United States in 1995. In contrast, only 11 per cent of Koreans and 15 per cent of Japanese who earned science and engineering (S&E) doctorates from US universities in 1990–91 were working in the United States in 1995.
>
> In the longer term, however, return flows of people and capital may not only offset some potential negative effects of international migration but also constitute an economic development strategy in its own right. In Chinese Taipei, for example, half of all the companies emerging from that economy's largest science park, Hsinchu, were started by returnees from the United States. And in China, the Ministry of Science and Technology estimates that returning overseas students started most Internet-based ventures.[28]

Until the late 1990s, middle-class Indians chose to live abroad if they had the option. The brain drain reached the depths with the advent of the global information technology (IT) and software revolution and the New Economy boom.

America's maniacal fixation with the Y2K bug opened up another huge window of opportunity for India's software engineers. With their strength in mathematics, they seemed perfect to fix the virtual virus as programmers. Hordes of Indians winged their way to the United States, courtesy of the H-1B visas issued by the American government to professionals with skills not available in its country so that they could work there.

Indians, especially south Indians from Hyderabad and Bangalore, where the pressure is highest to graduate as engineers, pursued the American dream. Almost everyone wanted to go to the United States on a H-1B visa, which could later be converted into a green card. Everyone saw a huge stack of greenbacks in front of their eyes: dollars they would earn while working in the United States. Indian firms left no stones unturned to recruit and ship thousands of software engineers.

Read a few anecdotal experiences to soak in the software craze of those days.

Hyderabad became a H-1B visa hotbed. Hundreds of staff recruitment shops mushroomed, which were willing to give a commitment to potential and prospective visa seekers. The city was full of computer training schools that promised lucrative jobs in the United States. It was obviously at a price. City dwellers spent their life savings, and sold their assets, including land, hoping to find employment in America. The same happened in Bangalore, but in a more restrained manner.

The greed for greenbacks was clearly visible in both cities. There are quite a few amusing stories that point to the desperation to fly to the United States. A ticket seller in the city's public bus service managed to get employment with a software firm in the United States. Since the American firms insisted on telephone interviews to test for communication skills in the English language, a person with command of the English language would give the interviews on behalf of his or her friends to their prospective employers.

Those who got the visas had no idea of the work they were supposed to do. So many of them learned software books by rote on the long flight. Their Indian colleagues protected others until they had learned enough about their responsibilities and work. Staff brokers, mostly nonresident Indians (NRI) in the United States, opened sweatshops to help people get H-1Bs. Many Hyderabadis sought the help of their NRI family members, who opened fake software firms in America to grab a bunch of H-1B visas. Using these visas, they helped people reach the United States, and also found jobs for them.

It was the first step for many Indians, especially Brahmins and middle-class individuals, on the entrepreneurial path. In many ways, they became staff traders. To gain respectability, some of them opened credible software firms.

For many Indians in the United States, it became a passion to become an entrepreneur during the New Economy boom, and the era in which the Internet became the new tool to shape business strategies. As a sunrise sector, technology was considered the economic nirvana for anyone—Indian, Chinese, or American—to become wealthy instantly. Almost everyone who had the ambition, nerve, and audacity toyed with a startup.

Not too long ago, in December 2000 and January 2001, I was in Silicon Valley, the epicenter of rapid changes driven by the

Internet. At a New Year's Eve party, I met scores of educated, middle-class, perceived-to-be-conservative, and nonmaterialistic Indians and NRIs. My interactions with them were surreal.

Everyone talked about the new New Economy companies they had launched. They went on to predict the possible valuation of their firms, which, obviously, were in millions of dollars. Many arrogantly spoke about how they had already sold three or four firms they had founded in the past two or three years and made millions of dollars. The talks were all about valuation, selling of firms, and becoming wealthy.

The next day, my friend who had harbored similar dreams—and launched a couple of companies over the next two years—took me for a ride around the so-called millionaire hill. Most houses there had been sold for huge sums, and Indian Americans and NRIs owned many of them. Each one was a New Economy founder. Out there, I saw how the traditional values and attitudes of middle-class India had changed.

As I witnessed the birth of this new genre of Indian Brahmin and middle-class startups in Silicon Valley or the Bay Area, I dubbed them the Bay Brahmins. They were all over Silicon Valley in cities such as San Jose and Santa Clara.

Probably the best way to sketch their character and attitude is through an example. Meet Rakesh Mathur, who was involved in half-a-dozen startups in the late 1990s, and came into the limelight when he sold one of them, junglee.com, to amazon.com. Rakesh and seventy others were absorbed by Amazon, and became millionaires. But Rakesh had become famous a year earlier, and it had nothing to do with his "idea."

In 1998, the junglee co-founder appeared on the cover of *Upside* magazine wearing a tiny black dress. The "crossdressing" idea was part of a well-thought-out PR campaign to create a buzz about junglee. It was a take-off on an earlier ad, where the founder, president, and CEO of CrossWorlds, Katrina Garnett, wore a black evening outfit for an ad campaign that ran in *Vanity Fair* and *The New Yorker*. The apocryphal story is that when Amazon's Jeff Bezos saw *Upside*, he said, "With a CEO who looks that good in a dress, that's a company I want to go to bed with."

Rakesh's black dress gives a clue about one of the traits of Bay Brahmins. They were audacious, almost brash. During my trip to the Bay Area, the Indian Americans I met only spoke about money. They were obsessed with the millions their neighbor had made, and what they could make. They were loud, and boasted about their successes, existent and nonexistent. There was no humility, which was shocking because middle-class Indians are generally believed to be soft-spoken and to underplay their achievements.

That these entrepreneurs were attached to a string of startups hints at their underlying ambition and confidence. Even the Indian employees in various technology firms displayed these very same characteristics. The friend with whom I had stayed in California said that he was going to launch a new firm that would make routers that were better than Cisco's. He had worked with Cisco, and he was sure he knew what was wrong with their routers, and also knew how they could be improved. He told me that he was seriously looking for venture capital for the first-round funding.

Nothing was taboo, and the sky was the limit for these businessmen. They could do anything—everything. In an interview in March 2000, Rakesh said that Purple Yogi, a venture he set up after selling junglee and leaving Amazon, would be "the highest-trust Internet company." He added: "What we are creating is a scenario where we know nothing about the customer, unless they choose to let us know. I'm confident I have a product that does not violate anybody's trust and privacy."[29]

When asked about the software's in-house trials, he sang its praises. "Everybody has been blown away by it—absolutely." He claimed, "I try and improve by a factor of ten each time I do a startup... " It is a different matter that Purple Yogi flopped, and had to reinvent itself on a much smaller, and more sober, scale. In an environment in which networking was crucial to access finance, gain credibility, and be in a position to woo takeover giants and make millions, the Bay Brahmins got to know anyone, everyone, who was important. The technology firms knew the venture capitalists (VCs), who knew the smart guys, who had the smartest ideas and, in turn, knew the VCs. And the VCs knew the tech giants.

Going by the many studies on the evolution of social networking in Silicon Valley, it seems that what the Bay Brahmins did was follow their predecessors from different nationalities; the latter were responsible for a system that is unique, and has not been successfully replicated in other area in the United States or elsewhere.

A study by Emilio Castilla, Hokyu Hwang, Ellen Granovetter, and Mark Granovetter—which was published as a chapter in *The Silicon Valley Edge,* published in 2000—started with the axiom that "the most crucial aspect of Silicon Valley is its networks."[30] It added that "in Silicon Valley, networks have special importance in the movement of labor, the evolution of influence and power, and the actual production of innovation."

However, according to a 1998 paper by Stephen Cohen and Gary Fields ("Social Capital and Capital Gains, or Virtual Bowling in Silicon Valley"), Bay Area networking was distinctly different from the traditional socioeconomic framework, which was termed "networks of civic management," and popularized by Robert Putnam.[31] In his book, *Making Democracy Work,* Putnam suggested that in

> these locales of tight civic engagement people know one another and one another's families; they meet frequently in non-work related organizations and activities. They constitute a dense and rich social community. Business relationships are embedded in community and family structures. They reinforce trust in powerful and multidimensional ways.[32]

However, Cohen and Fields felt that "Silicon Valley is notoriously a world of strangers, nobody knows anybody else's mother there. It is a world of independent—even isolated—newcomers."[33] So the networking system that came into being in the Valley was vastly different. It was the result of "collaborative partnerships that emerged in the region owing to the pursuit by economic and institutional actors of objectives related to innovation and competition." More importantly, these collaborations were largely driven by commercialization (read: profits and finance).

The lack of any historically driven social networks in the Valley spawned several attempts to formalize them. During the technology and New Economy boom in the 1980s and 1990s, many loose-knit structures were born. Stated an article in the *Mercury News* ("Schmoozing in Silicon Valley") in 2007:

> Eager to keep up with the fast-forward industry, techies have banded together in affinity groups. SD Forum, for software developers, was

founded in 1983, originally under the name Software Entrepreneurs Forum. The Silicon Valley Association of Startup Entrepreneurs began in 1995. Immigrants have also organized. In 1992, Indian immigrants founded TiE, for The Indus Entrepreneurs, which now claims 2,000 valley members and chapters in many states and 10 countries ... Collectively these groups produce a staggering schedule of events, from a small breakfast to huge conventions. Former Stanford provost William Miller, a co-editor of *The Silicon Valley Edge*, said it is possible to attend some sort of business-related meeting for breakfast, lunch and dinner for an entire week.[34]

In 2000, I went to one such meeting held at the Marriott Hotel. The conference room was packed with hundreds of people—VCs, lawyers, budding founders bubbling with ideas and laptop presentations, senior executives of large technology firms, and so on. They were all sporting a large-ish badge so that anyone could figure out who was who. It just made it easier for people to figure out whom they wanted to meet and interact with.

But the real action was in the lobby. People were sitting on the floor, hanging on to sofa armrests, or finding whatever place they could. New founders, who thought they had the next big idea, cornered VCs or technology firms' managers to give an instant presentation. VCs were anxiously interested in finding the killer applications. But everything was driven by money. The new entrepreneurs wanted funding, VCs wanted that idea that would make hundreds of millions of dollars, and tech firms hoped to partner with an idea that would help them stay ahead of competitors. Some people knew each other, most did not. The only reason they were meeting and talking to each other was because they knew there was a pot of gold at the end of one of those rainbows.

American-Indians, who traditionally stuck with their kith and kin, especially from the same state or region, became a part of these networks. Many of them already had some form of relationship with the Americans, since they worked in tech firms as software engineers or R&D experts. It also became easier because many American-Indians had become VCs or worked with such firms, or were employed with accounting and law firms. Thus, the Indian entrepreneurs had an informal network or networks to tap in to.

Simultaneously, the software and the New Economy revolution in the United States offered business opportunities to the middle class and the Brahmins (especially south Indians). Many started as body shoppers, or those who provided staff for IT-related work in the United States. They recruited in India, organized H-1B visas for their (middle-class) employees, and shipped them to the American sites where they would work for various vendors. After the completion of the projects (3-to-12 months), the software engineers would be shifted to another client, another project, another city, in the United States.

Within a few years, the smarter firms discovered the virtues of a hybrid onshoring–offshoring business model. They had a sizeable presence in the United States to interact directly with their clients, but they also shifted part of the noncritical project work to their campuses in India. So they could take some advantage of the lower staff costs in India and thereby boost their margins. The clients were happy too because the vendors passed on a part of their savings by charging lower labor rates.

The situation changed by the beginning of this century.

As the technology boom of the 1990s changed to bust, as stock-market valuations crashed, as easy funding and financing vanished in a jiffy, the American tech dream turned into a nightmare, and the U.S. firms had no option but to cut costs drastically. They pink-slipped thousands of employees (many of them Indian engineers), and cut costs; even the traditional manufacturing and services companies reduced their IT and software-related budgets. Suddenly, there was technology mayhem out there.

This is how a *Businessworld* cover story, in March 2001, described the pandemonium in the technology space, and the mania that gripped software engineers, mostly Indians. The article said that there was not much recruiting happening in those days; Indian software companies had drastically slowed down or frozen hirings, and even professionals were unwilling to risk a job move as they desired stability and security.

> It is in the e-mails, the answer lies there.
> "About 21 people just got laid off in my office yesterday."
> "Desperate situation. I and my wife (sic) are both without jobs. Can you please suggest a new sponsor for our H-1B visas?"

"How long can I stay back on an H–1B if I have lost my job? Is it one or two months? Any idea?"

"B2B: Back to Bangalore. Or, back to bench."[35]

Hundreds and thousands of Indian H-1B visa holders were forced to come back to India. Many of them joined universities and schools in an attempt to stay back in the United States on student visas. The H-1B was no longer a ticket to instant wealth.

Explaining the reasons behind this trend, *Businessworld* said:

> The slowdown in the US economy has forced companies to cut down on IT spends and defer projects that are not critical. This has had a ricocheting effect, impacting the fortunes of not only IT companies both in India and the US, but also of the legions of people they employ. US tech majors such as Nortel, Cisco, Intel, Hewlett-Packard and many others have slashed jobs, especially the contractual software workers. It is estimated that in the last month alone, some 30,000 jobs have been axed. And around 100,000 Indian IT professionals (yes, that's right) have been benched. A term used by body-shoppers to indicate the numbers of people they have, waiting and ready, for projects that could emerge. For example, Varun Khan, who works for a US-based consulting firm, has been on the bench for nearly three months. Others have been on the bench much longer. N.K. Venkatesh, a software professional who works in Massachusetts, says he has met people who have been there for four to five months. The once-unsinkable flotilla of IT workers has crashed on the reef of a global tech slowdown.
>
> For some of the H-1B visa holders, the long (and frustrating) journey back home has begun. A Hyderabad-based middleman talks of two professionals who were forced to come back home. "They were among the 44 people sacked by a Kansas-based body-shopper. I am trying to place them with a second-rung Indian software firm at a monthly salary of Rs 40,000 each, far lower than what they were making in the US," he explains. Then there is an instance of a husband-wife team; the husband has a green card while the wife was on H-1B. The wife lost her job and faces the bleak prospect of having to return to India ... the US laws state that a green-card holder cannot support an H-1B holder.[36]

Given this scenario, Indian businessmen had to change their models totally to survive. This led to the birth of the offshoring and outsourcing ideas.

Renowned Indian firms like Wipro, Infosys, TCS, Satyam, and HCL started a hectic process to convince their clients to shift entire projects to their Indian campuses. They said that this would reduce the cost of the projects by a factor of at least five (or one-fifth of the U.S. costs). Thus, offshoring, or doing the projects in India, will take care of the two critical issues—slashed vendor budgets, and the race to seek ever lower rates.

The only problem was to persuade the clients that the quality and timely delivery would not suffer. Initially, the clients experimented with greater proportion of offshoring; in time, it led to almost 100 percent offshoring. The Indian IT vendors, mostly middle-class entrepreneurs and founders, found a new lease on life.

As offshoring boomed, and led to outsourcing of most business processes to developing countries such as India, China, and the Philippines, it led to the rise of what I call the Bangalore Brahmins. It established the Brahmins and other middle-class businessmen firmly on the global map, and firms such as Infosys and Wipro as global brands.

The second coming of the Brahmin Businessmen, or Bangalore Brahmins, and the first coming of the educated middle-class entrepreneur were the direct result of the middle-class resurgence that India has witnessed since the 1980s.

In the past three decades, I wrote in an *Outlook* article,

> Brahmins, [the] educated elite and the power classes began occupying the corner rooms. Not as just CEOs, but as owners and founders. It signaled the rise of Narayana Murthy (Infosys), Jaithirth Rao (Mphasis), Ramesh Vangal. These were the unexpected and unusual promoters who suddenly occupied the top tier of the corporate pyramid. The most surprising among them were south Indian Brahmins, who many thought would rather die than turn entrepreneurs.
>
> Apart from the Brahmins, the past three decades have proved that [the] educated middle class can adapt to business like fish to water, it can make money instead of merely balancing accounting ledgers, it can lead and manage employees from the front rather than merely nudge the nation's destiny from the shadows, and it can become competitive, cut-throat and innovative, apart from just following the rules.[37]

The Brahmins and the middle classes have become the new cradles of entrepreneurship.

Over the next few years, I came to understand the factors that were responsible for this transformation.

But before I delve into them, let me give you a feel of the families that these modern Brahmin and middle-class businessmen belong to. Without exception, their stories were uncannily similar to legends like the garage-to-Google and apartment-to-Apple ones. Each one hints, consciously or subconsciously, at his or her modest beginnings. They were, in a sense, the twenty-first-century Bill Gateses and Jeff Bezoses.

Ramesh Vangal, for example, runs a global conglomerate, but his father was a Class II government officer for most part of his working tenure. He finally retired as a Class I public servant. Arjun Malhotra, head of the U.S.-based IT consulting firm Headstrong, was born into an army family; his father took part in the India–China war in 1962. Polaris Software's CEO Arun Jain's father worked with the central posts and telegraph department.

The story of Rana Kapoor is even more interesting. The founder of Yes Bank, a private sector bank, reveals that his father refused to run the family's traditional jewelery business, and decided to use his education to take up a job. He narrates how his grandfather sold his three jewelery stores, meant for each of his son, just before the Gold Control Act. "It was a bad move as most of the other traders made huge profits due to the restrictions imposed by the new Act. But my grandfather had no option as none of his sons wanted to get into the family business. But as a child, when I used to play chess with my grandfather, I would console him saying, 'Don't worry, one day I will become a businessman.'"

Ironically, even the old guard, the traditional Indian business families such as the Birlas and Tatas, had their own modest-beginning legends. Shiv Narayan Birla began trading in cotton in the 1850s. Nusserwanji Tata was the first member to break out of the traditional priestly profession. H.P. Nanda of Escorts came to India during the post-independence Partition days with Rs 5,000 (US$125) in his pocket. He told friends that he still hired expensive cars to impress his potential clients, but told the car rental company that he would pay it later when he made it really big in the capital.

As is commonly known, Dhirubhai Ambani, who built India's largest private sector business house before its split in 2005, was the son of a teacher in a small village in Gujarat. Of course, the Bajajs and Mafatlals also boast of "humble" beginnings.

But that is where the similarities between the old guards and the neo Turks end.

The major difference between the two was education. Almost every businessman in the latter category went to a premiere college or institute. Many of them went to renowned IITs and IIMs. With no social or financial protection, with no external props to help them succeed in a society that was fast becoming intensely competitive, their parents forced them to focus on studies. The parents believed in India's fascination and passion for higher education, which seemed like a panacea for individual success and also to change the destiny of a fledgling nation.

"Nehru made many mistakes but he got some things right. It was because of his attitude that the IITs were saved, and have become the biggest brand from India," says Arjun Malhotra.

Others agree that higher education helped them to jump the first few steps of the entrepreneurial ladder.

Elite academic backgrounds helped Bangalore businessmen to initially land "cushy," comfortable and well-paying jobs with top-notch Indian firms or MNCs. Such tenures enabled them to become what travel writer Pico Iyer called the "global souls." They became seasoned, global professionals, who lived and thrived in the globalization era when the world became wirelessly connected like never before.

As these professionals crisscrossed strange lands, as they personally witnessed the workings of new markets in Asia, Africa, Europe, and North America, as they learned about business practices in different markets, they acted more like entrepreneurs than managers. As they witnessed the technological and business changes across the globe, they became convinced that the traditional Indian business houses were unable to identify the sunrise sectors in which action was inevitable. Their international exposure gave them the confidence that they too could change things. Finally, it inculcated an inherent, almost blind, belief in India's economic story.

Ramesh joined Pepsi in the 1980s to kickstart its controversial, delayed, contentious, and much-criticized project in India. (The details of this project have been given in an earlier chapter.) According to him, the stint taught him the nitty-gritty of dealing with government officials, business and other critics, and operational, ground-level practicalities and realities. "It was a traumatic period, both personally and businesswise. We were the guinea pigs who got hammered around by all the interested lobbies and interest groups. But it was a fantastic, lasting, learning experience," says Ramesh.

Even before his Indian Pepsi experience, Ramesh worked at Proctor & Gamble in Geneva, where he handled the MNC's export markets.

> The experience was more entrepreneurial, it was quite unstructured unlike any other job in the company. I handled 22 nations, but the most striking was when we set up a joint venture in Egypt. I lived in Egypt for a year. I had to go deep to understand the local mindset and culture. We set up everything from scratch, and I realized that I really liked it.[38]

More importantly, their global observations enabled them to spot new opportunities that did not register on the radars of traditional business houses, which felt comfortable in their socialistic, protected, license-raj environment of the 1980s.

Arjun Malhotra accidentally stumbled into a job because of personal pressures:

> I wanted to study further. But then I wanted to marry this girl, my wife, and her parents were not willing to wait for another five years. So, I took up the job with DCM with the intention of getting married first and studying later. I kept my Stanford University admission open for five years. In DCM, under Shiv Nadar's leadership, we started this new division.[39]

He recalls how the DCM experiences led to the setting up of a new company:

> We were ready to launch our brand of computers. But apparently, the legal folks told the DCM promoters that they should not risk the future fortunes of the fourth largest business house for a division that was likely to contribute not more than Rs 2 crore [US$500,000] a year. We thought they were crazy to give up on such a huge opportunity. We understood the paradigm shift in the technology space. We knew we could screw the existing competitors. We knew the market, had the contacts, had done the designs ourselves.[40]

So Arjun and others in DCM, including Shiv, decided to do it themselves. Arjun reminisces:

> But we were completely naïve. For example, we did not know that you required a license to start one. Moreover, we had no money and did not know how to develop computers without it. I was born in a joint family and, hence, I was not too worried about financial security. But it did not apply to the others. So, we decided to trade in calculators initially as it required less money and was an easier option. All of us had the basic gut that technology would change the world.[41]

More than that, since they came from elite institutions, many of them also had a kind of brashness, an arrogance that they could succeed against all odds.

Arun Jain, whose family had no clue of what IITs were all about when his elder brother gained admission to one in 1972, says he decided to get into business because of a discussion with one of his brothers-in-law, who was settled in the United States and was visiting India in 1982. Says Arun:

> During his trip, he told me that nothing could happen in India. The country cannot get anywhere, it had only problems. It was a typical reaction from a nonresident Indian. Although I had the US green card, I felt hurt and decided to stay back. Three of us, including two IIT friends of my elder brother, joined hands together and formed our first company in 1983.[42]

Although Arun and his partners were in the software services space, they still dreamed of manufacturing-related ideas:

> Services were not considered a business at that time. So, we thought about making watches or electronic gadgets. On most weekends, we got together and threw up new ideas related to chip-making or manufacturing semiconductors.[43]

But the shift in Arun's mindset came when he visited America in 1985. During that trip, he went to a jobs fair to have some fun, and, surprisingly, landed a job instantly. "I was not even carrying a copy of my engineering degree, but got the offer letter for a short-term project. My brother-in-law was amazed." But at Wang Labs, Arun's perspective about the global software sector underwent a dramatic change. At this laboratory, he saw a thousand people working out of a single office.

In Ballarpur Industries, we were just 20 software engineers, and we were thinking of expanding the base to 40. At Wang Labs, a thousand people were working on internal software needs. Then and there, I took the decision to be in software.[44]

Like Arjun and his partners, Arun too was quick to spot global trends. In addition, they knew that the future in business lay in being a global, or glocal, player.

I wrote in *Outlook*:

But they were all thinking big and wanted to compete globally as that was what they had seen and imbibed. So, Kapoor (Rana) wanted his bank to be world-class and compete with the international brands. Explains Ramesh, "I want to carve and create a large vision, scale up the various businesses to a certain level, invite financial or technology partners to enable these to become truly global and competitive."

For traditional businessmen, the globalization urge dawned late. In the license-quota raj, they thought in terms of the protected domestic market, grabbing licenses to deter newer players, and competing with inefficient PSUs. They worked the system, policymakers and other lobbies to influence decisions in their favor. Even in the immediate post-reforms era, the Bombay Club (comprising several traditional promoters) clamored for slower reforms and a level playing field against the foreign onslaught.

Although there were a few visionaries, most groups became global only when it came to choosing between survival and death. The 1990s witnessed the decline of business families like the Modis and Dalmias. The ones who managed to thrive were those who became globally competitive. It was because of those efforts that we are now witnessing the making of the Indian MNCs, like Tata Steel ... who are gobbling up huge global firms or setting up the world's largest factories.[45]

However, it was the Brahmins and the middle class that understood the need for a globalized business outlook. Once they realized that, and also grasped the huge gaps in emerging sectors, the only change that was required was for them to become risktakers and give up the conservative, risk-averse attitude.

Personal confidence set in when they saw what was happening around them. Says Arjun:

In 1985, I went to Harvard. I realized I was not inferior to the whites. I was good at managing huge numbers of people. The whites knew

how to deal with finances. But I realized that their skill was easier to
learn; and I could do it from books. Mine was more experiential and,
therefore, could not be learnt easily.[46]

During his studying days, Rana also became convinced that
Indians could do what the Americans or Europeans had done, or
were doing. "During my MBA, I saw the beginnings of the success
of Indian Americans who bought houses and cars. I was convinced
that if Indians can make it in America, they can in India too."

Fortunately, while the earlier crop of Bangalore Brahmins did
struggle for cash, and, therefore, opted for businesses that needed
little financial backing, the later entrants could raise funds in innovative ways in the changing global economy. For example, in
the late 1990s after his Pepsi stint, Ramesh managed to raise
US$115 million as private equity to start his businesses. "But it
was wrong timing, as 1997 witnessed the Asian meltdown," he
says. Not to be deterred, he inked an unusual deal with Edgar
Brosnan Jr. of Seagram, and took charge of Seagram Asia's operations. Brosnan agreed to give Ramesh a stake in the Asian venture, and also advanced loans to invest in the initial years.

"Seagram's business was complicated. It had a huge debt, and
we cut costs very deep. The business turned around, we tripled
profits, and the Asia operations contributed 25 percent of
Seagram's global profits. I moved in when Brosnan sold the
business." Luckily, Ramesh made a killing by selling off his stake
in the company, and that provided an ideal platform for him to
become a venture capitalist later.

Another trigger for the increase in risk appetite, I wrote in
Outlook,

> is the conviction that India's is the next economic story, after China. "I
> believe India's arbitrage potential is enormous. There is something
> inherently strong in our economy. India today is like the US in the
> 1900s. It is in exciting times and there are several Wild West kind of
> business opportunities," feels [Ramesh] Vangal. Adds [Rana] Kapoor,
> "India is at the centerstage of the global economy. And its future will
> be driven by entrepreneurship."[47]

As well as thinking that they can make money in these adven-
turous times, the Bangalore Brahmins also realized that they
could give a lot back to society. In keeping with the tradition of

helping society, they used their money for considerable social work. Ramesh reveals that the inspiration for doing this came when his wife and he met the Dalai Lama.

> On our way back, we stopped at an orphanage. We decided then to set up a foundation to help children, and find ways of supporting it. My wife's brother suffered from an injured brain; my son has special needs. So we are familiar with such issues and empathize with them. We also realized that the more we could give, the more we could get to give. Our business is not about wealth creation only.[48]

The final word comes from (Arun) Jain, who thinks there is a huge social change happening right now in India.

For Arun, India is in the midst of a monumental social flux:

> In our society, the second-generation youth do not have too many responsibilities. Their parents are still young and may still be working. Under the two-kids system, the pressures on the youth are less. What they earn is like their pocket money. In our times, decades ago, we still had to think about money to manage our house and for our marriage. But now the working kids have more financial freedom. Hence, their risktaking abilities become higher. Today, two or three younger people can come together and take risks.[49]

One cannot really forget another socioeconomic change that reduced the downside to risks. Concludes Arun:

> In Chennai, the epicenter of Brahmin conservatism, the rise of the Brahmin Businessmen can be traced to a recent period when knowledge started having a value. The Brahmins were always the knowledge keepers of the world. But in the 1990s, the world allowed knowledge to be charged, knowledge got payments. The three elements of success in business are humility, hunger and smartness. The Chennai Brahmins had always had two of them. What was missing was hunger, but the Brahmins jumped this gap due to their experiences in Silicon Valley.[50]

Endnotes

1. Brandon Gary Lovested, "A Tale of Two Bostons," iBoston. http://www.iboston.org/mcp.php?pid=taleOfTwoBostons
2. ibid.
3. ibid.

4. ibid.
5. ibid.
6. "History of Saraswat Migrations," http://www.gsbkerala.com/gsbhistory.htm.
7. Anthony Mann, "How 'Poor Country Boys' Became Boston Brahmins: The Rise of the Appletons and the Lawrences in Ante-bellum Massachusetts," *Historical Journal of Massachusetts*, Winter 2003, http://findarticles.com/p/articles/mi_qa3837/is_200301/ai_n9184108/print
8. Aarti Maskeri, "Gaud Saraswat and Chitrapur Saraswat Brahmins of India," 1996, http://www.angelfire.com/sc/saraswat/bhanaps.html
9. Mann, op. cit.
10. ibid.
11. ibid.
12. ibid.
13. ibid.
14. David Kew, review of the book, *Merchant Prince of Boston: Colonel T.H. Perkins, 1764–1854*, by Carl Seaburg and Stanley Paterson, February 2004, http://capecodhistory.us/books/MerchantPrince.html
15. ibid.
16. ibid.
17. http://saraswat.aryashaadi.com/
18. "History of Saraswat Migrations" http://www.gsbkerala.com/gsbhistory.htm.
19. Francesca Trivellato, "Discourse and Practice of Trust in Business Correspondence During the Early Modern Period,") Department of History, Yale University, http://www.econ.yale.edu/seminars/echist/eh04-05/Trivellato 101304.pdf
20. Mann, op. cit.
21. Aarti Maskeri, "The Saraswats: Formation of Chitrapur Saraswats," http://www.saraswatsamajuk.org/roots/theSaraswats.html
22. Oliver Wendell Holmes Sr., "The Brahmin Caste of New England," *Atlantic Monthly*, 1860, http://www.slate.com/id/2096401/sidebar/2096424/
23. ibid.
24. Mann, op. cit.
25. Alexandra Hall, "The New Brahmins," *Boston Magazine*, May 2004, http://www.bostonmagazine.com/articles/the_new_brahmins/
26. "Spirit of the Skies," http://www.tata.com/0_about_us/history/pioneers/jrd_tata.htm
27. Vaishali Honawar, "Indian Middle Class Makes Mission out of Sending Children to College: Primary Focus on Engineering, Medical Studies," *Education Week*, 25, 13 (November 30, 2005), http://eric.ed.gov/ERICWeb Portal/custom/portlets/recordDetails/detailmini.jsp?_nfpb=true&_&ERIC ExtSearch_SearchValue_0=EJ739089&ERICExtSearch_SearchType_0= no&accno=EJ739089
28. Mario Cervantes and Dominique Guellec, "The Brain Drain: Old Myths, New Realities," *OECD Observer*, no. 230, (January 2002), http://www.oec-dobserver.org/news/fullstory.php/aid/673/The_brain_drain:_Old_myths,_new_realities.html

29. Shanthi Shankarkumar, "Rakesh Mathur's Karma Yoga," www.rediff.com, March 3, 2000, http://www.rediff.com/us/2000/mar/03us1.htm

30. Emilio J. Castella, Hokyu Hwang et al., "Social Networks in Silicon Valley," *The Silicon Valley Edge*, 2000 http://www.stanford.edu/group/esrg/siliconvalley/docs/siliconvalleyedge.pdf

31. *The Silicon Valley Edge*, Stephen Cohen & Gary Fields, *Social Capital and Capital Gains, or Virtual Bowling in Silicon Valley*, 1998, http://works.bepress.com/gary_fields/22

32. Eric L. Lesser, *Knowledge and Social Capital: Foundations and Applications*, (Butterworth-Heinemann, 2000), pp. 179–80.

33. Cohen and Fields, op. cit.

34. Scott Duke Harris, *San Jose Mercury Nag* "Schmoozing in Silicon Valley," July 20, 2007, http://www.accessmylibrary.com/coms2/summary_0286-32303375_ITM

35. Manish Khanduri and Alam Srinivas, "Software Hard Knocks," *Business world*, March 26, 2001, http://www.y-axis.com/bench/hardknocks.shtml

36. ibid.

37. Alam Srinivas, "In the Company of Chanakya," *Outlook*, August 20, 2007, http://www.outlookindia.com/full.asp?fodname=20070820&fname=SAlam+%28F%29&sid=1

38. Interview with author, August 2007.

39. ibid.

40. ibid.

41. ibid.

42. ibid.

43. ibid.

44. ibid.

45. Srinivas, op. cit.

46. Interview with author, August 2007.

47. Srinivas, op. cit.

48. Interview with author, August 2007.

49. ibid.

50. ibid.

Conclusion: Seven Ps of the Indian Middle Class

When I originally decided to write this book, I had planned to end it with a three-dimensional matrix for marketers, investors and corporate decision makers. The X axis would indicate price points, the Y axis the product category, and the Z axis the number of potential customers. The idea was to convey the idea that the number of Indian middle-class consumers depends on all these factors. There is a different number depending on price or product; for a luxury car, the size is only a few million buyers, but it can be a 100 million for a two-wheeler (motorcycle or scooter) or a mixer grinder.

But as I progressed with the manuscript, and as I reached the conclusion, I realized that the matrix would have to have nearly a dozen dimensions. Therefore, it would be an impossible task to depict it on two-dimensional paper. It was then that I realized that a better way of achieving the same objective would be to talk about the several Ps of Indian consumers. It would also be in a language that marketers and CEOs comprehend. So I am taking a shot at the "Seven Ps of the Indian Middle Class," four of which are akin to the traditional Ps of marketing and the rest have an Indian twist.

Product: The product is important, but not necessarily the brand. Both McDonald's and Kentucky Fried Chicken (KFC) were known brands as far as the Indian consumer was concerned. But the former has been successful in the country, while the latter has floundered several times. The reason: McDonald's got its products right, especially when it indigenized its menu (with Indianized products such as the McAloo burger) and catered to religious sentiments by refusing to serve its globally accepted product, the Big Mac, made of beef, which is considered wrong because the cow is a holy animal for Hindus.

Similarly, Toyota and M&M (Mahindra & Mahindra) special utility vehicles (SUVs) have sold well because of the quality of the products. The saying about Toyota is that its cars and SUVs never break down (which is probably why the Toyota SUV has become the preferred model for taxis that ply long routes). And M&M's Scorpio has become one of the hottest-selling vehicles in recent times because of its styling, looks, and performance. This also proves that the success of the brand has nothing to do with whether it is global or local, foreign or Indian.

This is even truer in the white goods and consumer electronics segments, where South Korean *chaebols* such as LG and Samsung coexist with the Japanese Sony, and with Indian giants such as Onida, Videocon, and Voltas. As long as a manufacturer or service provider fulfills a need, requirement, or wish, and offers a quality product or service, the consumer laps it up. He or she does not make a distinction on the basis of the brand. But the same may not be true in the luxury segments because the "snob" value of owning Swarovski, Chanel, Armani, or Esprit may become the overriding factor.

Price: The "Nano," or the world's cheapest car, which has been designed by Tata Motors, is probably the best example of how price can work in India. Because it is priced at a low Rs 100,000 (or US$2,500), experts believe that the model can easily sell a million units a year. One of the key ingredients for McDonald's success has been its pricing strategy. So has been the case with cola makers such as Coca-Cola and Pepsi, which have not reduced prices but have offered more for the same price. And the demand for second-generation mobile phones, or for those whose new variant is out, goes up immediately once its price is slashed by 30–50 percent by the manufacturer. Nokia has mastered this art of pricing.

However, the Nokia example also highlights the other end of pricing strategy. That is, in India, one can create a demand for a higher-priced product because of a willingness among a certain set of consumers to own a model or a brand at any cost. Such consumers, who are either rich or wannabes, or have been exposed to the Western lifestyle, will go to any extent to buy a certain product. So each time Nokia launches its latest model, there is a rush among certain sections to be the first to own it.

Or if Swarovski launches a new product range, there will be a few thousand people who will buy it instantly.

There's a third dimension to pricing in India, which is value-for-money pricing. This is most clearly visible in the automobile sector. Companies such as Hyundai and Maruti-Suzuki have successfully forced Indian consumers to buy more expensive models as their entry-level cars. So instead of the cheapest car being a family's first car, it can be a more expensive, more powerful, bigger model. In the case of the motorcycle segment, for instance, many first-time buyers are opting for more expensive, higher-powered bikes, instead of the cheapest 100 cc ones.

Looking at it from all possible angles, the one fact that emerges is that there are no rules about pricing in India. Each company, product, and brand has to discover and invent its own price points. McDonald's competes with street vendors on prices. Expensive fashion brands haven't done too well in India, nor have some of the lesser-priced ones. Despite the high ticket prices, people frequent PVR (a group that has built several cinema multiplexes in India) theaters, because they are like a picnic or an outing for families—watch a movie, have popcorn, eat out, and have fun. A cheap product sells but after some time stagnates as new consumers aspire to something that's not so commonly used and owned by thousands of other families.

Place: The demand for specific products at specific prices also depends on the region or the place where one is selling them. For example, a village in Punjab has 80 M&M Scorpio SUVs. The largest number of owners of luxury cars such as Mercedes-Benzs, Jaguars, and Bentleys are in the state of Punjab, and not in cities such as Delhi, Mumbai, or Bangalore. Similarly, more than 70 percent of the total sales of tea are in the northern states. More than three-quarters of demand for health drinks is accounted for by sales in east and south India. Nearly half the premium wine sold in the country is consumed in west India.

Therefore, as an investor or marketer, don't aim to be present across India within a few years. First, study the regional and location trends for each product and price category, and then finalize the expansion strategy. Let's consider a few examples in which companies got it totally wrong. The first was Domino's pizza, which was in a hurry to set up as many outlets as possible in a bid to spread across the country. The firm believed that pizza has become an accepted food product in all states. In a bid to be the first fast-food giant to reach 100 outlets, it even set up in small towns and cities.

Domino's did get it right in several places. Its outlet in the Infosys campus in Bangalore became the largest revenue-earning outlet. Swarmed with techies who worked 24/7, pizza sales zoomed. But, at the same time, there were dozens of outlets, especially in states such as Uttar Pradesh and Punjab, where daily sales were dismal. In the end, Domino's franchisee in India had no option but to shut down several outlets, and go slow on the expansion spree. In comparison, McDonald's is extremely choosy about the proposed location of its outlets, be it in India or any other country.

In a similar vein, Amway, the pyramid-marketing company, came to India wearing rose-tinted glasses about the potential of the Indian market. It initially targeted the metropolises and big cities, thinking that it would easily grab thousands of members, who would willingly sell its products or become consumers for them. But it didn't happen the way Amway had planned it. There was major criticism of the company; there were major debates about how Amway can kill personal and other relationships because of its ingrained aggressive policy to sell at any cost. There were several media reports about how the company destroys a society, and how that has happened in several markets.

So Amway changed its location strategy. It decided to expand into the smaller cities and towns, where the scope for criticism would be low, so the company would be able to pursue expansionist plans. The ploy succeeded, as thousands of the small-town middle class lapped up Amway's spiel in a bid to become millionaires. Only now, after several years, has Amway decided to get back to the bigger cities. However, this second coming is with a difference: Amway is not directly marketing itself; it has formed groups, which are roping in potential marketers and consumers for its products.

Positioning: This is a critical area, especially when one realizes that the Indian middle class comprises hundreds of subsets, who may look similar, yet are vastly different. So it is critical to target specific segments in most cases, rather than simply send out a universal positioning communication through advertising, promotions, and marketing strategies. For example, take a look at how Indian and foreign fashion designers have clearly tried to appeal to specific socioeconomic categories.

At a social level, Ritu Kumar, an Indian designer famous for ethnic wear (*salwar kameez*) believes in targeting the traditional, conservative, middle-class families. Her clothes make a fashion statement about Indian-ness and being distinct from the melting pot that the globalized world has become. At the other extreme of this spectrum are foreign brands such as Armani or Chanel, which appeal to a Westernized middle class, which is exposed to the American and European way of life, and has imbibed the so-called modern lifestyle and mindset.

Deliberately sandwiched somewhere between those extremes are designers such as Satya Paul, who offer a balanced combination of tradition and modernity. So while Satya Paul would offer traditional wear such as saris for middle-class women, the design would be contemporary, so that the buyer could even wear them to a corporate office. Manish Malhotra looks at the fashion market in a tangential manner; he designs only for Bollywood celebrities, or stars and starlets of the Indian movie industry. So a Manish Malhotra would be a part of the heroine's wardrobe in a much hyped movie or in a real scene when it comes to Bollywood events and parties.

If one looks at the economic segments of the middle class, one realizes how fashion brands have positioned themselves. The high end belongs to globally known names, which price their products quite expensively. The Benettons and Tommy Hilfigers appeal to the middle middle-class segment with their affordable price tags. Among the Indian designers, David Abraham and Rakesh Rathore price their products so that they can be purchased by the Neo Middle Class (NMC), or the young yuppies, who are single or DINKs (double income, no kids), and have money to splurge on themselves.

People: The four Ps mentioned until now point to a major conclusion: marketers need to know the people (consumers) they are selling to. And their experiences in India can be different from their home or other markets. Take the case of Pizza Hut, which is perceived to be a fast-food firm, but has come to be associated with fine dining in India. Or consider the case of McDonald's, which is known to be a stopover eating place, which has started home delivery in India. India is the first market in which McDonald's has pursued this strategy of directly reaching out to consumers.

Whether they have been forced to, or they have intuitively realized it, or they have learnt their lessons the hard way, managements have come to know that they cannot have the same appeal and image across the socioeconomic, caste, class, and religious categories of the Indian middle class. Brands have to be content with selling to only a few of these categories. As I have mentioned several times, the Indian middle class is divided into hundreds of subsets, and is not homogeneous at all. Let me quote from an article that appeared in *The Hindu* newspaper in 2005.

> The region-wise brand preferences compiled by Perfect Profile and KSA Technopak give an idea of what styles and which brands dominate different regions. Nike is the market leader, followed by Reebok in three of the income segments, except for Adidas in the Rs. 15,000 to Rs. 25,000 income segment, and Nike has an 8.3 per cent share. While Duke is the most popular brand in the wardrobe of the lowest income group of customers, it is second in the next higher income slab to Lee and third in the Rs. 50,001 to Rs. 1 lakh income group. The top five in the highest income segment is dominated by Wills Sports followed by Lacoste, Allen Solly, Lee and Classic Polo in that order.
>
> Benetton is the second most popular brand in the Rs. 50,001 to Rs. 1 lakh income segment and occupies fifth rank in the Rs. 15,000 to Rs. 25,000 segment. Peter England is among the top five favorites in the lowest income bracket and Crocodile gets similar endorsement in the Rs. 25,000 to Rs. 50,000 income segment. In the next higher income group, Allen Solly and ColorPlus are in the running. The income analysis of women shows that Reebok is the top women's "active wear" T-shirt in the lower income segment, Nike in the middle income segment and Adidas dominates the highest income bracket.[1]

Posturing: Given the fragmentation of the Indian middle class, it is important for both foreign and Indian brands to posture themselves in a particular way to woo consumers. For instance, in the soft-drink market, both Coca-Cola and Pepsi have carefully crafted a promotional strategy to appeal to young middle class Indians. Their brand ambassadors are smart, cool, suave, street-smart, and, obviously, young. The latest Pepsi ad shows the protagonist who makes a fool out of his girlfriend's father by behaving as if he was an alien who has come from "Young-istan" (the land of young people).

At the other extreme is another beverage, Sprite, which has invariably projected itself as a contrarian brand, one that is neither Coca-Cola nor Pepsi. So the Sprite ads always take on the ads launched by the latter two; the latest Sprite ad is a spoof on "Young-istan" and shows the "alien loser" who says he is from "Junglistan" (the land of unruly people). In a bid to distinguish itself from other brands, Thums Up, an Indian brand that was purchased by Coca-Cola, tries to project itself as a he-man drink, with action hero Akshay Kumar (who is a black belt in karate) as its brand ambassador.

Since India is getting younger, and the Westernized nuclear families in urban areas have imbibed a trait for parents to become friends with their children, the kids have a considerable say in the choice of products and brands. Therefore, advertisers and marketers have targeted kids in a bid to promote their products. This is evident from advertising campaigns launched by Unilever (Surf Excel) and Airtel (Bharti Group's telecoms services venture). Both feature kids and talk to them.

One of the Surf Excel ads showed two kids fighting in dirt and grime, mimicking their fathers who were caught in a bout of road rage. The punchline: *"Daag achche hain"* (Dirt marks on clothes are good), because they can be removed by this detergent, Surf Excel. Airtel featured an ad about two kids on either side of a barbed-wire fence. In this case, Airtel communicated that boundaries vanish when people talk. Another telecoms service provider, Hutch (now Vodafone) constantly featured a child with a pug following him. Its punchline was that the Hutch network follows you, wherever you go.

Post-mortem: In a country where the middle class or the set of consumers is fast changing and constantly evolving, companies need to have the ability to learn from either their, or their competitors', mistakes, or their, or their competitors', successes. So when Tata Motors rewrote the rules of the passenger-car game by launching a diesel version of its Indica model, competitors were quick to grasp the importance of the trend. Almost every car company, Indian and foreign, has several diesel variants in its portfolio. Similarly, the car firms learned from each other to introduce new price points consistently.

In the case of Tata Motors, the company understood the importance of lower price points and that included diesel variants, for which running costs are also low. So for its revolutionary model, the Nano, the company kept in mind the need to launch a diesel variant quickly, immediately after showcasing its petrol version. After Hyundai Motor changed the concept of an entry-level car with its more-expensive-than-the-cheapest car, the Santro model, it came out with the i10, which created a new segment of entry-level consumers, who wished to buy a car that was even more expensive than the Santro.

Haier, the Chinese white-goods maker, is one of the few firms that has tried to learn from its own mistakes. Before it launched its products in India, the company knew that Chinese brands were perceived by Indian consumers as cheap and low quality. In a bid to change this mindset, Haier introduced high-quality models, and pitched itself as a premium brand. However, the strategy did not work because South Korean brands such as LG and Samsung and several Japanese firms had already occupied the premium platform. Haier also learned the lesson that, as did LG and Samsung, foreign firms have to indigenize their products to suit the needs and requirements of local buyers.

Therefore, Haier has decided to design its products in India, and even to manufacture them at a local plant. This will enable Haier to catch up with competition in a bid to introduce "Indianized" products, and also to cut costs in an effort to improve profit margins. It is also changing its promotional strategy to convey the "premium" message to prospective consumers. More subtly, Haier is trying to tell prospective buyers that it is more of a global brand, and not the "cheap" Chinese one.

Armed with these minimum seven Ps, and maybe more that a firm or its managers can learn from their own experiences, one has some ammunition to deal with Indian consumers and India's middle class. But as I have repeatedly said earlier, there are no neat endings to this story about the rise of the Great Indian

Middle Class. This is just the beginning. One has only to remember that the realities about this class or segment are changing fast. No one can even begin to claim that he or she knows everything there is to be learned about its consumption behavior. In many ways, these people are half blind and they are making sweeping conclusions about the Indian elephant based on the part of the body that they can see. As I said, even if we collate all such observations, the sum of parts is not a simple, straightforward addition.

Endnote

1. "T-shirts Are Hot in Corporate World," *The Hindu*, July 29, 2005, http://www.hindu.com/2005/07/29/stories/20050729145 20200.htm

Index